Practical Observations on the Treatment of Strictures in the Urethra, and in the Oesophagus
by Sir Everard Home

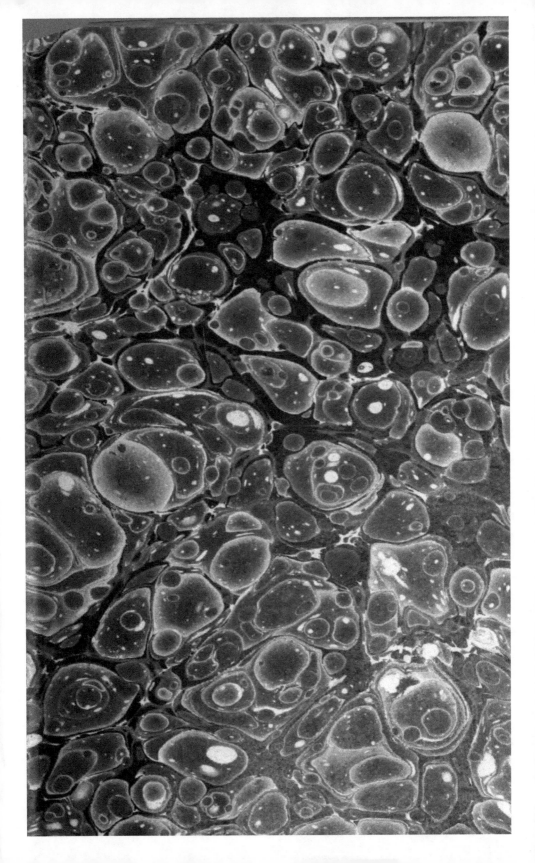

PRACTICAL OBSERVATIONS

ON THE

TREATMENT

OF

STRICTURES IN THE URETHRA,

AND

IN THE ŒSOPHAGUS.

BY

EVERARD HOME, ESQ. F. R. S.

SURGEON TO ST. GEORGE'S HOSPITAL.

VOL. I.

——————Omne per ignem
Excoquitur vitium.——————   VIRG. GEORG.

THE THIRD EDITION.

LONDON:

PRINTED BY W. BULMER AND CO.
CLEVELAND-ROW;
FOR G. AND W. NICOL, BOOKSELLERS TO HIS MAJESTY,
PALL-MALL;
AND J. JOHNSON, ST. PAUL'S CHURCH-YARD.
1805.

From you they will receive the indulgence of a Friend, and your protection will give a favourable bias to the public opinion.

My dear Sir,
believe me to remain,
with the highest esteem,
your sincere Friend,

Leicester-Square,
Nov. 3, 1795.   **EVERARD HOME.**

PREFACE,

TO THE SECOND EDITION.

WHEN the first Edition of this Treatise was laid before the public, the doing so appeared to be justified by the experience then acquired of the mode of treatment which it was intended to explain.

The reception it met with, has afforded me extensive opportunities of confirming my former observations, and of making many additions. It has also brought before me a greater variety of cases, in different stages of this disease, than could have been collected in any situation, except in the metropolis of a great empire.

Having derived from my former publication those advantages, by which my knowledge of the disease, and of the mode of treating it, have been materially improved, it became a duty to render a work, which has been marked by the public approbation, as far as it was in my power, deserving of it.

It has been objected to the first Edition, that the cases are all favourable, and that, in most of them, the patients were stated to have recovered in a short period; whereas some of those which have been since met with, have been much more tedious, and others unattended with success.

To this truth there is a very plain answer. In the first Edition, were published all the cases attended with difficulty, which had at that time come under my care, and the circumstances, whatever they were, that occurred.

My being now enabled to give a more ample detail of cases, has arisen in part from this; that the former publication induced many patients to apply to me for relief, who had found all other means of treatment ineffectual.

Among those, there are cases more obdurate than any that had been before known to me, more difficult to remove, and some few in which, though relief has been afforded, the cure has not been completed.

The difficulties that have been met with, the delays which have occurred, and the failures experienced, all have a place in the present Edition, equally with the successful cases; and even more stress is laid upon them, since they will convey to the minds of practitioners much useful knowledge, and must tend materially to improve this important branch of surgery. It will however appear, that the unsuccessful cases bear a very small proportion to the rest; and that the practice has been fully and completely confirmed by very extensive experience.

Leicester Square,
  Nov. 3, 1797.

PREFACE,

TO THE THIRD EDITION.

In laying before the public a New Edition
of this volume, no pains has been spared to
render it more perfect than the former,
both by giving a continuation of the histories of the cases up to the present period,
where it could be done, and by adducing
such new facts and observations as have
since occurred to me. These have been so
numerous as to fill a second volume, and
considerably to enlarge this edition of the
first.

All that has been done forms but a very
imperfect investigation of so extensive a

subject; it is howeve no inconsiderable attempt for an individual to make, and is sufficient to point out the principal varieties of the disease, and to convince every impartial reader of the utility of the practice which is recommended.

Sackville Street,
  Nov 3, 1805.

CONTENTS.

CHAPTER VI.

CHAPTER VII.

CHAPTER VIII.

CHAPTER IX.

INTRODUCTION.

In laying before the Public the following observations on the treatment of a very painful and distressing complaint, and endeavouring to obviate the objections that have been thrown out against the use of caustic, as a remedy, there are two motives which actuate me; the desire of rendering a service to my Profession, and that of paying a new tribute of gratitude to the memory of Mr. Hunter; to whose ingenuity the world is indebted for the original proposal of such a mode of practice, and the invention of a safe and easy method of conveying the caustic to the seat of disease. These tasks cannot be better performed than by attempting to elucidate and extend his very useful discoveries.

B

Mr. Hunter is universally allowed to have been a skilful anatomist, nor has any one been hardy enough to deny that he excelled his cotemporaries in an intimate knowledge of the changes in structure, which are met with in different parts of the body, in consequence of their having been diseased. In these acquirements he was unrivalled; and in pursuing them, he brought to light the information we at present possess respecting the nature of Strictures in the Urethra.

The account he has published of the different stages of this disease, taken from actual observation in the dead body, and illustrated by engravings, contains a connected body of evidence, established upon facts, to which no one can refuse an assent. There are, however, practitioners who are unwilling to give more credit to these facts than is absolutely necessary. They admit such cases to occur, but at the same time do not choose to give up the opinions they had formerly imbibed; and this they reconcile to themselves, by supposing the appearances mentioned by Mr. Hunter to arise only in extraordinary cases, while those taken notice of by former writers, are more commonly met with; but in support of this no anatomical facts can be produced.

In surgery, as in other practical arts and professions, attempts at improvement are considered by many as hasty and unwarranted innovations. This caution, when restrained within proper bounds, answers a good purpose, by inducing men qualified for the task, to examine with accuracy whatever improvements in the art are proposed; and to prevent all those which do not bear the test of their inquiry from being obtruded on the world.

This salutary care degenerates, however, in less liberal minds into mere jealousy, and leads the prejudiced to condemn improvements without putting them to the trial, or even making themselves masters of the intentions for which they were proposed.

These observations have been made from the following circumstance, which happened when the mode of applying caustic to strictures was first introduced into practice. At that time a gentleman who had many years laboured under the disease, and had in vain tried every other mode of treatment then in use, upon hearing that some improvements had been proposed by Mr. Hunter, was desirous of availing himself of them ; he consulted four of the professors of one of the first universities in Europe upon this subject : he stated, that in the present stage of the disease no bougie could be passed ; that the symptoms were of a very distressing nature : and he requested their opinion respecting the use of the caustic, or any other mode by which they thought he might obtain relief. These gentlemen subscribed their names to the following written opinion.

" That they had no mode of relief to recommend ; but that the application of caustic was a practice which they did not hesitate to condemn; since they thought *the* disease, bad as it might be, was more supportable than so violent an application, which must be productive of the worst consequences, both on the urethra and bladder."

This was their opinion, with which they were so well satisfied, that a number of facts, stated by a surgeon high in practice, higher in reputation, and unimpeached in veracity, had not sufficient weight to raise a doubt in their minds. This opinion, so *signed*, was afterwards put into my hands by the patient, who had the courage, notwithstanding this declaration, to submit to the use of the caustic; from which he received considerable benefit, without experiencing any of the dreadful effects they had so strongly predicted.

That practitioners should not hastily adopt a mode of practice of which they were afraid, and the effects of which they could not reconcile to the doctrines they had been taught, is natural and right; in justice to their patients, as well as to themselves, they were to wait till the practice was sufficiently established to authorize them in their acquiescence.

This is the line of conduct impartial men would naturally pursue; but to form an independent judgment requires more resolution than many possess; and to investigate an intricate disease demands more opportunities, as well as professional acquirements, than fall to the share of every practitioner.

To approve or condemn without a knowledge of the subject, must be the result of caprice or prejudice; by such prejudice Mr. Hunter's opinions have been too often estimated, and any opposition to which they were liable from this mode of judging, his natural warmth of temper, and want of knowledge of the world, made him ill qualified to avoid or to repel.

Mr. Hunter has been held out to the world, by his cotemporaries as a man of ingenuity, and of a speculative turn, who indulged himself in forming theories, and advancing opinions whose chief merit was their novelty and singularity. This character has been artfully applied, by affecting to give him a certain degree of credit, but in reality to take from his professional labours their full value, which arises from their being the result of deductions from facts, either developed in the progress of disease, or brought to light by experiments instituted for that purpose.

His real character was directly contrary to the representation above mentioned. So far from being of a turn for fanciful speculations, his mind was exclusively fitted for the investigation of practical and experimental truth ; he had ever an aversion to all hypothetical reasoning ; and in disquisitions of every kind, the only part that interested him was the authenticated facts which they contained. Hence it was, that he had little taste for works of imagination or poetry ; his attention being so much absorbed in considering the combination of the facts, that he overlooked the other beauties of the composition.

This turn for research formed the most prominent feature in the character of Mr. Hunter; it never left him; it never could be said even to be dormant, and he was always happy when allowed to indulge it. To this natural bent of his mind, the world is indebted for his uncommon exertions in promoting medical science, and extending experimental inquiries.

In the investigation of whatever engaged his attention, he not only formed no theory of his own, but even disregarded the observations of those who had preceded him; leaving his mind unbiassed, to make use of its own powers in considering the various facts from which his future observations and conclusions were to be drawn.

This mode of prosecuting medical inquiry, upon the model of the great Lord Verulam, which is seldom so strictly employed, required the genius and talents of a Hunter to insure its success. His education under his brother allowed him to lay in a stock of anatomical knowledge, and made him familiar with the changes its structure undergoes from different diseases; this formed a solid foundation for his future acquirements : his natural industry made him unwearied in his labours, and unremitting in his pursuits; and his zeal for improvement, which amounted to enthusiasm, supported him under the difficulties and disappointments, which in researches of that nature so frequently occur.

Anatomical and medical facts collected and registered by such a man must prove of infinite value; they are materials of which every one may avail himself, who is enaged in the same pursuits, independent of any opinions whatever. Some of his conclusions, from the fallacy of human reasoning, may prove erroneous : others, although just, may have been extended beyond their proper limits; but the facts themselves will remain, and in the course of progressive improvement, may materially assist in exploring those laws of the animal economy, both in health and disease, with which we are at present almost entirely unacquainted.

That part of Mr. Hunter's labours which is connected with the subject of the present observations, consists wholly of facts, nothing rests upon opinion, either with respect to the nature of the disease, or the mode of treatment.

In his works we have a detail of the symptons and appearances in the different stages of stricture in the urethra. Where the stricture was impervious to the bougie, he was led, from the nature of the obstruction, to see the inefficacy of that instrument; he therefore considered himself warranted in resorting to other means, and had recourse to the application of the argentum nitratum, or lunar caustic.

This mode of treatment he found, upon trial, capable of destroying the stricture, without doing any material mischief to the urethra; he made use of this application in a number of cases, and finding it successful, was led to adopt the practice, and lay it before the public.

These remarks have not been made from a wish to pass censure on those who differ in opinion from the late Mr. Hunter; but to do justice to his professional abilities, which although generally admired, are not sufficiently understood.

The consideration of being too nearly connected with him to be admitted as an impartial judge, has prevented me from going more at length into this subject; and the event of his death is still too recent to allow the passions and prejudices of his cotemporaries to have subsided, and his merits to be held in their due estimation.

When called upon to give a short account of his life, the same motives led me to confine it to bare facts, and simple events; reserving such observations as might be thought to rest upon opinion, to some more distant period. It would however, have been improper to offer to the public the remarks contained in the following pages, without having previously stated what Mr. Hunter had done on the subject, the additions he had made to our knowledge of the disease, and the improvement he had brought forward in the manner of treating it.

OF STRICTURES, &c.

CHAPTER I.

OF STRICTURES IN THE URETHRA.

IT is proposed in the following pages to consider the common mode of treating Strictures in the Urethra; to point out cases in which that method is not found to answer; and recommend a practice which, in those instances, affords a more favourable prospect of success.

It will be necessary, before it is attempted to fulfil any of these intentions, to explain the nature of the disease itself, and distinguish it into its different stages; that the principle upon which the mode of treatment depends may be the better understood.

Concerning the nature of this disease, much cannot be added to what has been published by the late Mr. Hunter; and it was originally my intention to have referred the reader to his work. This, however, upon consideration, appeared liable to many objections. There is an evident impropriety in not laying before the reader at one view, the observations and practical remarks, and the data from which they were deduced.

In explaining the nature of strictures, facts alone will be attended to, nor will any be noticed that have not come immediately within my own knowledge. If at the same time, cases recorded in Mr. Hunter's work are mentioned, they will be only those with which there was an opportunity of making myself perfectly acquainted.

SECTION I.

OF THE NATURE OF THE MEMBRANE OF THE URETHRA

THE internal membrane of the urethra in men, lines the canal, which is destined to carry two very different fluids, the urine and the semen, and in very different quantities. When the urine passes, the canal is large; when the semen is thrown out, it is small, the membrane having a power of adapting itself to these two different states; and this power of action within itself, is similar to muscular contraction and relaxtion.

It may be difficult, and perhaps impossible, to prove this membrane to be muscular, either from its appearance, or from examination of its texture; since the peculiar structure upon which the contraction of a muscle depends, has not as yet been ascertained. It may be sufficient to observe, that other structures, apparently membranous, and equally unlike the fasciculated fibrous texture commonly met with in muscles, are endowed with a power of contracting and relaxing, in a much greater degree than is ever found to take place in the membrane of the urethra. The Tænia hydatigenia ovalis, an animal consisting of a semi-transparent membranous bag, met with in the brain, liver, and omentum of sheep, when taken from its natural situation, and kept in warm water, contracts and relaxes the different parts of its bag to a considerable extent.*

That the membrane, which forms the lining of the urethra, does occasionally contract when irritated, may be illustrated by a variety of instances, both in health and disease. In hot weather, when the

* An account of this animal is given by the Author, in the Croonian Lecture, for the year 1790, and published in the First Part of the 85th Vol. of the Philos. Trans.

urine contains a large proportion of salts, more of the watery parts of the blood than usual being carried off by perspiration, the stream is rendered smaller than common, by the irritating quality of the urine producing a contraction in the internal membrane of the urethra. When a portion of this membrane is in an inflamed state from gonorrhœa, it is rendered so irritable that the urine passing over it, causes it to contract, and sometimes the urine comes away only in drops. In this state of the parts, if the penis be immersed in warm water, the membrane of the urethra frequently becomes relaxed, and the water is allowed to pass more freely. After the inflammation of gonorrhœa is gone off, and injections are used, with a view to stop the discharge; in many instances where the injection irritates the urethra to a great degree, so strong a contraction takes place in its internal membrane, that the injection is not only obstructed in its course, but is frequently forced back with a considerable degree of velocity.

C

SECTION II.

OF THE FORMATION OF STRICTURES.

THIS natural power of contraction, which has been explained in the last section, is common to the whole canal of the urethra, although probably not equally great in every part of it, and as the bladder is the only antagonist muscle, when the contracted state has once taken place, it must continue till counteracted by that viscus expelling its contents, and forcing open the passage.

This contraction and relaxation forms the natural and healthy actions of the urethra; but this membrane, like every other muscular structure, is liable to a spasmodic action, which produces a degree of contraction beyond the natural; and in that state the canal loses the power of relaxing till the spasm is removed. When this happens, it constitutes disease, and is termed a spasmodic stricture.

While a stricture is in this stage, it is only a wrong action of the membrane of the urethra; and if the parts could be examined, in their relaxed state, there would be no appearance of disease.

When a portion of the urethra is disposed to contract beyond its natural easy state, this disposition commonly increases till the part becomes incapable of falling back into a state of complete relaxation, and the canal remains always narrower at that part.

In this stage it is both a permanent stricture, and a spasmodic one. It is so far permanent, that it is always narrower than the rest of the canal; and so far spasmodic, that it is liable to contract occasionally in a still greater degree.

A stricture in the urethra, whether in the spasmodic or permanent state, is a contraction of the transverse fibres of the membrane, which forms that canal.

When this contraction is in a small

degrees, it appears, upon examination after death, to be simply a narrowing of the canal at that part ; but when the contraction is increased, it becomes a ridge projecting into the canal : this last is the appearance of what is understood by a permanent stricture.

The thickness of a stricture is a subject on which there are many different opinions, and some have supposed it to be of considerable extent. It is, however, commonly no more than the thickness of a single fold or doubling of the membrane of the urethra. The ridge which projects into the canal can only be a single fold, with the cellular membrane between the two portions ; it will become thicker as it approaches the side of the urethra.

This is the appearance the parts have exhibited in the cases examined after death, and my opportunities of seeing it have been so frequent, as to make me consider such contraction the most general cause of strictures.

There is a circumstance which readily accounts for the opinion of strictures being of some thickness; this is, two strictures forming within an inch of each other, and the space between them becoming narrower than the rest of the canal, although not so much so, as at either of the strictures. This is frequently met with.

The stricture is generally all round equally, the ridge projecting to the same distance, from every side of the urethra. It sometimes happens that it only projects from one side. Cases have occurred where there were three strictures, and all on the same side of the urethra, the other being perfectly smooth. This is a fact which cannot be ascertained after the canal is laid open in the dead subject, but is readily discovered in the living body, by passing a soft bougie through the stricture, which takes an exact impression of it.

In the first edition of this work, strictures were divided into spasmodic and permanent, to express two very different stages of this disease. It is now to be understood, that all permanent strictures which are not impervious, are capable of being more contracted at one time than another; so that a stricture having arrived at that stage which renders it permanent, does not prevent it from having also a spasmodic contraction. This, however, in many instances is in a less degree after the disease has been of some years continuance, than at a more early period; for we find patients who have been subject to occasional suppressions, afterwards entirely free from them, the disease in its encrease having rendered the parts more indolent, and therefore not so readily affected by accidental causes; but when the aperture in the stricture becomes very small, the occasional suppressions return, and become more serious.

SECTION III.

OF THE SITUATION OF STRICTURES.

As a necessary step towards ascertaining the situation of strictures in this canal, its natural size should be pointed out. This has not hitherto been done; it is therefore necessary to be more particular in my statement of the dimensions.

To determine with precision the length as well as width of the urethra, exact casts of it were taken in wax stretching it in the dead body as much as it would readily bear; in this way a bougie was formed of the size of the urethra. The subjects from which these casts were taken were of different ages, one was between 70 and 80, the other 30. In both of them the penis was of a small size, and the external orifice at the glans unusually small in the collapsed state.

The length of the canal cor-responded exactly in both casts. From the external orifice to the neck of the bladder was — 9* Inches.

From the external orifice to the bulb of the urethra — 7

The membranous part, extending from the bulb to the prostate gland $1\frac{1}{2}$

The canal passing over the pro-state gland — — $\frac{1}{2}$

The width of the urethra varies in different parts of the canal, and is every where much larger than had been supposed, exceeding the size of the largest bougie in use in a very great degree. It will make the diameters of the urethra in its several parts more clearly understood to contrast them with those of bougies.

The diameter of a common sized bougie — — — $\frac{4}{20}$ Inch.

Of the largest sized bougie in use. — — — $\frac{5}{20}$

* The canal in a relaxed state is in common about $8\frac{1}{4}$ inches long.

The diameters of the casts of the Urethra, in different parts.	years old. 80. 30.
At $\frac{3}{4}$ of an inch from the external orifice – – –	$\frac{9}{20}$ $\frac{7}{20}$ $\frac{1}{2}$
At $4\frac{1}{2}$ inches from the external orifice . – –	$\frac{7}{20}$ $\frac{7}{20}$
At the bulb of the urethra, 7 inches from the orifice –	$\frac{11}{20}$ $\frac{13}{20}$
In the membranous part, directly beyond the bulb, $7\frac{1}{2}$ inches from the orifice* – –	$\frac{7}{20}$ $\frac{4}{20}$
In the membranous portion near to the prostate gland, $8\frac{1}{4}$ inches from the orifice .–	$\frac{9}{20}$ $\frac{7}{20}$
Where the membraneous part terminates, and the prostate gland begins, $8\frac{1}{2}$ inches from the orifice	$\frac{7}{20}$ $\frac{6}{20}$
In the middle space of the prostate gland, $8\frac{3}{4}$ inches from the orifice – –	$\frac{11}{20}$ $\frac{10}{20}$
At the neck of the bladder, 9 inches from the orifice† –	$\frac{9}{20}$ $\frac{8}{20}$

* In the man 30 years of age there had been a stricture at this part.   † Vide Plate I. Fig. 1. and 2.

From these measurements the urethra appears not to be uniformly of the same width, and the narrowest part is $\frac{1}{20}$ of an inch wider in its diameter than the largest sized bougie. It is a fact of no small importance, that the two parts that are naturally the smallest are those most liable to stricture.

These dimensions are to be understood as much beyond those of the easy state of the urethra; they do not, however, exceed the size to which the canal is sometimes enlarged in the living body, when circumstances occur that require it. They give us a more extensive idea of the powers of contraction and relaxation possessed by this membrane, than has been commonly imagined.

Strictures occur most commonly just behind the bulb of the urethra; the distance from the external orifice being $6\frac{1}{2}$ or 7 inches; the situation next in order of frequency, is about $4\frac{1}{2}$ inches from the orifice of the glans ; they do occur at $3\frac{1}{2}$ inches, and sometimes almost close to the external orifice.

In some cases the external orifice itself is contracted; when this happens it is sometimes the source of considerable errors, since it misleads the surgeon, who supposes the whole canal to be naturally formed of the same size. When the orifice of the urethra has a pouting appearance, it is almost always in a contracted state, and appears smaller than it really is.

The prepuce is also very often contracted, which is called a natural phymosis ; this happens more frequently in those who are disposed to strictures than other men ; at least it is often met with in patients who have strictures.

In almost all the cases which have come under my care, there has been one stricture about 7 inches from the external orifice, whether there have been others or not; that part of this canal would therefore

appear to be much more disposed to contract than the rest of the urethra.

This is a fact long known, but could not
be accounted for till casts were made of
the urethra ; from them it is seen that there
is a natural contraction in the urethra, just
behind the bulb, probably intended to prevent the semen which is collected there
from passing back at the time the acceleratores urinæ' muscles are acting, to propel it
along the canal.

This particular part of the urethra in the
natural state has an uncommon degree of
irritability ; a proof of this is its being affected by blisters, and contracting spasmodically, so as to produce strangury. Whether the contraction is confined to that part,
or also takes place at the neck of the bladder,
it may be difficult to determine, but that
it is at that part, was ascertained in the
following case. A young gentleman in a
fever had a blister applied to the chest ; a
strangury came on. Under these circum-

stances a bougie passed readily $6\frac{1}{2}$ inches, but could not, although of a small size, be passed further; the strangury went off with the effects of the blister.

SECTION IV.

OF THE CAUSES OF STRTICTURES.

STRICTURES in the urethra have been generally considered to arise from some new formation of parts in the canal, in consequence of disease; and have been supposed to have their origin in a previously distempered state of the membrane, either from gonorrhœa itself, or the effects of some violent application made use of in the treatment of that disease.

From what has been said of the internal membrane of the urethra, it will appear evident that a constriction of any particular part of the canal, may be brought on by an unusual or preternatural degree of action in the membrane itself, without any new formation whatever; and therefore, when this is the case, the complaint may be considered as a diseased action of natural parts, which may be brought on by a variety of causes.

In some constitutions the natural disposition for contraction in this membrane, will be much stronger than in others, and in some may be so strong, as to take place at a very early age, and in consequence of a degree of irritation so slight as not to have been noticed.

An instance of this kind has occurred at ten years of age.

The stone is, in many instances, a cause of stricture; this happens sometimes in infancy. Cases of this kind are met with at six years old, and very frequently at a more advanced age, as will appear in the Cases.

As strictures of long standing put the bladder under the circumstances most favourable for the formation of stone, and stones are sometimes met with which appear to have had their origin from that cause, it might, at first view, be supposed, that wherever the two diseases are combined,

this had been the case. We might, however conclude, when the stricture is very
slight, and easily overcome, and the stone of
considerable size, that the stricture was the
effect, not the cause ; this is also strengthened, by the urethra in most patients who
have the stone, being in a very irritable
state, and readily affected by spasm.

There is reason to believe, that in many
instances the inflammation in the venereal
gonorrhœa is the cause of this complaint.
It appeared to have been so in the following
case.

A gentleman, twenty-five years of age,
who had resided many years in Spain, returned to this country, and almost immediately on his arrival contracted a gonorrhœa.
The urethra was extremely irritable ; the
inflammation very violent, and it extended
itself over the surface of the glans penis
and prepuce. Injections of milk and water
gave pain ; mercury disagreed with his constitution, bringing on heat, uneasiness, and
symptoms of general irritation, so that it

was left off. No local application that could be devised gave the smallest relief; even oil was unpleasant; but fresh cream was, by accident, discovered to have a soothing effect, and was the only thing used during the inflammatory stage, which lasted for three weeks. The discharge continued, and bark was given internally, but could not be persevered in, as it disagreed with the stomach. Steel also heated him. The balsam copaiva had the same effect: in short, no plan that was tried seemed to answer; they were therefore all given up.

Two months after, the discharge still continued; and upon passing a bougie it was discovered that a stricture had formed near the bulb of the urethra, which readily yielded to the use of the bougie; and in two months more the patient recovered.

There are so many instances where the symptoms of stricture have been immediately preceded by a severe gonorrhœa, from the effect of which the membrane had never recovered, that there has long been

D

little doubt in my own mind of gonorrhœa
being a very general cause of strictures.   It
may be remarked, that when this has been
the case, the venereal imflammation has not
been confined to the space near the glans,
which is most commonly the seat of it, but
has extended itself along the canal, and
brought on a great degree of irritation in
the membranous part of the urethra ; which
has probably given a disposition to the
canal at that part to form stricture. This
opinion is corroborated by a gentleman
who has had a high situation, for sixteen
years, in the Maratta army in the East
Indies, and who, from being entirely do-
mesticated among the natives, had ample
opportunities of gaining accurate knowledge upon this subject. He assures me,
that three-fourths of the natives of rank are
troubled with strictures, which is entirely
attributed to the effects of gonorrhœa, for
the cure of which no local applications are
in use. There prevails, however, a strange
depravity among the natives in India,

which may justly be considered as disposing the parts to form strictures. This
is toying with women, and prolonging the
venereal act for a very unnatural length of
time ; taking medicines which are supposed
to contribute to the possibility of that continuance. That keeping the parts in such
a state for a very great length of time, must
bring on irritation is self-evident, and the
frequent repetition of such acts must dispose
them for spasmodic affections, the fore-
runner of strictures. The extent to which
this strange abuse is carried among the
native Indians, is such as could not be
believed without the strongest testimony.

An improper indulgence in venereal pleasures, by which is to be understood a more
frequent repetition of that act than the
parts are able fully to accomplish, is in
Europe productive of great irritation, even
where there is no stricture ; and when that
disease has previously taken place, often
brings on suppression of urine. Are we to
wonder then at its producing much more

D 2

serious consequences in the irritable, debilitated constitutions of the natives of a hot climate, whose excesses in pleasures of this kind fill up a principal part of their time?

It is necessary to observe, that in warm climates strictures, as well as all other spasmodic diseases, are much more readily brought on than in Europe, the climate disposing the parts to fall into such actions.

Injections have been charged with being the cause of strictures; how far this is true it may be difficult to determine. For as a stricture frequently comes on after a gonorrhœa, where no injection has been used, its appearance after a gonorrhœa cured by injection, cannot amount to a proof that this application contributed to the effect. It appears, however, highly probable, that where there is a disposition for stricture, injections may increase it; and the following case is one of those which have tended to give currency to that opinion.

A gentleman from the West Indies

twenty-three years of age, had a gonorrhœa, the symptoms of which were by no
means severe ; an injection of saccharum
saturni, in the proportion of a scruple to
eight ounces of water, was used, and made
stronger as the symptoms abated : the discharge, however, continued, and after trying
the bark, the balsam copaiva, and using the
cold bath, for three months, without the
smallest benefit, on passing a bougie, it was
found that a stricture had formed near the
bulb of the urethra ; this was dilated by
the use of the bougies.

Since the first edition of this work was
published a number of cases of stricture
have come under my care, that were considered by the patients themselves, to be
the immediate effects of injections ; in many
of these it might be attributed to prejudice,
and therefore it was improper to draw
any conclusions from them. However, two
or three instances have occurred where
from using injections less diluted than they
ought to have been, the irritation was almost

immediate, in the middle of the canal, where the injection stopped ; and the formation of a stricture in that part, which is not commonly the seat of the original disease, could be actually traced to the use of the injection. The internal membrane had become thickened in consequence of inflammation forming a swelling, which was felt externally through the common integuments.

These instances, which do not admit of a doubt, led me to pay more attention to this subject, and induced me to believe, that many of the accounts before discredited, were not unworthy of attention. In those cases of stricture, attributed to injections, it is to be observed, that the application had generally given unusual pain, and brought on an irritation in the membranous part of the urethra, or at the neck of the bladder, as it is more commonly termed ; which proved both tedious and troublesome before it could be removed.

That injections injudiciously used, have

in some individual cases disposed the canal to stricture, is supported by facts beyond the reach of controversy. There is, therefore, in all irritable habits, some danger of an injection producing this effect; since whenever the strength of the injection is greater than the membrane of the urethra in that person can bear, which cannot be *a priori* ascertained, a state of irritation is the consequence.

The idea that injections do sometimes produce strictures, and that we are unable beforehand to determine in what cases they may be used with impunity, have induced me entirely to forego their use in the treatment of gonorrhœa, rather than incur a risk, however small it may be, of producing so seriously distressing a complaint.

That no specific complaint is necessary to bring on stricture, cannot be more strongly proved than by cases in which it has arisen from accidental violence, even when applied to the external parts. Of this two

instances were immediately under my own
observation, and several others, have been
stated to me. That any violence com—
mitted upon the perinæum brings on a
suppression of urine, is a fact requiring no
proof : but as this effect may by many be
referred to inflammation of the neck of the
bladder, rather than stricture in the urethra,
the following account of a case of this kind,
in which there was an opportunity of examining the parts after death, and ascertaining the nature of the obstruction, will
shew that it was exactly similar to the
strictures commonly met with.

A. B. a seaman, aged about thirty, in
stowing the hold of a ship of war, received
a violent blow upon the loins from a piece
of wood, which knocked him down, and he
fell upon the edge of a cask which passed
between his thighs, and struck him on the
perinæum. For some time he was insensible, and when he got up, the parts were
exceedingly swelled, and he was for several
months unable to make water without first

using the warm bath. An enlargement and hardness continued upon the whole perinæum, from the time of the accident. He continued in this state for a considerable time, and at last grew something better, passing matter with his urine, and having a violent straining to make water, which continued till the bladder was completely emptied.

After four years had elapsed, he was re-received into the Royal Naval Hospital at Plymouth, at which time he was exceedingly reduced, and had great difficulty in making water, constantly straining, and being in the greatest agonies on every attempt. When he became my patient, he never made more water than a tea-spoonful at a time.

A bougie stopped at seven inches from the external orifice, the catheter stopped at the same place; and from that part the whole perinæum was swelled and hard: the bladder also was distended and enlarged, and reached nearly to the navel. He was put into the warm bath, where he staid above a quarter of an hour, and a catheter was again attempted to be passed, but with no better success.

In about a quarter of an hour he felt something come away, and the urine continued to pass, till he was quite fatigued, in a small stream, in all about three pints. After this, he felt very much relieved, and slept that night exceedingly well; next day, however, he was obliged to strain as before, without bringing any thing away.

He took the Canada balsam and æther; but rather got worse, from not having his water drawn off.

The day following, being the 10th of August, he was no better, and took an opening medicine, which relieved him much; and he passed some water, without straining very violently through the day.

12th. He was much worse; went into the bath, but was not relieved by it; remained exceedingly weak and exhausted, and died on the following day.

After death the body was examined and

a stricture was found about seven inches
from the external orifice, which rendered
the canal nearly impervious at that part.
Its thickness did not exceed the tenth of an
inch ; ulceration had taken place over the
whole surface, between the stricture and the
bladder, without having formed a passage
outwards at any one part. The stricture, in
its appearance, was exactly similar to those
found in other cases.

Strictures may be caused by any irritation
which affects the membrane of the urethra.
Blisters in some instances produce them ;
of which the following case is an instance.

A gentleman, sixty years of age, has an
irritable stricture at seven inches, which
has been very troublesome for seven years,
attended with frequency in making wa·er,
a discharge of mucus from the bladder, and
occasionally pain in the perinæum. He
was free from complaint in these parts till
forty years of age, when he was attacked
at Bristol by a fever, in which he was de-
lirious for seven days ; during that period

he was blistered on several different parts of his body, so as to be a whole week under the influence of blisters.   When he came to himself, he found a very violent irritation at the neck of the bladder, and in the perinæum ; this continued very severely for a year, after which it diminished, but did not go off; for the next year it was less violent. At the end of two years the constant uneasiness subsided ; but from that time, upon riding, drinking freely, or any exertion, he has been subject to occasional returns ; and for the last seven years has had a permanent stricture.   A surgeon whom he consulted, told him, that he himself, when a boy at Westminster school, had an irritation in the urethra, brought on in consequence of the effects of a blister, which lasted several years.

When once a stricture is formed in the membranous part of the canal, it produces two effects; it renders the urethra in general more irritable ; and it prevents all that portion of it between the stricture already formed and the external orifice, from being dilated to its usual extent; and consequently deprives it of its natural healthy actions. Under these circumstances it becomes more disposed to the formation of strictures.

This is so much the case, that when the original stricture, at seven inches, has been of long standing, there is almost always another formed about an inch further on, in the anterior part of the urethra, and too often a third, about three inches from the external orifice. Whenever strictures are met with in these situations, there is reason therefore to consider them as the consequences of one which has been formed for a longer time, nearer the bladder.

SECTION V.

LOCAL SYMPTOMS OF STRICTURE.

In the commencement of the disease, a stricture in the urethra is seldom discovered; the only symptom it produces being a diminution of the stream of urine, which cannot be ascertained, unless the patient has before attended to the natural size of that stream, which is hardly ever the case.

The disease is therefore unknown, till the expulsion of the urine is attended with difficulty, and this seldom happens till the contraction has been of some standing, and has made considerable progress; but when the mind of the patient has once taken the alarm, and the nature of the complaint is explained, he becomes enabled to recollect several circumstances, to which he had not before attended, and to trace the disease nearly to its origin.

According to information, in this manner collected, the first progress of the contraction is in general very slow ; but when once it has so far increased, that the urethra is not wholly relaxed by the force of the urine, its subsequent advances are more rapid, and new symptoms are perceived. The urine is voided more frequently, does not pass without a considerable effort, attended with pain, and a straining continues after the bladder is emptied. If the patient accidentally catches cold, drinks a glass of spirituous liquor, acid beverage, or punch, commits an excess in drinking wine, or removes quickly from a warm to a cold climate, the urine will perhaps pass only in drops, or be entirely obstructed ; these causes inducing, in the contracted part, a spasmodic action, by which it is closed. Cold externally applied to the body, has so great an effect upon spasmodic stricture, that a patient who can make water without the smallest difficulty in a warm room, upon attempting it in the open air, shall be entirely unable to pass a drop; but even under this difficulty, if he return to a warm room, and sit some little time, the urine shall flow as before. It is a curious fact, that the symptoms of stricture are more frequently brought on when the patient is living a sedentary life than an active one : of this there is a variety of instances.

When these last symptoms occur, and a stricture has not been known previously to exist, the disease is not unfrequently mistaken for an inflammation on the neck of the bladder, and treated accordingly; but the symptoms not yielding to internal medicines, and an absolute necessity arising to draw off the water, the attempt to perform that operation by a catheter, discovers their true cause.

In this stage of a stricture, it is very liable to be affected by an action of the parts, which is very little suspected. When this happens, both the patient and surgeon are misled, and the disease is very improperly treated.

The action alluded to, is that which takes place in the membrane of the urethra during copulation, to reduce the size of the canal, and fit it for throwing out the semen with the necessary velocity ; in doing which it sometimes also increases the stricture. This does not, however, often happen, unless the action of the coitus is repeated two or three times, at short intervals, or when the act itself is lengthened beyond the common period.

Under these circumstances, the membrane is kept longer in a state of contraction, and the part disposed to stricture loses the power of relaxing again; the passage is not completely closed but very much narrowed at this part, and remains in an extremely tender state, so that it is irritated by the urine passing through it, and in a few hours a discharge of matter comes on, similar to that from gonorrhœa. In some instances, and those not a few, the contraction is so great as altogether to stop the emission of semen, and force it back

E

into the bladder : in others, it passes through
the stricture, after the orgasm has taken
place, but with little or no force.

A gentleman in the act of copulation felt,
at the instant the emission should have taken
place, considerable darting pain in the urethra, and found afterwards a few drops of
blood upon his linen. About an hour after,
he had occasion to make water, and in preparing to do so, the semen which should
have been emitted, appeared upon his shirt
in considerable quantity.

When consulted upon the cause of such
very unusual and distressing circumstances,
the patient was informed that there must
be a stricture in the urethra, which alone
could explain what had happened. This
he was inclined to doubt, as he made
water very well ; but upon passing a bougie
an obstruction was met with, just beyond
the bulb of the urethra ; and upon allowing
the bougie to remain, with a slight pressure
against the stricture, for a few minutes, it
was capable of being passed on to the bladder.

The discharge and pain in making water brought on under the circumstances above mentioned, at a time when no previous disease is known to exist, and most commonly after a connection between the sexes, which leaves a suspicion of infection, are naturally concluded to be the symptoms of gonorrhœa; from which, however, they will be found to differ very materially. They come on a few hours after the connection; the degree of inflammation is very slight; the discharge is the first symptom, which is more violent at the commencement than at any other period. The inflammation, after remaining a few days, begins to subside, leaving nothing but the discharge, and that also frequently disappears in five or six days, whether any means are employed or not for its removal. The course of these symptoms differs so much from that which takes place in gonorrhœa, that if the attention of the surgeon is called to it, there is little danger of his being mistaken in his opinion.

E 2

The mistake is however sometimes made, and not only with impunity, but even greatly to the credit of the surgeon, raising him high in the opinion of his patient, for his skill in curing gonorrhœa ; yet the mistake is sometimes attended with serious consequences ; for the use of strong injections, with a view to stop the discharge, brings on in particular cases, a state of irritation, which is carried to an alarming height, and continues for a considerable time.

The circumstance which has in the greatest degree tended to make strictures mistaken for gonorrhœa, is that the pain in making water is confined to the same spot in both diseases, which it is impossible for patients to comprehend. They understand the seat of gonorrhœa, and therefore naturally consider any pain in that part as a proof of gonorrhœa being present.

The fact is, that a stricture in the membranous part of the urethra does not render the part itself uncommonly sensible, but all the painful sensations are felt an inch and a half from the orifice of the glans penis. This does not happen in particular cases, but is a general fact : whether this is to be accounted for from the nerves that are spread over the canal terminating there, or from a sympathy between the parts, it may be difficult, at present to decide. It will, however, be rendered less surprising than it otherwise might be, when it is compared with the symptoms of stone in the bladder; in that disease there is a burning pain in the glans penis, without any part of the canal of the urethra having much unusual sensation.

The pain in the seat of gonorrhœa is so common a symptom of stricture, that in several letters of consultation from the country, the patient states that he has a stricture several inches down the canal, but there is also an ulcer an inch an half down, which must be cured previous to the removal of the stricture.

This fact appears to me so well established, that if in passing the bougie to ascertain the real state of the urethra, a great degree of unusual tenderness is felt when the bougie passes over that part ; that circumstance alone, leads me to conclude that there is a stricture in the canal further on ; and do not recollect to have met with an instance to the contrary. The following case explains the similarity of the symptoms of stricture to those of gonorrhœa.

A gentleman, seventy years old, had a connection with his own servant maid, of whom he had no cause of suspicion, respecting infection ; but finding in the morning, a discharge and pain in making water, in the usual seat of gonorrhœa, he concluded it to be venereal, and applied for assistance to a surgeon, eminent in that branch of surgery, and under his treatment found himself perfectly well in a week. He now ventured upon a second connection, and in the morning had a return of his complaint : upon which he applied to me, relating all the circumstances, to know if his case could be venereal. There was no difficulty on my part in declaring, that neither of the complaints had been so, but had been occasioned by a stricture, which upon examination proved to be the case; and the stricture, although it had never been discovered, was so far advanced as to require the use of the bougie for several months, to dilate the passage to its natural size.

When the stricture is in a more advanced stage, the contraction has so established itself, that at all times the seat of the stricture is much narrower than the rest of the canal. The strictured part still, however, possesses the power of contracting and relaxing; in the contracted state, closing up the passage; in the relaxed state, allowing the urine to pass through it in a small stream. In this state the stream is so small, and the exertion necessary to empty the bladder so great, that the patient can seldom be wholly ignorant of his complaint.

The spasmodic contraction is very great, and acts with considerable force. This is known by the urine being unable to pass in a stream, and a small bougie, which, in a

relaxed state of the urethra met with no resistance, can scarcely be passed through
it ; and, if allowed to remain for a few minutes, is not unfrequently grasped so tight
by the spasmodic contraction, that when it
is attempted to be withdrawn, some force
is required to overcome it. The bougie,
when examined, puts on an appearance
exactly resembling what would have been
produced if a piece of packthread had been
tied round it. In this stage the spasmodic
contractions, although more violent, occur
less frequently than while the stricture was
in a more recent state. When the stricture
has been of some years standing, the bladder becomes thickened in its coats, to increase its power of expelling the urine,
which is rendered more difficult by this
obstruction ; the bladder in this thickened
state does not admit of the usual dilatation,
so that the patient at all times makes water
frequently, every three or four hours, if not
oftener. He is unable to go through the
night without once or twice making water.

An inquiry into this circumstance often leads to a knowledge of the disease. Besides the symptoms of stricture which have been taken notice of, and which occur in the more common cases of this disease, being the immediate effects of mechanical obstruction to the urine, there are others, both local and constitutional, arising from peculiarities in different patients, which are equally deserving of attention.

One very common symptom of stricture is nocturnal emissions; and there are patients who have no other cause of complaint, neither pain in making water, nor discharge from the urethra, and upon examination by a bougie, a stricture has been met with, the removal of which has carried off this complaint. In such cases the stricture had no disposition to spasm, and the patient, while awake, was insensible of any disease : but when asleep, the diseased state of the urethra conveyed sensation to the mind, at a time when the other parts in health did not; and the effect of this sensation was dreams respecting the actions in which those organs are usually employed.

In very irritable patients there is, in the seat of the stricture, in [the membranous part of the urethra, a variety of unusual sensations, conveying to the mind the idea of something in motion; and thus have enquired " if it were possible that a maggot could " have been crawling there ?" Some have compared it to the fluttering of a bird. This sensation has been removed with the stricture.

In many cases of stricture there is a periodical discharge, brought on by cold, or any occasional cause; when this comes on, the inflammation extends to the bladder, the frequency of making water is very much increased, and the urine very turbid; it is voided for twelve or twenty-four hours, once an hour, or even twice in that period; and when allowed to stand, it deposits a substance in the form of powder, not very unlike common hair powder, and is made up of coagulable lymph in that form. This is the slightest kind of attack, and it very seldom stops there; sometimes the bladder is inflamed in a greater degree, and secretes from its inner membrane matter or pus, which passes out after the urine. When the irritation on the bladder is prolonged, or the attack more violent, the discharge is glary, and like the white of an egg; it is so adhesive, that after it has stood some time in the pot, it is scarcely possible to separate it. This glary discharge is the vitiated secretion of the prostate gland; it was discovered to be so in the examination of the parts after death; for while one part floated in the bladder, it could be traced to its origin in the ducts of the prostate gland. It is produced by the inflamed state of the coverings of the prostate gland, brought on by the pressure of the urine upon those parts in the necessary efforts of the bladder to discharge it.

This discharge of pus and gelatinous mucus, have been considered as the symptoms of an ulcer, or a calculus in the bladder; they are, however, by no means peculiar to such causes; they arise from any irritation in the bladder, and are met with very frequently in cases of strictures of long standing. When the bladder is attacked in this way, from stricture, the urine loses its natural smell, and acquires a peculiar flavour; it has a faint smell, in a slight degree similar to the odour communicated to the urine from eating asparagus. This is often a first symptom of the attack, coming on some days before the discharge from the bladder takes place.

These symptoms, when they increase to a very great degree, bring on inflammation upon the peritonæum lining the abdomen, and the patient is carried off.

In two cases this has taken place. As there is no immediate communication between the bladder and abdomen, this effect must arise from sympathy.

A stricture in this state, as it impedes the passage of the urine every time an attempt is made to evacute it, increases also the action of the bladder, in proportion to this resistance. A constant irritation is thus kept up in the stricture, by which it acquires a stronger disposition to contract; in this way the canal is gradually diminished, and, in some uncommon cases, is rendered impervious at that part.

As the evacuation of urine is necessary for carrying on the functions of life, this last stage, or complete obstruction, cannot take place without destroying the patient, unless another outlet is formed; complete strictures are, therefore, only met with where fistulæ in perinæo have previously been produced. By their means an artificial passage is formed for the urine; but it is in general so imperfect, as only to diminish, and not to remove, the irritation at the stricture.

SECTION VI.

CONSTITUTIONAL SYMPTOMS OF STRICTURE.

As a stricture is entirely a local disease, it may not appear capable of producing particular effects on the constitution, and it is natural to suppose, that any derangement of the general system which occurs is only accidental, not immediately connected with the local complaint. We find, however, in practice, that there are constitutional symptoms which very frequently take place in this disease, and these are no longer met with after the stricture is removed.

The most common symptom of this kind is a complete paroxysm of fever ; the rigor, or cold fit is extremely severe, agitating the whole body, and shaking the bed upon which the patient is laid with great violence ; this is followed by a hot fit, and afterwards a very profuse perspiration breaks out, the sweat is so profuse as to require several changes of linen before it goes off; the shivering lasts from fifteen minutes to an hour; the hot fit continues sometimes several hours, and the perspiration is also two or three hours before it ceases.

It very often happens that the first paroxysm is imperfect, and in the course of a few hours it is followed by a much more violent one, which completes the attack; so that, when the sweating fit of the first paroxysm is very copious, there is seldom a second; but if it is not, there will most commonly be another. In some instances the shivering is not accompanied with the sensation of cold. Sickness and retching generally take place in the cold fit. During this paroxysm, when the most severe, there is a frequency in making water, but seldom a strangury.

This attack differs from common ague, in the violence of the perspiration, which is in general much beyond what is met with in agues; the fits do not return at the same periods, and seldom more than twice.

This symptom is exceedingly common in warm climates, as in the East Indies, the West Indies, and Spain; but very rarely occurs in patients who have resided entirely in cold climates, although it is sometimes to be met with.

In those climates, when it has occurred, attended with frequency in making water, the constitutional affection has always been considered as the primary disease, and the irritable state of the bladder only as a symptom. A patient has been under my care, who for three years had this constitutional symptom of stricture, in the West Indies, which was treated in that country as an irregular ague. But not finding himself relieved, he came to this country; and it was discovered that he had strictures in the urethra, upon the removal of which, the ague disappeared, without the use of any internal medicine.

This symptom is brought on by exposure to cold, more than by any other cause; it may, however, be produced by any other acts of imprudence, as excess of fatigue, or eating and drinking so as to disorder the bowels. It is also an effect of passing a bougie, or applying the caustic.

This rigor, which so commonly occurs in cases of strictures of long standing, appears to arise from a sympathetic connection between the bladder and stomach; and, in some instances, the stomach alone is affected, without producing the rigor, and the patient has sickness and vomiting. In one instance this was mistaken for a symptom of gout; there had been several different attacks of this kind, one every two or three months, and the last, which was the most violent, brought on inflammation upon the bowels, and the patient died.

In particular people, more especially those who have been in warm climates, strictures produce an irritable uneasy state of stomach; this, in one case, came on

F

every night on going to bed, and continued several hours. It returned in this way for twelve years, and, upon the stricture being removed, went off. This state of stomach is accompanied with a degree of general irritation, quick pulse, loss of appetite, white tongue, thirst, heat in the skin, and restlessness, both at the time, and for some hours after the attack in the stomach goes off. In several cases, this state of irritation occurs without the stomach being particularly affected: it has been mistaken for nervous fever, and treated as such for a considerable time, without benefit : but upon removing the stricture it went off.

Inflammation of the tonsils and fauces, in two instances, came on periodically, at the times when the bladder was in a state of irritation, and went off when it returned to its easy state. One of these attacks was suspected to be venereal ; but it went away altogether upon the removal of the stricture.

CHAPTER II.

OF DISEASES WHOSE SYMPTOMS RESEMBLE THOSE OF STRICTURE.

As some of the symptoms of stricture are situated in the canal of the urethra, others in the bladder, any disease which affects either of these parts, may produce symptoms in some respects similar to those of stricture, and mislead the judgment of the surgeon. To render such mistakes less frequent, it is proposed to consider the diseases whose symptoms bear the greatest resemblance to those of strictures, and to point out the means by which they may be distinguished. An irritable state of the urethra, and an irritable state of the bladder, are of this kind. Diseased enlargement of the prostate gland is often mistaken for stricture ; but, on the other hand, strictures are much more commonly mistaken for affections of the prostate gland ;

on both these accounts it becomes necessary to explain the peculiar symptoms of each.

The stone, as it produces an irritable state of the bladder and urethra, has symptoms in common with strictures; but there are, at the same time, many peculiar to the stone, and any doubt that may arise can be removed by sounding the bladder. It therefore becomes unnecessary to say any thing upon that disease.

Ulcers in the urethra, and caruncles, were, till very lately, generally considered as causes of obstruction; and capable of producing all the symptoms of stricture. This opinion is still supported by many practitioners: which leads me to make some observations upon these supposed impediments to the urine.

SECTION I.

OF THE SYMPTOMS OF AN IRRITABLE STATE OF THE URETHRA.

THE membrane of the urethra is upon many occasions liable to have its natural actions disturbed, and rendered irregular; when this happens to any particular part, it is in many patients communicated over the whole canal : this sometimes follows upon the discharge being checked in the early stage of gonorrhœa, by means of irritating injections, and lasts for weeks; at the end of which period, there is little or no abatement; afterwards it may perhaps quite suddenly go off. This, though it differs in many respects from the common effects of inflammation, and does not give the same kind of pain to the patient, may be considered as a slighter degree of inflammation.

The readiness with which the natural actions of the membrane of the urethra are disturbed by slight causes, will be best understood by stating the effect produced on that canal by the influence of the mind.

If a person of much sensibility has had a suspicious connection, as sometimes happens, while in a state of intoxication, upon coming to his recollection of the past, he takes the alarm of having received an infection; the state of mind sometimes actually produces a number of painful sensations, and shooting pains in the membrane of the urethra; all which go off as soon as the time is elapsed in which he can suspect any danger of gonorrhœa.

This effect is so common, that multitudes must have experienced something like it; but the degree is ever proportioned to the state of mind. In one instance of a young gentleman, whose situation was of a delicate nature, and whose feelings led him to consider that his being discovered to have such a complaint might be absolute ruin to all his future prospects, the symptoms that were brought on by his apprehensions were so violent, as to deprive him of rest for several nights ; not from mental reflections only, but from the painful sensations in the urethra, attended with fever; all which were abated by opium. The truth was, that no infection had been communicated, and in a little time the alarming symptoms altogether ceased.

This irritable state of the canal, when it is the consequences of gonorrhœa, in many instances produces all the symptoms of stricture. There is a discharge of matter, a pain in making water, an irritation in emitting the semen, and the urine passess with difficulty, and only in a small stream.

The difficulty in this case differs from that met with in stricture; for although there is some exertion required, and the stream is small when the water begins to flow, the difficulty gradually decreases, and the stream becomes larger before one half of the urine has been evacuated, and afterwards as large as usual, which does not happen in cases of stricture.

These symptoms occasionally abate, and even go off, but after connection with women, return again ; so that the history of the symptoms may correspond with those of strictures, and nothing but an examination by the bougie can distinguish them; and still if the examination be imprudently made, it may confirm the deception.

Patients frequently consult me on account of symptoms not in the least suspected to arise from stricture ; and when the nature of the disease has been ascertained by examination, they have expressed their astonishment at what appeared to them so extraordinary a discovery.

On the other hand, in a variety of instances, the complaints had been previously decided upon as strictures; and yet upon examination they proved only to be irritable urethras. Some of the most remarkable cases of this last kind will now be mentioned.

CASE I.

An irritable State of the Urethra mistaken for
Stricture.

A gentleman who consulted me for some
symptoms supposed to arise from stricture,
confessed that he had, from a boy, a great
sensibility in the lining of the urethra, which
he thought was natural, and therefore had
taken no notice of it, till after a gonorrhœa,
when it had so much increased as to give
him considerable alarm, and had never afterwards gone entirely off. He had occasionally a discharge like a gleet, always a small
stream of urine, often a frequency in making it; and these symptoms were brought
on or increased after having connection
with women. Upon passing a full sized
bougie, the canal was found of the natural
size, but in a very irritable state.

CASE II.

An irritable State of the Urethra mistaken for Stricture.

A gentleman with an irritable urethra, consulted his surgeon on account of the following symptoms; a discharge from the urethra, and pain in making water. A bougie of a small size was passed, which met with an obstruction at six inches from the external orifice; this was considered by the surgeon as a stricture, and the use of the caustic was recommended. The gentleman was a little afraid of this mode of treatment, and wished to consult me before it was adopted. On passing a full sized bougie it went readily into the bladder. By this means it was discovered that the former bougie, from the smallness of its point, had stopped at the curve of the canal, which led to the opinion of there being a stricture; and had nearly been productive of a very improper mode of treatment.

CASE III.

An irritable State of the Urethra mistaken for Stricture.

A gentleman who had a deficiency in his powers with respect to women, at an earlier age than he thought he had reason to experience it, consulted a surgeon of character; who passed a small bougie, and met with an obstruction at the curve of the urethra. He explained to the patient that the complaint was a stricture, and put him on a course of bougies; these the patient passed himself daily for three months without benefit, not being able to get into the bladder. The patient had heard of the treatment by caustic, and mentioned it to his surgeon, who declined adopting it, which induced him to consult me. To make myself master of the case, a full sized bougie, of a very soft composition, was passed, which stopped at the curve of the urethra; and when it was withdrawn, the end had a fairly rounded appearance, except on the lower surface, which had a small projection, not thicker than a knitting needle, that appeared to have gone for one tenth of an inch into a hole. This led me to believe that there was no stricture; but that the point of the small bougie had been stopped by some little irregularity, and by repeated applications, had made a way through the internal membrane. To ascertain the true state of the parts, a flexible gum catheter of the full size was used, with a stilet which had previously the curve of the canal given to it, so that the end might not be caught upon any irregularity on the lower surface of the urethra.* This instrument went without any obstruction into the bladder, and the water passed through it.

In this way it was ascertained that there was not the smallest obstruction in the urethra, only an irregularity on the lower surface; and upon inquiry it was found that

* See Plate II. which represents the curve of the urethra.

he retained his water during the whole night, made it in a full stream, and had only a slight irritation in the canal, which was encreased by the use of the bougie.

His principal complaint was a diminution of his powers respecting women, which he had attributed, without reason, to a complaint in the urethra.

CASE IV.

An irritable State of the Urethra mistaken for Stricture.

A gentleman twenty-three years of age, while living in the country, had an irritation in the urethra, and the urine passed in a small stream. The surgeon who was consulted introduced a small catgut bougie, which went along with difficulty, and stopped at the neck of the bladder. From this examination it was decided that he had a stricture, if not several, and an enlarged prostate gland.

This, to a very nervous man, increased all the symptoms, and he came to London to consult me.   In stating his case, he mentioned the small stream of urine, inability to pass the semen, and pain and uneasiness in the perinæum.   A full sized bougie, passed with ease into the bladder.   This proved that there was no stricture, and no enlargement of the prostate gland, as the canal at that part had its usual curve.   The whole of the complaints had their origin in the piles ; which in this particular instance had brought on considerable irritation upon all the neighbouring parts, but particularly the urethra.— After this explanation he had a connection, and found the semen was emitted without irritation or difficulty ; so that a great part of the symptoms appeared to be brought on merely by agitation of mind.

SECTION II.

OF THE SYMPTOMS OF AN IRRITABLE STATE OF THE BLADDER.

THERE is such a connection between the bladder and the urethra, they sympathize so readily with each other, in their natural actions, and the diseases of the one have so great an influence upon the other, that there is scarcely any complaint to which the urethra is liable, that does not more or less derange the functions of the bladder; and on the other hand, the diseases of the bladder produce uneasy sensations and morbid actions in the urethra.

The bladder is not only rendered irritable by strictures in the urethra, diseases of the prostate gland, and calculous concretions contained within its cavity, but it is very frequently diseased without any apparent connection with these causes; and as the

irritable state of the inner membrane of
that viscus must produce in some measure
the same symptoms, in whatever way it is
brought on, it will require some discern-
ment to distinguish this complaint from
strictures.

The diseased state of the inner membrane of the bladder, by producing spasmodic actions in the urethra, may be mistaken for stricture; and this mistake is by
no means uncommon in practice.

The disease of the bladder which most
commonly occurs, is a thickening of its
coats; the muscular coat does not relax,
or admit of the usual extension, and consequently the inner membrane is thrown
into rugæ; these are also thickened, and
have not their natural, soft and membranous
texture; they are at the same time extremely sensible to any pressure that is
made upon them.

Whether the disease originates in the
muscular coat or internal membrane it
may be difficult to determine; it is, how-

ever, most probably in the inner membrane, which from its situation is much exposed to irritation, and upon many occasions liable to inflammation.

This inflammation of the internal membrane of the bladder may take place from any irritating substance passing into its cavity, or it may arise from the urethra, by contiguity of parts; it does not unfrequently happen in both ways, and when it has once taken place, it leaves that viscus liable to future attacks, from much slighter causes than were necessary to bring it on at first.

In many instances of severe gonorrhœa, the inflammation is found to extend to the bladder, and to produce a great degree of irritation for a considerable time. It sometimes does occur from the effects of injection, and oftener than we are willing to believe. The following case is an instance of this kind.

G

CASE I.

Irritable Bladder from the Use of Injection.

A gentleman, thirty-four years of age had a gonorrhœa six months ago; for this complaint he made use of an in—jection, with the composition of which he was unacquainted; it stopped the discharge for which it was employed; but almost im—mediately brought on an irritation upon the bladder, which has continued ever since. The attacks are periodical, with short in—tervals; sometimes of a week, at others only a few days. The symptoms are an uneasy feel in the region of the bladder, extending at times into the neighbouring parts, but principally felt directly behind the os pubis. A pain runs along the urethra to the glans, and in that part is very severe. There is a straining after making water, attended with pain, which goes off in a few minutes. In the urine there are small portions of coagulating lymph in the form of flakes and threads. The urine is voided more frequently than in health. These symptoms for the first three months were very severe, they are now less violent, and appear to be gradually going off.

Two months ago, a full sized bougie passed readily into the bladder ; and he had been sounded by another surgeon, who had felt nothing hard in the bladder. From this investigation, it could neither be stricture nor stone that caused the irritation. The prostate gland is in a natural state ; so that the disease must be confined to the inner coat of the bladder, which had suffered so much from the irritating effects of the injection, as to be inflamed, and to produce all the symptoms that have been mentioned.

Similar effects of an injection, but in a much more violent degree, are taken notice of in the 3d section of the 5th chapter of this work, in a case of stone adhering to the bladder.

CASE II.

Irritable Bladder from Injection.

A gentleman twenty-six years of age, in September, 1786, immediately after having returned from India, caught a gonorrhœa, which was treated in the common way, by using an injection of saccharum saturni diluted in water. The discharge suddenly disappeared three days after this treatment was commenced, and a violent pain was felt in the perinæum, a frequency in making water came on, with a violent spasmodic affection of the sphincter vesicæ, and in the rectum. These symptoms increased to a most insufferable degree ; opiates were employed, both in clyster and by the mouth ; but although above a dram was administered by the anus, and two grains of the extract of opium by the mouth, every four hours, it seemed to have no effect on the spasms, or the irritability of the bladder, which continued with nearly equal violence; warm applications in the form of bladders filled with water, flannel, fomentations, and poultices were tried in vain. Musk in doses of one scruple every four hours gave no relief, although continued two days; after which camphor was tried. During this time the patient could not retain his urine above ten or fifteen minutes; when the urine came away the pain in the glans penis was violent; this seemed to be a little alleviated by immersion in hot water. The irritation in the bladder brought on an increased secretion of mucus, which followed the urine; the camphor julep seemed to make the spasms less frequent; but whether that was really the case could not be ascertained, as after two days continuance the symptoms were equally violent. At this time the complaint was of a fortnight's standing; a bougie was now passed for some inches up the urethra, but this produced no effect: it was then tried covered with oil and one fourth part balsam copaiva; this gave a little pain in the glans, but different

from that brought on by the complaint : it
continued for some time after the bougie
was withdrawn, and next day a discharge
of matter from the urethra came on, and he
found himself easier. In a few days he got
well.

SECTION III.

OF THE SYMPTOMS OF A DISEASED ENLARGE-MENT OF THE PROSTATE GLAND.

THE prostate gland, when enlarged, obstructs the urine in its passage from the bladder.——This disease, when examined in the dead body, is more obvious than stricture, it has been therefore more generally known, and better understood.

As the seat of stricture and enlargement of the prostate gland is not the same, it would appear difficult to confound the two diseases, where the parts have been examined by a bougie; and yet, from want of an accurate knowledge of those parts, this is very often done. The length of the canal is by no means accurately known to many practitioners, nor has it been commonly believed that strictures are met with beyond the bulb of the urethra. Any obstruction which the bougie or catheter meets with, lower down in the urethra than the curve, is therefore supposed to be an enlargement of the prostate gland.

This remark would not have been made had it only been found true in a few instances; but having known the mistake to be made in so great a variety of cases, it is of importance that it should be corrected.

The prostate gland has been accused, very unjustly, as the cause of many distressing symptoms of irritation, which are really brought on by strictures. It has been considered as a very sensible part, and the least violence committed upon it has been supposed capable of producing stoppage of urine, with every circumstance of aggravation that can attend that distressing complaint.

This opinion, when combined with the idea that every stoppage beyond the bulb is produced by an enlargement of the prostate gland, has been productive of alarms in the mind of many surgeons, which have prevented them from administering relief to their patients in cases that would have admitted of it.

The prostate gland, when it enlarges and brings on a stoppage of urine, certainly does produce distressing symptoms, which do not always attend an equal degree of suppression from any other cause; these even continue after the bladder is emptied, but are not kept up by any preternatural sensibility of the prostate gland.

They arise from the membrane which covers the gland being in an inflamed state, and rendered highly sensible by the pressure of the urine against it, which is rendered more violent from the indurated state of the gland behind it. This inflammation also extends itself into the bladder, when the parts are much irritated, but more commonly is continued into the urethra, and effects the orifices of the seminal vessels, keeping up in that part of the perinæum so much sensibility that the patient is unable to sit down without great uneasiness. When these symptoms are violent they are attended by a glary discharge, which has already been noticed as a symptom of stricture, and stated to be a vitiated secretion of the prostate gland, not from the gland itself being diseased, but from its covering being inflamed. This symptom so frequently occurs, and comes on so very regularly with every attack of irritation, upon these membranes, although there is no apparent change in the size of the gland itself, that it must be referred to this cause.

· The following case, which is of rare occurrence, appears to elucidate some of these observations, although the symptoms were in the rectum instead of the urethra.

A gentleman about 50 years of age had an irritation in the rectum, which occasioned him great uneasiness; it produced little disturbance during the night while he was at rest, but came on immediately after having a motion in the morning, and lasted the greater part of the day; the sensation was of the most distressing kind, began at a particular spot a little way within the sphincter ani, and from that part extended itself along the rectum to some distance, varying in this respect at different times. On examination by the finger, the prostate gland could be readily felt in the rectum, and the left portion of it decidedly more prominent than the right ; on this prominent part there was a small eminence, which when pressed by the finger gave pain of the same kind as that of which the patient complained after going to stool ; this pain, even when the pressure was increased, did not extend through the substance of the gland, but along the membrane of the gut. He never had any uneasiness in the urethra or neck of the bladder, and from his sensations believed his complaint to be entirely in the bowel.

This case, though a solitary instance, should no others be met with upon record, was to me very satisfactory in proving that the effects of an enlargment of the prostate gland were not symptoms in the gland itself, but in the sensible membranes which surround it, not being fitted by nature to bear the pressure of a hard substance against them.

In this case suppositories of opium and hemlock passed up the fundament, and allowed to dissolve there, gave more relief than any other mode of treatment which was adopted; they not only lessened the irritation, but they produced a diminution of the projection of the gland.

So little has the sensibility of the prostate gland to do with these symptoms, that in many instances it has been perforated by the end of the catheter, in attempting to draw off the water, and this accident has brought on no symptoms whatever; it has not even been discovered till after death, that such an accident had happened. Of this fact I shall adduce two instances.

CASE I.

A gentleman, aged sixty-six, had an enlargement of the prostate gland, and in consequence of it, a suppression of urine; several ineffectual attempts were made to draw off the water, and it was proposed to puncture the bladder. While the instruments were preparing for that purpose, one more attempt was made with the flexible gum catheter, made firm by means of a stilet, assisting it by a finger in the rectum. The catheter went on into the bladder, and the urine flowed; it was therefore supposed to have taken the right course. The patient was relieved, and the catheter was afterwards passed several times; but it always required to be guided in the same manner. From the diseased state of the bladder, it was subject to violent spasms and irritation, and in seventeen days the patient died.

Upon examining the body after death, it appeared that the end of the catheter had forced a way for itself through the prostate gland into the bladder, making an artificial canal; this had not brought on inflammation or thickening of the surrounding parts, and the hole was covered with a membrane, like any fistulous orifice of long standing.

CASE II.

A gentleman, sixty-five years old, travelling in a post-chaise, was so circumstanced as to be prevented for several hours from making water; and when he attempted it, none would pass. The common means in cases of strangury were made use of, but it was found necessary to pass a catheter. The want of power to expel the urine without the use of the catheter continued, and he was obliged to have the water drawn off till his death, which was five years. The instrument was found for the first year to pass with much difficulty. It was therefore left in, and only changed occasionally. This was attended with some difficulty, requiring the instrument to have a particular curve to carry it, as was supposed, over the point of the prostate gland.

In the course of time its passage became more easy, and the bladder much freer from irritation, but still no water passed when the catheter was withdrawn. This complaint was not the cause of his death, which was the consequence of an affection of the bowels.

Upon examining the parts after death, the prostate gland was found much enlarged, firm, and solid in its texture, and projecting into the bladder, with an appearance not unlike an os tincæ; and what is to the present purpose, in the lower part was a round hole large enough to admit the catheter, through which that instrument had been passed for five years. It was rounded

off at the edges like a natural opening. The
bladder was nearly in a healthy state.

These instances are sufficient to prove
that the substance of the prostate gland is
not sensible when injured, nor does it suffer
materially from accidental violence.

The prostate gland in its enlargement
does not diminish the size of the passage
into the bladder, but rather increases it.
The lateral portions of the gland, as they
swell, widen the passage between them,
rendering it of an oval form; it is therefore the projecting portion from the lower
part which prevents the urine from flowing, and obstructs an instrument in its
passage into the bladder. The obstruction
in some instances arises from the two sides
of the gland enlarging unequally; the
larger portion pressing against the smaller,
which is made hollow to receive it, so that
the passage winds round the projecting part,
and this winding cannot be followed by an
instrument.

A diseased enlargment of the prostate

gland is not nearly so common as is generally believed, and very seldom occurs but at an advanced age.

A stricture may be distinguished from an enlargement of the prostate gland in the following manner :

The distance of the obstruction from the external orifice is to be determined by passing a soft bougie, which is to be left in the canal for a minute, so as to receive an impression from the obstruction. If the bougie does not pass further than seven inches, and the end is marked by an orifice of a circular form (it is immaterial as to the size of the orifice), the disease is certainly a stricture ; but if it passes further on, and the end is blunted, a disease in the prostate gland is to be suspected. This in general can be ascertained by a flexible gum catheter with a stilet, very much curved, passing into the bladder, which it will do in most cases of enlargement of the gland.

Strictures by impeding the urine become

H

the cause of injury to the prostate gland, as will be stated, but the cure of such consequent affections of this part, depends upon the removal of the stricture, and the symptoms are to be included among those of that disease.

SECTION IV.

OF THE SYMPTOMS SUPPOSED TO ARISE FROM CARUNCLES IN THE URETHRA.

IT is to be observed that there are still many surgeons of eminence who retain the opinion, that other causes of obstruction to the passage of urine often occur, which are mistaken for strictures. These are caruncles or excrescences from the membrane of the urethra, and venereal ulcers in different parts of the canal.

To say that such affections of this membrane seldom take place, may appear to some a rash position; but it is founded on never having met with them; and were they of frequent occurrence, it must have been peculiarly unfortunate to miss them, having had more than common opportunities of inspecting the appearance of these diseases in the dead body.

H 2

There is a circumstance attending all strictures of long standing, which has been already explained, and which may have given rise to the opinion of caruncles existing in the passage. The circumstance alluded to is the anterior part of the urethra becoming irregularly contracted; and so irritable, that any attempt to pass a bougie brings on a spasmodic increase of this contraction.

When this is the case, a small bougie conveys the sensation of passing over little eminences, or forcing its way through soft parts that obstructed it; and when this is attended with hæmorrhage, the idea of having broken down some fungous excrescence is very much strengthened; while, in fact, all these impediments arise from the irregular contraction and irritable state of the membrane; and when the canal is a little more dilated, they are no longer to be met with.

The idea of ulcers and caruncles in the urethra has been very general, and in tracing the origin of this opinion, the following appears to be the foundation upon which this erroneous doctrine has been established.

When gonorrhœa was first introduced into Europe, the discharge from that disease was believed to arise from ulcers upon the inner membrane of the urethra ; as it was not at that time known that any surface could form matter, without being previously in the state of ulceration. All the symptoms of obstruction in the urethra were frequently found to come on, soon after the cure of gonorrhœa, and in general had been preceded by that disease, although at very different periods of time ; the obstructions were therefore naturally referred to the ulcers formed in the time of the gonorrhœa. When they were attended by discharge, they were supposed to arise from the thickened edges of the ulcers filling up the canal ; and when the parts bled upon being touched by an instrument, this was considered as an excrescence from the ulcer. If the

obstruction was unaccompanied by discharge, it was conceived that the ulcers
were healed, but the contraction of the
cicatrix had become callous.

This theory, in its full extent, was generally believed, till Petit and several other
surgeons of eminence, as Dionis and M. De
la Faye, found, upon opening patients who
had died while labouring under obstructions
in the urethra, that there were no caruncles,
but an appearance which they considered
as the cicatrices of the ulcers formed in
gonorrhœa.

Monsieur Daran, when he introduced
into use his suppurating bougies, probably
from a belief of the old doctrine, insisted on
the presence of caruncles; of which he has
given no other proof, than that he knew them
by the feel which they gave to his bougie;
which when applied brought them into a
state of suppurtation, and destroyed them.

Some years after this, it was discovered
that secreting membranes, of which the
lining of the urethra is one, are capable

of producing a discharge, without a breach of their substance; this doctrine was published by Mr. Sharpe, in his Critical Inquiries. But although he takes much pains to prove it, he does not venture to deny the existence of either ulcers or caruncles, but assents to the doctrine of Daran, and believes that they arise from both these causes. At the same time he says they also arise from a simple tightness in the canal, especially where they occur, as they sometimes do, without being preceded by gonorrhœa. He considers gonorrhœa as a discharge from the surface of the membrane, and the ulcerated orifices of the lacunæ. He mentions instances of caruncles and ulcers near the verumontanum.

Since the time of Mr. Sharpe, it has been ascertained by Mr. Hunter, that in gonorrhœa there is not necessarily any ulceration, and that it is rarely if ever to be met with in that disease; that the seat of gonorrhœa is in one part of the canal, the more usual seat of stricture is in another, at a distance of several inches. These facts being established upon the most solid ground, namely, that of actual observations made in a great variety of cases, the whole theory of ulcers and caruncles from gonorrhœa proves to be erroneous.

Ulcers have, however, been found by Sharpe, and something like caruncles ; ulcers have also been met with by others, and almost always at the verumontanum. These have only been noticed in the worst cases, where the patients have died from the violence of the obstruction. Such appearances are still met with, but they are now known not to be the cause of stricture, but a consequence of it, and an effort of nature to relieve the bladder, by giving a passage to the urine behind the stricture, by means of ulceration, which, when effected, is called a fistula in perinæo.

In proof of the truth of these remarks, and to shew how the mind is misled by previous theory, if any one will take the trouble to compare Daran's cases with those mentioned in this treatise, he will find that they correspond in the number and situation of the obstructions, and only differ in the names given to them. Daran calls the first a caruncle, the second a callosity, and the third an ulcer; the last being the worst, and always at the verumontanum; or he found three or four ulcers, in the same relative situations.

The same number of obstructions are here described, and the last always the worst. The whole of them, in every instance in which they have been examined in the dead body, have proved to be thickened contractions of the internal membrane; and the cases of stricture treated in the living body, from the impressions they make on the bougie, during the progress of the effects of the caustic, prove that they are of the same nature.

It is stated that the seat of the last stricture is near the neck of the bladder, a part of the canal most subject to this disease; that the others are only secon-

dary strictures, in consequence of the urethra being, by this obstruction, deprived of
its natural dilatation ; and the ulcer with
thickened edges, mentioned by Daran, the
disease which required so long a continuance of the application of bougies, is exactly
in the same situation, so that there can be
no doubt of the obstructions so differently
described being the same.

Where the patient dies from the effects
of stricture, the symptoms are almost always
so violent, that ulceration takes place between the stricture and the bladder some
days before death. This appearance, when
cursorily examined, may readily be mistaken for the original disease : and is the
ulcer described by Daran ; but more frequently supposed than actually found.

It is proper to mention that the membrane of the urethra, like the membrane of
the mouth, is not disposed to throw out
fungous excrescences, after ulceration has
taken place on its surface, but readily skins
over,

CHAPTER III.

OF THE TREATMENT OF STRICTURES.

In the foregoing account, the symptoms and appearances which occur in the different stages of strictures, have been noticed so far as they are necessary to assist us in our treatment of the disease, by means of local applications.

The applications made use of for the removal of strictures are employed with two different intentions; to bring back the contracted part to its original state, by dilating it; or to destroy it.

For the first of these intentions, the bougie is the instrument in general use. For the second, besides the bougie, the application of lunar caustic is also recommended.

It has hitherto been thought adviseable to have recourse to this last mode, only where a bougie cannot be passed through the stricture; and in all other cases to attempt the cure by dilatation.

As these observations will be confined entirely to the treatment of those strictures which admit a small bougie to pass into the bladder, it will be necessary, before any other mode of treatment is proposed, to consider whether that instrument is, in such cases, always capable of effecting a cure; and what are the disadvantages attending its use; after which the caustic will be recommended and the reasons given for preferring it, in many cases, to the bougie; both as less distressing in the application, and more permanent in its beneficial effects.

SECTION I.

OF THE USE OF THE BOUGIE.

THE bougie has long been in common use among surgeons, for the cure of strictures; and all other means have been generally considered as very inferior in their effects.

In the early stages of the disease, where the membrane of the urethra is not in a very irritable state, recourse is had to the bougie with every advantage; and if the stricture admits of dilatation, and allows the constricted part in a few weeks to be enlarged to the common size of the canal, a cure may be effected. But as the dilatation only overcomes the effect, the same disposition which induced the first contraction, may bring back the complaint; and a second, third, and fourth time, recourse to the same mode of treatment may be required.

From this circumstance of the return of strictures, after they have been dilated by the bougie, which too frequently happens, several physicians, some of them very high in the profession, have been led to condemn bougies altogether; conceiving that they cannot effect a cure, and by their application to the internal membrane of the urethra are injurious.

A physician in London carried his prejudice against bougies to so great an height, that he left a legacy at his death to a particular friend, upon the sole condition that he would never use a bougie for the cure of a stricture he had in the urethra. The friend complied with the dying request of this physician; and afterwards died in the greatest misery, from the effects of a single stricture, which might have been palliated by the use of bougies. In this case it was found after death that the urine, prevented by the stricture from coming forwards, had forced its way backwards into the intestine, instead of coming through the perinæum; and the first symptom that gave alarm was that of the fæces coming through the penis, with the urine.

Whatever objections may be made to the use of the bougie, its effects are certainly more salutary than those of internal medicines. No internal medicine appears capable of stopping the progress of a stricture, much less of producing even a temporary cure; and these objects are evidently gained by the bougie.

The injury which the urethra is supposed to receive from a bougie being long applied to it, has in no respect been proved. We have no fair opportunity of determining this in cases of stricture, because a diseased state of the canal when met with, may with more propriety be attributed to the stricture, than to the application; conclusions drawn from such cases, cannot therefore be admitted, since it is the healthy membrane, not the diseased, which the bougie is supposed to injure. The information we receive upon this subject from

cases of diseased prostate gland, where the
urethra is in a more natural state, will be
less objectionable ; and in one instance, a
flexible gum catheter, which is a harder
instrument than a bougie, was in constant
use for five years ; nor was it removed in
all that period for more than a few hours at
a time.

When the parts were examined after
death, the membrane was found in a natural state. Were it necessary, several
facts of a similar nature might be adduced;
but none where the application had been so
long continued.

When the bougie brings on irritation,
which it often does, it will be found that
this effect does not arise from any injury
done to the healthy membrane, but from
the strictured part being kept in an uneasy
state while stretched by the bougie; which
brings on spasm, first upon the stricture, and afterwards upon the rest of the
canal, and sometimes even upon the bladder
itself.

As the bougie is required only to act mechanically as a wedge, its most important properties are, smoothness to allow it to pass through the stricture with all possible facility, and softness, to allow of its remaining there without bringing on irritation.

With respect to the use of the bougie, two points are principally worthy attention, the one is, that its size be gradually enlarged, till it has dilated the stricture as nearly as possible to the full size of the passage; the other, that when this effect has been produced, its use should be continued for some time, to destroy, as much as possible, the acquired disposition of the part to contract.

If the former caution be not observed, this part of the canal, being still narrower than the rest, must be more pressed upon by the urine, and cannot acquire its natural easy state, but suffers a repeated irritation, which is likely to bring back the stricture; whereas, if the seat of the stricture is brought upon a plane with the general

I

surface, the urine in its passage will tend to keep it dilated, and thus establish a cure.

The necessity of removing the cause, as well as the effect of a diseased state, sufficiently evinces the second rule.

Were we always consulted in the early stages of a stricture, the bougie would be liable to only one objection, that of not producing a permanent cure; but partly from ignorance of the nature of the complaint, and partly from an unwillingness to expose any defects in these parts, till it cannot be avoided, the surgeon is seldom applied to, till a considerable progress of the disease has made it less within the power of the bougie to give relief.

When the stricture to be removed is of some years standing, which must be always the case when it has originated in the East Indies, it does not admit of being readily dilated, nor does it bear, for any length of time, the application of the bougie. Any attempt to render the dilatation more rapid, or to continue the use of the bougie beyond the time in which it lies quiet in the urethra, brings on too frequently spasm, strangury, and abscess in perinæo. These symptoms often appear singly; but they are all sometimes met with in the same patient. In these cases the bougie will not do more than prevent the increase of the complaint, since it cannot be persevered in so as to effect a cure.

Where there are several strictures in the same urethra, there is more than common irritability in the membrane lining that canal, which circumstance becomes unfavourable to the use of the bougie; and in such cases we find the common bougie cannot be retained even for a few minutes; while those of a milder kind can be kept in without pain for an hour. Bougies which have preparations of lead in their composition, have an advantage here; but when made of wax and oil simply, they answer better than when made of harder materials.

In such cases, the number of strictures, and the irritability of the passage, make it almost impossible to succeed in dilating them with the bougie; the time required to overcome all the obstructions being longer than the urethra can admit of its application, without being irritated by it; and till the last stricture, or that nearest the bladder, is dilated, there can be no material step gained towards a cure.

In consequence of these disadvantages, strictures of long standing become very unfavourable for the use of the bougie, and are only palliated by it; not cured. By perseverance for months, a bougie, about one half the size of the canal, is made to pass easily into the bladder; but all attempts to introduce one of a larger size are vain. The patient in this state makes water without difficuly; but if the bougie is left off, in less than two months the contraction, which had never been wholly removed, begins to increase, and requires again to be dilated.

SECTION II.

OF STRICTURES WHICH ALWAYS YIELD TO
THE USE OF THE BOUGIE, AND IN WHICH
THE CAUSTIC OUGHT NEVER TO BE USED.

IT has been already stated, that all contractions of the urethra which admit of being
relaxed equally with the rest of the canal
by means of the bougie, require no other
means for that purpose ; and many such
occur in patients, where the parts have no
disposition to form a permanent stricture.
Strictures of this kind are removed by the
bougie being two or three times passed into
the bladder, the contraction having been
similar to a cramp in any other muscle,
which, when counteracted, relaxes completely, retaining no disposition to contract
again. The number of strictures of this
kind which occur in practice is very great;
they resist the passage of a full sized bougie

the first time, as much as any other stricture; and as the patient has laboured under
all the common symptoms of the disease,
the surgeon would be led to conclude the
complaint very difficult of cure; but on the
next tria , the bougie passes on   to the
bladder, and in consequence of its doing so,
all the symptoms go off, and when the
bougie is introduced at any future period, it
passes equally readily.   These are cases of
a spasmodic state of the urethra, in which
nothing is necessary but passing a bougie
two or three times to complete the cure,
and in which leaving it in the canal would
bring on irritation.

Strictures are also met with in young men
who have never had a severe gonorrhœa,
nor used injections, who have had no
appearance of gravel, nor any of the other
common causes of stricture ; and yet labour
under many of the symptoms of that disease,
such as making water in a small stream,
attended with difficulty, and a considerable
quantity of gleety discharge.

In several of these cases the urethra is found in a very contracted state, but the parts yield with the utmost readiness to the use of the bougie ; so that although on the first trial the smallest size cannot be introduced into the bladder, yet upon the next trial, one a full size larger passes with ease ; and although not retained there, in two days, one of an encreased size can be passed ; and in this way six or seven times passing a bougie and immediately withdrawing it, is found to be all that is necessary to bring the canal to its natural dimensions. On enquiring into the cause of these strictures which appear so formidable, and yet yield readily to the bougie, while others apparently less contracted are not to be relaxed by the same means, it was found that the patients, none of them beyond the age of 23 or 24, had been living very freely, indulging in wine to excess, at the same time that they were having connexion with different women. Under such circumstances spasmodic contractions can be readily accounted for ; and it appears to me that the quantity of wine contained in the urine has so much influence on it as to prevent it from acting with sufficient force to relax an urethra that had previously been in a state of spasmodic contraction, by the prolonged and imperfect act of copulation performed in a state of intoxication.

This statement would not have been made, had not the number of instances which have come under my observation induced me to believe it of importance, to make them generally known.

SECTION III.

THE KIND OF CAUSTIC TO BE USED, AND THE MODE OF APPLYING IT TO STRICTURES.

IF the bougie is found inadequate to the cure of stricture, in many cases, where it can be passed through the contracted part, it will be readily admitted, that the chance of success in those cases where it cannot go beyond the stricture, must be still less. It has been recommended to press the bougie against the stricture, and by producing ulceration, to remove the disease.

This may have succeeded in particular instances; these, however, are not many in number; and the danger of making a false passage, forms a strong argument against this mode of practice.

This is carried still further by some surgeons, who make use of a silver cathether, to encrease the pressure, and more effectually produce ulceration. Where this practice does not succeed, it appears to do harm, by disposing the parts to become still more callous, and thus to increase the disease it was meant to remove.

In those cases that are wholly impervious, or where the orifice is so small that the end of the bougie cannot be made to pass through, Mr. Hunter proposed to enlarge it by the effects of caustic. He was led to this idea from the appearance of the disease, when examined after death ; the thinness of the membrane forming the obstruction, making it highly probable that a few touches would destroy it. The particular caustic employed, the success attending the practice, and the instrument made use of to convey it to the stricture, are in the hands of the public. But as that mode has been since found capable of great improvement, some objections to it will be mentioned, and the mode he afterwards adopted and used for several years before his death, will be explained.

The argentum nitratum or lunar caustic is peculiarly adapted to the present purpose, from its having a solid form, and being less active than many of the others, therefore more under the management of the surgeon; its not dissolving readily, allows of its being passed over a moist surface without injuring it, and its coagulating the substance it destroys, prevents the effect being extended beyond the immediate surface to which it is applied.

Such properties give this caustic an essential advantage over those that destroy by exciting so great a degree of inflammation as to produce death in the part, of which kind are arsenic and corrosive sublimate, or those which dissolve the parts they come in contact with, as the alkalies. The alkalies, can never completely destroy a stricture; for however compounded at the time they are used, they must be dissolved, and the solution will rest upon the under surface, and injure it; the blood vessels destroyed by it must always bleed, since there is no time for inflammation to produce contraction in them. This hæmorrage is almost instantaneous. The difference in this respect between the lunar caustic and alkalies cannot be better illustrated than by the following account. After having removed a large superficial tumour, composed of blood vessels, from the neck of an infant, on the first dressing the exposed surface had not a perfectly healthy appearance, it was therefore thought right to destroy it by caustic; the lunar caustic was tried, but did not succeed, the effects were too superficial; the lapis septicus, or caustic alkalie, was therefore employed, but the hæmorrage was so great that it became necessary to apply the lunar caustic to coagulate the surface, and restrain the bleeding, which it immediately effected, and in two or three days, by the use of the two kinds of caustic, the one immediately after the other, the object was obtained, healthy granulations were produced, and the child got perfectly well.

The instruments Mr. Hunter made use

of for passing the caustic, consisted of a silver canula, and a stilet; one end of the stilet has a small bulb, that filled up the end of the canula, and made it pass more easily down to the stricture; the other end was a portcrayon, that contained the piece of caustic to be passed down through the canula, and applied to the stricture as long as might be thought necessary: the portcrayon then being guarded within the canula, the whole was withdrawn.*

* This idea had been taken up an hundred years ago, for Wiseman says, when the obstruction is a caruncle, and you cannot pass it, you may well conclude it is callous: " In which case you may pass a canula into the urethra to that caruncle, and whilst you hold it there steady, you may convey a grain of caustic into the canula, and press the caustic to it; and whilst you hold it there, you will perceive its operation, by the pressing forward of the canula." He does not say this is the common practice, or his own particular mode, nor does he give an instance in which it had been tried.

This observation of Wiseman's Mr. Hunter was not acquainted with; he would not have passed that author in silence, had he known that the idea of applying the caustic originated with him.

This method was found in practice to be liable to many objections. The silver canula could not be adapted to the flexible canal of the urethra, through which it was to pass; when, therefore, the caustic was applied, and any degree of pressure made use of, the effect of the caustic was necessarily produced upon the angle between the stricture and the side of the urethra, and not in the middle of the stricture, the part intended to be destroyed.

In consequence of being thus applied, the side of the urethra was liable to be injured; and where that did not happen, the orifice made in the stricture was often oblique, and could not be followed by the bougie; so that the effect of the caustic on the stricture was only to be judged of by the increased stream of urine, as the bougie could not pass, either to ascertain the size of the aperture, to enlarge it, or prevent it from contracting again.

The unyielding materials of the canula were attended with another disadvantage;

for in many urethras, those particularly which require the application of the caustic, the internal membrane is so irritable, as not to allow a hard body to pass along it without inducing spasm, while a softer substance gives no uneasiness ; the silver canula was often prevented, by the degree of irritation it produced, from reaching the seat of the stricture ; and sometimes when it had been carried down to it, was not allowed to remain there ; so that a doubt very often arose, whether the caustic was really applied to the stricture or not.

This fact of the urethra not allowing a hard substance to remain in it, cannot be better illustrated than by mentioning the effects of the wire bougies : so named from having a small wire in their centre, to give them firmness. These are to appearance exactly like other bougies ; but when passed into the bladder of a patient with an irritable urethra, he will generally, from the sensation, discover that they contain a wire, and is unable to allow one of them to remain in the passage. Of this sensibility of the urethra, the following is a remarkable instance a patient on whom one of these bougies was passed unintentionally, it having by accident been laid with the common ones. The patient immediately said, the bougie was not to be borne, for there was a wire in it: this was declared not to be the case. But he still persisted, and said that he could not be mistaken. Upon withdrawing the bougie and examining it, the wire in its centre was discovered.

The state of the urethra in this disease being such as to allow a bougie to pass, and at the same time not to admit a metal instrument, is not peculiar to stricture; but appears to take place whenever the passage is much irritated, without having a reference to the particular cause of irritation. It occurs where the membrane of the urethra is the immediate seat of inflammation, as in gonorrhœa; and likewise when it is affected by sympathy, the disease being in the bladder.

The following cases are instances of this.

A patient who had a gonorrhœa, attended with chordee, by catching cold, brought on a suppression of urine: ineffectual attempts were made to draw off the water by means of the silver catheter; the flexible gum catheter, inclosing a metallic stilet, was also several times introduced, but could not pass. After remaining twenty-seven hours without making water, and in much pain, the patient was brought to town, from a distance of twelve miles, and arrived in a state of great irritation. The flexible gum catheter without a stilet was readily introduced into the bladder, and drew off three pints of urine.

The surgeon who accompanied the patient expressed his astonishment at the ease with which this instrument passed; as the one he had brought with him was of the same size, and he had never before heard of there being any advantage in passing it without the stilet.

A gentleman had the symptoms of an irritable bladder and urethra, supposed to arise

K

from stone : attempts were made at different
times to ascertain the nature of the disease
by sounding him ; but no solid instrument
could be passed, while a bougie of a middling size went on to the bladder. The case
was now considered as a spasmodic stricture,
and the bougie recommended. Under this
course the complaint grew worse, and the
desire to make water came on every five
minutes. A flexible gum catheter was now
introduced into the bladder, and retained
there two days. After the passage had been
accustomed to the flexible catheter so long
a time, a sound of the same size passed with
little difficulty, and a stone was very distinctly felt in the bladder. The irritation
from the stone had so much increased the
irritability of that part of the urethra, as to
make it contract whenever the sound was
attempted to be introduced into it.

A gentleman, aged seventy-four, had a
suppression of urine from an enlargement
of the prostate gland ; a flexible gum catheter passed readily down to the projecting

part of the enlarged gland, but could not
go over it into the bladder ; an iron stilet
was therefore put into the catheter, to give
the instrument the necessary curve, for it
to get into the bladder ; but now it could
not be passed lower than $6\frac{1}{2}$ inches, the
urethra contracting so as to stop it at that
part. On withdrawing the stilet, it could
be passed on to the prostate gland ; upon
introducing it again, it was stopped as before : after repeated failures, it was found
necessary to give up the attempt of passing
it with the stilet, and it fortunately got into
the bladder in its flexible state, the end accidentally slipping over the gland.

Some days after, when the urethra had
become more quiet, it admitted the catheter
with a stilet to pass ; but at the end of four
weeks, when the parts had been irritated in
consequence of a journey, the canal again
refused the instrument with the stilet, but
let it pass readily without it.

This will account for the difficulty which
often occurs in passing the staff in the

K 2

operation for the stone, and which is sometimes hardly to be surmounted.

These objections to the use of the silver canula did not escape Mr. Hunter's penetration. He not only saw them, but devised a mode by which they might be removed, the application of the caustic rendered more simple, and directed with more accuracy to the centre of the stricture.

This improved mode of applying the caustic is as follows : take a bougie, of a size that can readily be passed down to the stricture, and insert a small piece of lunar caustic into the end of it, exposing the surface of the caustic, but surrounding it every where laterally by the substance of the bougie. This should be done some little time before it is used ; for the materials of which the bougie is composed, become warm and soft by being handled in inserting the caustic ; and therefore the hold the bougie has of the caustic is rendered more secure after it has been allowed to cool and harden. This bougie so prepared, is to be oiled, and made ready for use; but previous to passing it, a common bougie of the same size is to be introduced down to the stricture, to clear the canal, and to measure exactly the distance of the stricture from the external orifice: this distance being marked upon the armed bougie, it is to be passed down to the stricture immediately upon the other being withdrawn. In its passage the caustic is scarcely allowed to come in contact with any portion of the membrane, for as it forms the central part of the point of the bougie, it always moves in the middle line of the canal; and indeed the quickness with which it is conveyed to the stricture, prevents any injury to the membrane, where it is accidentally brought to oppose it.

By this mode the caustic is passed down to the stricture, with little or no irritation to the lining of the urethra; it is applied in the most advantageous manner, and can be retained in that situation the necessary time to produce its effects.

This method Mr. Hunter adopted several

years before his death, in preference to that which is published in his work.

It has been mentioned publicly ever since that period in my lectures, and the manner of passing it has been explained.

By this mode of arming the bougie, strictures in the curvature of the urethra, which is their more usual situation, may have the caustic applied to them, which cannot be done by a silver canula, unless made flexible; and even in that state it is liable to many objections.

SECTION IV.

THE EFFECTS OF THE CAUSTIC ON STRICTURES.

THE application of the lunar caustic to strictures was thus introduced into practice by the late Mr. Hunter, in those cases only that did not admit the smallest sized bougie to pass; in which, therefore, no mode of relief, without having recourse to a very severe operation with the knife, was at that time known.

Under these circumstances, if it relieved the symptoms of stricture, and procured a freer passage for the urine, it was certainly a discovery of great value.

Against this practice, however, objections have been formed, and many bad consequences have been attributed to it, which it certainly does not produce; for whatever, *a priori*, might be supposed, the effects of so violent an application to a membrane so sensible and irritable as the urethra, and it is very natural to conceive they would be very severe; the result of experience, the only thing to be relied on, evinces the contrary. The pain that is brought on is by no means violent; and neither irritation nor inflammation is found to take place.

That cases do occur, in which strictures have produced so much mischief, and rendered so great an extent of the canal diseased, that the use of the caustic has proved unsuccessful, is certainly true; and several of these cases have fallen within my own knowledge. But when it is stated, that none, even of these, were made worse by its use; that no bad consequences attended it; and that no other mode, at present known, is equally efficacious; any occasional want of success cannot be considered as an objection to this mode of practice. It has also been found that after the use of the caustic for a considerable time, the common bougie is resorted to with advantage, and those strictures which could not before be dilated by it, in consequence of the use of the caustic more easily yield to its pressure.

But if the apprehension of violent effects from the caustic, however ill-founded, cannot be removed, let the alternative be considered; namely, the only operation previously in use, where a stricture cannot be dilated by the bougie.

In those cases we are obliged to have recourse to means certainly more severe and violent, laying open with a knife the diseased urethra, and passing through the divided parts a flexible gum catheter into the bladder. This has frequently been performed by Mr. Hunter and by myself, and it always succeeded; neither bringing on so much inflammation as was expected, nor being attended with any symptoms of irritation.

This practice has by other surgeons been carried still further; the portion of diseased urethra has been dissected out, and entirely removed; nor has so severe an operation always brought on untoward symptoms; and patients have recovered.

If the membrane of the urethra when diseased, is capable of suffering so much injury, without any consequent symptoms of irritation, it cannot be doubted that it will bear with impunity, to be touched in a very partial manner, several different times with lunar caustic.

As the following observations are published with a view to extend the use of the caustic to a greater variety of cases, and in some measure upon a different principle from that upon which it was applied to impervious strictures, by the late Mr. Hunter, it is thought necessary, before any new opinions upon the subject are made known, to mention the source from which they were derived; and to place the merit of the invention, as well as the mode of applying it, where it is due; reserving to myself that of the attempt to render it more generally useful.

Having met with a number of facts, from

which a general principle appears to be established, that the irritable state of a stricture is kept up, and even increased, by the use of the bougie, but lessened and entirely destroyed by the application of lunar caustic; made me desirous to communicate my observations upon these facts, and to recommend the use of the caustic, in many cases of irritable stricture, in preference to the bougie.

As the use of the caustic upon this principle is entirely new, and is contrary to every notion that had been formed upon the subject, it will require something more than general assertion, to gain even the attention of many of my readers, still more their belief; the circumstances which tend to establish the propriety of this practice shall therefore be detailed as they occurred, and afterwards some observations will be made upon the principle on which it depends.

My connection in practice with Mr. Hunter, afforded me opportunities of attending to cases of stricture, in all their different stages ; many of them brought on during a long residence in India, attended with great irritability, and exceedingly difficult of cure.

One case of this kind, which will be presently related, admitted the passing of a small bougie ; but in the course of three years, very little was gained by a steady perseverance in the use of that instrument, either in dilating the canal, or palliating the symptoms of stricture ; this made me see the inefficacy of the common bougie in this case, which was considered as an uncommon one, depending more on the peculiarities of the patient's constitution than on the nature of the disease ; but on a particular inquiry, it was found that several other gentlemen from India were under circumstances nearly similar ; the bougie only preventing the increase of the stricture, but being unable to dilate it beyond a certain size ; and when left off, the stricture in less than two months returned to its former state of contraction.

What plan ought to be followed in such cases was then unknown; but that the bougie could not be depended on was evident. During this suspense, the following case came under my care.

In August, 1794, a gentleman consulted me for some symptoms which had been considered as indicating the presence of gonorrhœa; but as they did not yield to the common treatment in the usual time, he was induced to take my advice respecting the nature of his complaint. In the necessary inquiry to obtain a perfect history of the case, among other things it was stated, that nineteen years before, there was a stricture which became very troublesome, and that Mr. Hunter, by the desire of the patient, had applied the caustic, by which the stricture was removed, and never after returned. He said that he was one of the first persons on whom the caustic had been used. This account naturally led me to believe that the stricture had gradually returned, and was now increased so much as to produce the

present symptoms; a discharge being almost always a symptom of stricture, when
it is much contracted; but upon examining
the canal, a bougie of the full size passed on
to the bladder without the smallest impedi-
ment. The case was therefore taken up as
an inflammation in the urethra; and the
balsam copaiva, given internally, effected a
cure.

The circumstance of a stricture having
been removed nineteen years before, and not
returning, made a strong impression on my
mind; and made me desirous to ascertain
whether this practice could not be employed
in cases of stricture in general, and the cure
produced by it equally permanent. A short
time after, the following opportunity of
trying it occurred.

A captain in the East India Company's
service, in September, 1794, applied to me
for assistance. His complaints were, great
irritation in the urethra and bladder, constant desire to make water, and an inability
to void it, except in very small quantities.

These symptoms had been at first supposed to arise from gonorrhœa, afterwards
rendered more severe by catching cold ;
but not yielding to the usual remedies for
gonorrhœa, they were investigated more
minutely, and a stricture was discovered in
the urethra. The mode of treatment was
now changed, and the bougie employed ; but
its use aggravated all the symptoms, and
brought on so great a degree of irritability
on the bladder and urethra, that there was
an alarm for the patient's life, which was
the reason of applying for my assistance.

Besides the local symptoms, this patient
had those of quick pulse, white tongue, hot
and dry skin, loss of appetite, and total
want of sleep, with frequent attacks of
spasm on the bladder and urethra. A very
small flexible gum catheter was passed, and
the water drawn off, in quantity about a
pint, which gave him great relief ; this was
repeated morning and evening to keep the
bladder in as easy a state as possible ; but in
other respects he continued much the same.

As the present symptoms were brought on by the use of the bougie, little good was to be expected from that instrument; and where the urethra had been so easily irritated, and was disposed to continue in that state, there was no prospect of the use of the bougie afterwards effecting a cure. These circumstances were explained to the patient; and in confirmation of them the preceding case was mentioned, in which so little had been effected in three years.

It was proposed to make trial of the caustic, with a view to deaden the edge of the stricture, as the only probable means of effecting a cure. The degree of irritation was already great; there was, however, reason to believe, that the application of the caustic would not increase it; since by destroying the irritable part, it might lessen, and even remove the spasmodic affection; but if, contrary to my expectation, the irritation continued, we still should be able to draw off the water, as the slough formed by the caustic would prevent the edge of the stricture from acting, and obstructing the instrument.

The application of the caustic was, upon these grounds, determined on; and it was applied in the following manner.

A common bougie, nearly the size of the canal, was passed down to the stricture, to ascertain its exact situation, and to make the canal of the urethra as open as possible. The distance was then marked upon a bougie armed with caustic, of the same size, which was conveyed down as quickly as the nature of the operation would admit. It was retained upon the stricture with a slight degree of pressure; at first there was no pain from the caustic, but a soreness from pressure; in less than a minute, a change was felt in the sensation of the part, it was at first a heat, succeeded by the burning pain peculiar to caustic: as soon as this was distinctly felt, the bougie and caustic were withdrawn, having remained in the urethra about a minute altogether. The soreness, he said, was entirely local,

L

by no means severe, was unaccompanied by irritation along the canal, and he thought the uneasiness in the bladder diminished by it. He described the pain as resembling very exactly the first symptoms of gonorrhœa. This sensation lasted half an hour after withdrawing the bougie.

The caustic was applied about one o'clock in the forenoon, and he passed the day more free from irritation than he had been since the beginning of the attack, which had lasted six days. In the evening the water was drawn off with more ease than the night before. He passed a tolerable night, and the next day continued free from irritation. On the third day the caustic was again applied in the forenoon; the painful sensation was less than on the former application, lasted a shorter time, and in an hour after the armed bougie was withdrawn, he made water freely for the first time since the commencement of his indisposition. He said the irritation in the bladder was removed, and he felt very well.

His appetite returned, he slept well, and continued to void his urine with ease.

In this state nothing was done till the fifth day, leaving always a day between the applications of the caustic.

On this day a common sized bougie went readily into the bladder; it was immediately withdrawn, and the cure was considered as complete; no bougie was afterwards passed, lest it might bring back an irritation upon the passage.

This gentleman returned to India, where he died six years afterwards of a fever, but never had any return of the stricture.

From the result of this case, there was encouragement to hope that the caustic might be applied to strictures in the urethra with more confidence than had hitherto been believed, since it evidently did not bring on or increase the general irritation; but on the contrary, seemed to allay it.

In this case it had taken off the disposition to spasm, which appeared to me, as has

L 2

been already stated, an object of the greatest importance in the treatment of stricture in all its stages. One instance by no means afforded sufficient evidence to establish the general propriety of this practice; it justified, however, further trials, and induced me to prosecute the inquiry.

The case already alluded to, as having discouraged me more than any other in the use of the bóugie, appeared to be a very proper one for the trial of the caustic, and for comparing its effects with those of the bougie, particularly as it had been of very long standing, and the bougie had been persevered in with great patience, for a sufficient length of time, without any considerable benefit. An opportunity of trying it, was afforded me, and the following is an account of the case.

The gentleman was a lieutenant-colonel in the East India Company's service, forty-two years of age, had been many years resident in India, and during twelve of them had more or less difficulty in making water.

He came to England, in 1791, and put himself under the care of Mr. Hunter. Upon passing a bougie, there were found to be two strictures in the urethra, one three inches from the external orifice, the other at the bulb. The canal was extremely irritable, and a bougie, if allowed to remain in it for several minutes, produced uneasiness. The first stricture was, after a considerable time, gradually dilated; and then a small bougie was passed through the second into the bladder; after this had been continued daily, a few minutes at a time, for about a week, one a single size larger, was introduced. This larger bougie had been used for two days without any pain; but on the third, the patient, immediately after it was withdrawn, walked nearly a mile; he felt a little uneasiness, which he attributed to the walk. This was followed by a spasmodic irritation in the urethra and bladder, and in the evening a complete suppression of urine took place: in this state he remained all night, taking opium, and using other modes of relief, but without effect.

About four o'clock in the morning a bougie was passed down to the stricture, and allowed to remain there, pressing against it. This application was continued for fifteen minutes ; the spasm began to abate, allowing a few drops of urine to pass, and in a few hours it went gradually off.

The bougie was now laid aside : some time after it was again tried, and things went on tolerably well for about ten days, when an uneasiness was felt in the perinæum, and a hardness discovered there, which made it necessary again to leave it off. This hardness increased, and formed a very large abscess in perinæo, which was opened. It contained about three ounces of matter, but had no communication with the urethra ; and in two months healed up. When the parts were perfectly recovered, as there seemed to be no alternative, the bougie was again resorted to ; and as the common sort did not lie in the passage without giving uneasiness, those of a softer kind were tried, and found to answer better ; but unfortunately whenever they were regularly persevered in, they brought on, in less than two months, a local irritation, attended with constitutional indisposition, which made it necessary to omit them for a week or a fortnight. From these circumstances, at the end of three years, a bougie of no considerable size, composed of the softest materials (white wax and oil, in nearly equal proportions), could only be retained for ten minutes without irritation ; but if used regularly longer than a month, irritation came upon the parts.

After having suffered so much under the course of bougies, the patient was willing to make trial of the caustic, and on the 20th of November, 1794, it was applied to the stricture, nearest to the orifice of the urethra, which at this time did not admit a bougie of half the common size ; the effect of the caustic, after remaining a minute on the stricture, was local soreness, but no irritation ; the soreness continued a quarter of an hour, and went off. The sensation was totally different from the uneasiness he had always experienced while a bougie was retained in the stricture, and although more acute, was by no means so difficult to bear ; this was so decidedly his opinion, that as soon as the caustic was removed, from which he had expected very severe effects, he declared that he would at any time prefer the application of the caustic to *having* a bougie passed through the stricture. It was applied again on the 22d, and produced the same effects in a less degree. On the 24th, a full sized bougie was readily passed through the first stricture, down to the second. The caustic was now applied to this stricture ; after using it three times, with the interval of a day between each application, a full sized bougie could be pushed on to the bladder, but did not pass with ease ; the caustic was therefore used a fourth time, and then the bougie went into the bladder, and he made water freely. Thus, in fourteen days, by means of the caustic, a full sized bougie was passed into the bladder without the smallest degree of irritation; an object which could not be effected by dilating the passage with a bougie for three years together. As the urethra had proved to be so very irritable, it was not thought prudent to use a bougie, the parts were therefore left to themselves.

In the beginning of February, 1795, this patient caught cold, and was confined to his bed with a fever, and symptoms of oppression upon his breast, from which his life was considered in danger. For these complaints he was twice bled freely, and otherwise much reduced ; during the whole of this illness there was no return of his stricture, or irritation in the bladder; but while he remained in the weak state in which it left him, on the 14th of February, he had in the night a frequent desire to make water, which passed in small quantities, and towards the morning he had some irritation in the bladder. He sent for me, a good deal alarmed at this return, after having been ten weeks free from the complaint. From his account of the symptoms, the bougie was objected to, as it had always increased the irritation when employed.

The application of the caustic to the stricture appeared to be a preferable measure, since in its present contracted state, it would be more certainly opposed to the caustic, and more effectually destroyed. This was immediately agreed to; and in five minutes after it had been used the spasm went off, and he made water with ease to the quantity of half a pint, which emptied the bladder, and entirely removed the irritation. As the stricture had evidently in some degree returned, and as the only chance of a permanent cure depends upon the contracted part being equally dilated with the rest of the canal, or nearly so, his making water freely was not enough, and the use of the caustic was necessary to procure so desirable an effect. It was again applied, twice to the first stricture, and twice to the second ; after which a full sized bougie could be passed readily into the bladder. As this return might be attributed to leaving the urethra entirely to itself, after the use of the caustic, it was now judged proper to pass a bougie once a day, five minutes each time, for a fortnight, and then once a month, to ascertain the state of the canal ; at the end of four months there was an opportunity of passing a bougie, and at that time the stricture had not in the smallest degree returned. This gentleman went to India, and has had no return of the symptoms of stricture.

From the result of this case, in addition to the preceding, the evidence was so far satisfactory that an effectual mode of treating those strictures, which do not admit of being relieved by the use of the bougie, having been discovered, that from that time, this mode of treatment, has been adopted by me as a general practice. What has been already stated, is to be considered as the ground-work upon which this practice was taken up; and there is no mode of conveying to others, more distinctly, the facts collected from these different trials, than by detailing the cases in the order in which they occurred. Having done this, it remains to draw some conclusions from them, respecting the principle upon which the caustic produces this effect; and to annex the varieties which occur in the disease, and the different symptoms that are brought on by the use of the caustic.

SECTION V.

TO SHEW THAT SPASMODIC AFFECTIONS ARE
MORE READILY BROUGHT ON BY SLIGHT
IRRITATIONS, THAN BY THOSE THAT ARE
VIOLENT.

THAT the delicate and vascular internal membrane of the urethra should admit of a portion of its surface being destroyed, without any symptoms of consequence being produced by this violent application, is so curious a fact, that it almost staggers our belief; and any one is excusable who at first view may condemn this practice as unwarrantably bold.

For this reason it becomes a duty to be minute in detailing the proofs upon which this practice is built, in order to reconcile it to practitioners, and incite them to make trial of it. It is rendered, indeed, the more wonderful by the knowledge of the fact, that the most distressing symptoms do frequently follow very slight degrees of irritation affecting the same membrane.

Although at first we are unable to reconcile this to our minds, from being too strongly impressed with an idea of the delicacy and sensibility of the organs of generation, whose functions are so peculiarly under the influence of our imagination; yet if we divest ourselves of that influence, we shall find it perfectly conformable to the effects that take place in other parts of the body, and to the general laws of sensibility and irritability.

It is a general fact, that wherever a slough is produced, there is less inflammation, both in degree and extent, than from any other injury, of the same or even a less degree of violence. This is well known to all military surgeons, who are daily seeing illustrations of it; a bruise from a spent ball brings on violent inflammation over the whole limb; but if the ball passes with velocity, and goes directly through the limb, it acts like a caustic upon the surface to which it is applied; and destroys the parts to a certain depth, producing no more inflammation than is necessary to separate the slough. This inflammation is slower in coming on, and is almost wholly confined to the neighbourhood of the ball's passage. Is it then, we may ask, extraordinary that an analogous effect should take place in the membrane of the urethra, or is there more difficulty in accounting for it? The caustic deadens the surface it injures, and takes from it the power of conveying irritation; the surrounding parts therefore have only the degree of inflammation induced upon them that is necessary to remove the slough, which is very superficial, and extremely small; but where the parts are not destroyed by the violence, the natural actions are disturbed, and the symptoms of irritation may be carried to any degree, according to the sensibility and irritability of the parts.

An effect similar to this of which we now

treat in the urethra, takes place on the tunica conjunctiva of the eye.   If a mote or hair gets between the eyelids and the eyeball, it sometimes brings on a violent irritation, and the whole surface inflames ; but this by no means is the case when the lunar caustic is applied to any part of the same surface, as may be illustrated by the following case.

A man about forty years old, had a film beginning to grow upon the cornea of one of his eyes ;   and this newly formed part was supplied with blood, by a plexus of vessels dictinctly seen through the tunica conjunctiva.   With a view to destroy these vessels, lunar caustic was applied three different times to the tunica conjunctiva, about a quarter of an inch from the edge of the pupil ; it gave him a good deal of pain, but brought on no general inflammation or irritation upon the membrane.

Spasmodic actions in general, both constitutional and local, are brought on by slight degrees of irritation, and are usually relieved by violent applications. The locked jaw and other affections of the tetanus kind, are the consequences of wounds and fevers; but the time of their coming on is either when the wound has not begun to inflame, or after it is in an healing state; and the fever is going off or entirely removed when they arise from that cause. The shock, from plunging into the cold bath, a very violent application to the surface of the body, has been found of advantage in this disease.

Spasms in particular muscles, as in the intercostals, diaphragm, muscles of the arm, or leg, come on from slight constitutional irritation, or local injuries, attended with little violence; the cause is often so slight as entirely to escape discovery, and the treatment most generally found to succeed is blistering the surface nearest to the part affected, which is one of the most violent applications we are enabled to employ.

In surgery it is a fact too well ascertained to require any illustration, that local inflammations are more commonly removed

M

by irritating applications, than by those that are mild ; and here they are applied directly to the part affected. Sores in different parts of the body are often attended with extreme sensibility, and this symptom is frequently aggravated by poultices of bread and milk, preparations of lead or opium ; but poultices of arsenic, or the solution of caustic, applied to the whole surface, in many cases give ease, after being used some time, and in the end produce a cure.

This general principle of spasmodic affections and local inflammations yielding more readily to irritating applications, is now found equally applicable to affections of the urethra.. This not only appears when the irritating application is made to the part itself, but also, in a less degree, when it affects a neighbouring part ; for the inflammation arising from gonorrhœa, in one part of the canal, will sometimes take off the spasm from a stricture in another part, some inches distant ; the same effect is occasionally produced by irritating applications.

Of this the following is a very curious instance.

A gentleman of fortune who had a spasmodic stricture, was a considerable time under the care of Mr. Hunter, without receiving any benefit from the different modes of treatment that were used for his relief; finding no benefit from the regular practice, as it is termed, he applied to a well known empiric, who examines the water of his patients, and in general discovers that they have had gonorrhœa, which, according to his cant, has been too suddenly stopped, and from this virulent matter being locked up, accounts for their present complaints, whatever they may be. He therefore proposes to bring back the discharge, which is effected very ingeniously by passing an irritating bougie three or four inches along the urethra; and after promoting this discharge for some time, he leaves off the use of the bougie, and the discharge soon disappears; the complaints either do or should disappear along with it. This, his common

M 2

practice to all patients, was made use of in this case of spasmodic stricture : he passed a bougie, smeared with balsam copaiva, a few inches up the urethra, and by this application had the good fortune to remove the disease; the violence done to this part of the membrane, took off the spasmodic action from that nearer the bladder, and the patient got perfectly well.

SECTION VI.

OF THE COMPARATIVE EFFECTS OF THE BOUGIE, AND OF THE CAUSTIC, UPON STRICTURES.

THE bougie, it has been already observed, in recent cases, is sometimes sufficient to produce the cure of stricture, and then no other means are necessary. Where the bougie is capable of dilating the urethra to its natural size, it is to be preferred, as being not only more simple, but less alarming to the mind of the patient. Were the bougie capable of producing this effect more generally than it is, there would be less occasion to have recourse to the caustic.

It is not my intention by any means to discourage the use of the bougie, which is certainly a very useful instrument; but as it is found to be limited in its powers, it becomes important to point out a more active application, which may be capable of producing a cure, where that shall have proved inadequate.

In comparing the effects of the bougie with those of the caustic, strictures only that have been of long standing are here to be considered; and it has been already stated that, either from ignorance or bashfulness, too many strictures in the urethra arrive at that state before any thing is done for their relief.

It appears, from the observations which have been made, that these strictures commonly admit a small bougie to pass into the bladder, but will not allow of its being gradually increased, so as to dilate the passage at that part to a tolerable size; in all such cases the cure cannot be effected by that instrument. This is so obvious that it cannot be denied.

There are other cases, in which there is less irritation, that admit of being dilated by the bougie to a certain degree, but never to the natural size of the canal; when this is effected, the bougie is left off, as no further benefit can be derived from its use; and it has been erroneously believed, that no advantage would result from the canal at this part being made wider.

The patient, as his water passes tolerably well, is supposed to be cured; but unfortunately in less than two months the symptoms return, and the bougie must again be employed, which, after its application, leaves him only in his former state, and as liable to relapse as before.

This cannot be considered a cure, it is only a temporary relief,—for the stricture still exists, although in a less contracted state; and the relapse is brought on, most probably, from the urine still having a greater resistance to overcome in passing through the narrow part, which keeps up an irritation there, and brings on a spasmodic action; so that in a short time it becomes as much contracted as before.

In both these stages of stricture, where it cannot be dilated by the bougie, and where the dilatation can only be carried to a certain extent, the caustic has a manifest advantage, being capable of effecting what the bougie cannot do, namely, removing the stricture entirely, and making the canal of the same size, or nearly so, in every part. When this is accomplished, the urine, in passing along the canal, must press every where equally, and dilate the whole passage to the same extent; and by doing this, will prevent, as much as possible, a return of the disposition for forming a stricture.

In this comparison of the effects of caustic, with those of the bougie, upon strictures, there is an advantage seldom to be obtained in similar investigations; which is, that both modes have been tried, in almost every instance adduced in favour of the caustic. The trials of the bougie have in general been made for a considerable length of time, by several different surgeons, and upon patients whose situations in life enabled them to do justice to the plan that was laid down for their relief. The conclusions which are drawn from the results are therefore the more to be depended on.

Upon the whole, in estimating the advantages of the caustic, in the more advanced stages of stricture, from what has been stated, we may safely infer, that it is a mode of treatment more extensively useful, milder, quicker in its operation, more effectual, and more permanent than the bougie.

SECTION VII.

THE SYMPTOMS PRODUCED BY THE CAUSTIC IN THE PROGRESS OF THE CURE.

IT may be proper to mention some general directions for applying the caustic to strictures, and the effects which it produces on the parts.

In arming a bougie, it will be attended with some difficulty to get the piece of caustic of a proper shape and size for the purpose, unless it be cast in a small cylindrical mould.

In this state it is to be procured from Mr. Savigny, instrument maker, in King-street, Covent-Garden ; and if these pieces are thicker than the bougie can readily inclose, by putting them in water the outside quickly dissolves, so as to diminish their size as much as is required. The piece of caustic so prepared is to be cut into small portions, about a quarter of an inch in length, and an orifice being made in the end of a bougie, the caustic is to be inserted into it, and the bougie rolled, so as to be made perfectly smooth, taking care that the sides of the caustic are every where covered, and only the end exposed.

This was the mode in which bougies were armed, when this practice was first taken up; but it happened that, in two or three instances, the caustic was left in the urethra; that canal when in a very irritable state grasped the bougie, and pulled the caustic out; this led me to consider how such an accident might be prevented, and to apply to the makers of bougies for that purpose. Mr. Pass, the beadle of the surgeon's company, who deals in bougies, discovered a very ingenious and effectual mode of securing the caustic. In forming the bougie, a piece of wire, the size of the caustic, is rolled up along with it, passing into the substance for half an inch; when the bougie is nearly finished, the wire is withdrawn, and the caustic inserted in its place ; after this, the bougie is rolled again, so that the sides of the caustic become firmly cemented to the linen, by means of the composition of the bougie, and when cold, cannot be separated by any force. In this way bougies are now generally armed.

After the bougie has been thus prepared, the distance of the stricture from the external orifice is to be measured, and the canal cleared by passing a common bougie, fully as large as that which is armed. The armed bougie, with the distance marked upon it, is then to be introduced, and applied to the stricture ; when it is brought in contact with the obstruction, it is to be steadily retained there, with a moderate degree of pressure at first, and less as it is longer continued, since the bougie becomes soft by remaining in the urethra, and readily bends, if the pressure is too great. The time it is to remain depends a good deal upon the sensations of the patient, and the length of time the parts have been diseased ;

but on the first trial it should be less than a minute, as it then commonly gives greater pain than on any subsequent application. The pain produced by the caustic is not felt so immediately as it would be natural to expect; the first sensation arises from the pressure of the bougie on the stricture; a little after, there is the feeling of heat in the parts; and lastly, that of pain.

As soon as the caustic begins to act, the surgeon who makes the application is made sensible of it by the smaller arteries of the parts beating with unusual violence, which is very distinctly felt by the finger and thumb that grasp the penis.

The pain that is brought on by the caustic lasts for some time after it is withdrawn; but this period differs in almost every patient, being sometimes extended to half an hour, and sometimes only a few minutes.

The kind of pain is heat and soreness, which is not severe, not being accompanied

by the peculiar irritation, upon so many
occasions experienced by patients who have
strictures; an irritation that cannot be described, which is most insupportable, and
is too often brought on by dilating strictures with the bougie. After the caustic
has been withdrawn, it is desirable that the
patient should have made water before he
uses exercise, as the parts are commonly
more tranquil after having done so; but
sometimes no water will flow at the first
effort. When that is the case, it should not
be urged, as it is not of any material consequence. It happens not unfrequently, that
at the first time of making water, some blood
passes along with it. This is rather favourable; as when the parts bleed, the stricture
usually proves to be so far destroyed that
at the next trial the bougie passes through
it. Every other day, appears to be as often
as it is ever prudent to apply the caustic.
Nor can any thing be gained by applying it,
oftener, since the application would only be
made upon the slough, which takes that time

to separate in ordinary cases. In some cases the slough remains three or four days, and then the caustic should not be applied during that period. In others, once a week is as often as it can be used with advantage.

The bougie which is passed down to prepare the way for the caustic, and measure the distance for the armed bougie, must be made of soft materials, that it may readily receive an impression from the part against which it is pressed, and its colour should be light, so as to admit of those impressions being more distinctly seen. With the assistance of such bougies, the size and shape of the orifice of the stricture can be discovered; the progress of the caustic upon it accurately ascertained; whether it is on one side of the canal, or equally all round, distinctly determined; and the mode of applying the caustic, most judiciously managed.

When the soft bougie passes through the stricture, by leaving it in the canal a few minutes, it can be known whether the stricture is completely destroyed or only relaxed; in the last case, there is an impression on the side of the bougie; and the surgeon should never proceed further till it is ascertained that the first stricture is removed. When he finds that he has been deceived by a contraction again taking place at this part while the caustic is applied to another stricture, he must again return to it, and rest there till it is completely destroyed.

So necessary is the information which is acquired in this way, to enable the surgeon to prosecute the cure of stricture by means of the caustic, that without it this mode of practice could not be pursued. The necessary confidence, which nothing but an accurate knowledge of what has been already done can give, is in no other way to be procured.

In cases where, from long continuance of the stricture, there is so much induration, that the caustic makes very slow progress, which sometimes happens, the parts in time become so much accustomed to it, that it gives little or no sensation when used, but afterwards brings on the same irritation and irregular contractions in the urethra that follow the use of the common bougie ; whenever this takes place, it should be for a time left off.

This remark is less applicable to strictures that admit of a bougie passing on to the bladder, than to those of a worse kind, in which a bougie of the smallest size cannot pass.

In cases of stricture, attacks of inflammation frequently come on the passage after connection with women; in this state of the parts the caustic should not be applied, for the pain is infinitely greater than at other times, is of longer continuance, and seems considerably to aggravate the inflammation along the canal, but does not bring on spasm or suppression of urine. It is more prudent to defer the application of the caustic till the inflammation subsides, which it generally does in a few days.

The effects of the caustic, as it is natural

N

to suppose, vary in different men. In some men the pain is so little attended to, that they continue their former amusements, and do not even refrain from excesses of every kind, and yet pass with impunity; that such patients, however, are not always so secure, will appear from the Cases.

The pain is sometimes not felt at the time; the length of the application, in such cases, can only be determined by experience; but the pain comes on a few minutes after the caustic is removed, is very severe, and lasts for hours.

Where the stricture produces uneasy symptoms, the patient is often freed from them on the day when the caustic is applied, but they return on the following day; so that in such cases, the application of the caustic, instead of giving pain, produces ease. In some instances there has been a considerable hæmorrhage from the parts to which the caustic was applied; this, as will appear from the Cases, has generally been brought on by imprudence, but in no in-

stance has been attended with bad consequences.

There is a substance which in some
cases comes away after the application of
the caustic, either the same day or the day
following ; it is dark coloured on the outside, and of a light colour within, is tubu-
lar, and of different sizes. In general the
portions are too small to afford any information respecting it; but in one instance a
portion was procured an inch long, which
admitted of being preserved upon a bougie
in spirits. It is evidently the cuticular lining
of the urethra, and generally comes off
where a portion of that canal has been in a
contracted state between two strictures, and
one of them being destroyed, this part is
dilated, and the cuticle thrown off. The
surface is more tender next day, but that
symptom quickly goes away. There is sometimes a succession of these cuticles brought
away; when they come from the space close
to an old stricture, they have a conical form,
and obstruct the urine, till thrown out. When

N 2

these cuticular portions separate, the caustic should only be passed every third day.

If there is any peculiar symptom which comes on whenever the patient is guilty of irregularity, it will commonly also be produced by the caustic, till the parts are accustomed to the application, the patient is therefore to be directed to follow the same modes of relieving himself, should such symptom occur, as he was in the habit of employing before.

If he has been accustomed to suppressions, which were relieved by passing a bougie, or large doses of opium, they may happen the day after the caustic is employed, and will be readily relieved by the same means.

If a paroxysm of fever, or an ague fit, as it is termed, has frequently come on, it will most probably do so under the use of the caustic. In many instances it occurs upon the destruction of a stricture; and where strictures have been of long standing, a regular attack has followed upon any of them giving way. The only mode of treating this symptom which appears necessary, is giving opening medicines. Some uncommon instances of these paroxysms of fever are mentioned in the Cases. They most commonly occur in patients who have been in warm climates, but are by no means confined to them.

It often happens that when there are several strictures, the application of the caustic to that which is nearest to the external orifice affects all the others, and makes them relax ; so that the stream of urine which before had been very small, shall now be large and free ; but after this stricture has been destroyed, and the caustic is applied to one nearer the bladder, the very contrary effect is produced. This sympathy between strictures is sometimes the cause of patients and even surgeons forming too favourable a prognostic.

The effect of the caustic when applied to the first stricture in taking off the spasmodic contraction of the others, is well illustrated in the following case.

An officer in the navy who had been troubled with strictures for many years, was taken ill at Portsmouth with a suppression of urine; this did not go off, and an operation was thought necessary to relieve the bladder. Mr. Lynn was sent for from London to take charge of the patient; on his arrival he found the bladder very much distended; but by the means which he employed, an involuntary discharge took place, which prevented any increase of the distension, and made an operation not immediately necessary : he therefore ordered the patient to London. When he came to town, Mr. Lynn desired to have a consultation. At the meeting, it was stated by the patient that no bougie could be passed into the bladder since this attack began, although several attempts had been made before Mr. Lynn got down to him. At this time the bladder continued much distended, the integuments above the pubes inflamed, and in a state of suppuration. Mr. Lynn wished to know my opinion whether these attempts ought to be persevered in, or whether the use of the caustic might be attempted with safety.

After considering all the circumstances, it was my opinion that the caustic was a much safer instrument than the bougie, more likely to remove the spasm than any other mode, and its use attended with less risk than passing small bougies in that state of the parts. Mr. Rush and Mr. Lynn concurred in this opinion, and a bougie was immediately passed down to the first obstruction about four inches from the external orifice at the glans penis, and afterwards an armed bougie was applied to it; the pain was sharp, and continued during the rest of the day. After an interval of one day, the caustic was again applied, and he made some water in a natural way; this he continued to do at intervals of two hours. The use of the caustic was continued, and in the course of five months a passage was procured into the bladder, and he was cured of all his symptoms. In this case a strangury of near four

days, and the disease which produced it,
were removed by caustic.

Some pains has been taken to explain
that it is necessary for the cure of strictures,
that the canal at that part should be brought
to the same width, or nearly so, with the rest
of the passage. This is so obvious that it
cannot require being insisted upon; and
yet in very many instances in which strictures have been removed by caustic under
the direction of different practitioners, it
has not been sufficiently attended to, the
patient has been disappointed, and the mode
of treatment has been hastily condemned,
from being injudiciously used.

This imperfect mode of applying the
caustic by which the stricture is only partially removed, has arisen from two causes;
the most common of these, has been a want
of confidence in the practice, rather choosing
to do too little, than take further responsibility. This may be thought prudent, but
it is neither just to the patient, nor to the
mode of practice employed. The second cause

is, that the orifice of the urethra, in cases of stricture, contracts in consequence of the stream of urine being too small to keep it of its natural size ; and the surgeon mistakes the apparent size of the orifice for that of the urethra, which is commonly much larger. These observations are made from having been very frequently deceived in this way, and after the strictured part was rendered equally wide with the apparent size of the orifice, having considered my patient as cured ; but the symptoms not going completely off, or returning soon after, led me to try a bougie of a larger size, and in that way find out my mistake, which was corrected by making use of a larger sized bougie, after which the symptoms have gone entirely away.

There are instances of strictures returning after they have been removed by the caustic, and several of these are noticed in the first section of the following chapter. It would appear that in such cases the stricture has not been completely removed, either from one of the causes already stated, or the following circumstance, which may mislead the surgeon, although in a very different way.

Many strictures in which the permanent contraction has either originally been small, or has been diminished by the effects of the caustic, have a considerable spasmodic action ; this effect the caustic has a power of subduing, and by doing so is admitted to pass through ; by which means many strictures of this description elude the effects of the caustic, and are prevented from being wholly removed.

To give cases illustrative of every rule of practice that is laid down, would prove unnecessarily tedious ; but the following will explain the disadvantages attending the use of the caustic, when too small for the size of the urethra.

A gentleman had three strictures, for which he put himself under the care of a person in considerable practice ; who recommended the use of the caustic. It was

applied a great number of times, and at length
a bougie was passed into the bladder. He
was now told he was cured; but unfortunately all the symptoms remained with
little abatement. Medicines were then given
to relieve the inconveniences which the
caustic had not removed; but at the end of
four months, he said he was tired of having two evils, the disease, and the course of
medicines: he therefore got rid of the one,
which was in his power, and made up his
mind to bear the other as well as he was
able. Under these circumstances he consulted me. Upon examining the parts, the
orifice of the urethra appeared very small,
and was in some measure contracted. It was
stated, that the cure had not been accomplished, from the surgeon having believed
the size of the urethra was the same with
that of the orifice, which was a deception;
as the orifice had contracted itself to the
size of the stream of urine, in consequence
of the stricture lower down preventing the
urine from keeping it stretched to its natural

size. It was therefore proposed to apply the
caustic to the orifice ; and when that was
made larger, to proceed to the other strictures as they occurred. As soon as the caustic had enlarged the stricture next the bladder, the patient felt relief, made water with
more ease, and in a larger stream, and the
discharge and other symptoms began to
abate. Three or four applications allowed a
bougie of a full size to pass into the bladder, and the symptoms went off. In this
case, the former treatment had reduced the
strictures, but not removed them, and kept
the canal in a state of irritation, so that
the symptoms were not even palliated;
for though the canal was absolutely larger
than before the caustic was applied, the
strictures which remained were rendered
more irritable.

The same thing has happened to other
patients from the injudicious use of the
caustic, very much to the discredit of this
mode of practice.

CHAPTER IV.

CASES ILLUSTRATING THE APPLICATION OF THE CAUSTIC TO STRICTURES, UNDER DIF-FERENT CIRCUMSTANCES.

THE number of cases of stricture which have come under my care, since the first edition of this work was published, has been so great, that it now enables me to give instances of this disease under a great variety of circumstances; and to state the effects which the caustic has produced on different patients, upon a very extensive scale.

To make the detail of cases necessary for this purpose as little tedious, and as instruc-tive as possible to those who consult them, they are divided into separate Chapters, and these are subdivided into a number of Sec-tions.

Many of the cases are given in the words of the patient, with little or no variation, particularly the previous history. This might be inadmissible in a work which depended on the excellence of the composition; but in one like the present, which has for its principal object the conveying to the public facts and observations on a particular disease, with perspicuity and fidelity, there did not appear to be the smallest objection to it.

The present chapter contains the different circumstances under which the strictures have been met with, and the effects of the caustic in removing them.

SECTION I.

COMMON CASES OF STRICTURE REMOVED BY THE EFFECTS OF THE CAUSTIC.

THIS Section contains cases illustrating the common effects of caustic, and the number of applications which were made before the cure was completed; these will be found to have varied very much in different patients.

Having found that cases in which the bougie had been long used were very difficult of cure by the caustic, it led me to suppose the continued use of the bougie was disadvantageous to this mode of treatment; this however, a more extensive experience has shewn is by no means true, since in some instances where no bougie had ever been passed, the cure has been as difficult as in many of the others.

CASE I.

A gentleman, about forty-six years of age, who had resided many years in India, discovered a stricture in the urethra, which was treated in the common way by the bougie; and as soon as the dilatation had been carried to the extent the parts would bear, the bougie was left off, and the patient considered as cured. He was however put upon his guard, that probably after some time there might be a return; and whenever that happened, the bougie must be again employed. He found that two months was the longest time that the stricture remained in the state in which the bougie left it; beginning after that period to contract, and require dilatation. He went on in this way for four years, when he consulted me. It was proposed that he should endeavour to carry the dilatation further, and bring that part of the canal nearer to its full size, which there was reason to believe would make the returns less frequent. He did so; but found that little was to be gained beyond what he had before effected. In December, 1794, finding the bougie incapable of producing a cure, he consented to make trial of the caustic. It was applied in the manner already described, and gave pain almost immediately on being introduced; it was therefore only allowed to remain in contact with the stricture for a minute: the pain continued some hours, but was not severe. Next day some blood was discharged, and a degree of uneasiness was felt in the part. This made him suppose his case unfavourable for the use of the caustic; but on the following day, a common sized bougie passed readily into the bladder without any pain, or producing the smallest degree of irritation; nothing more was done, and the parts were left entirely to themselves. In May, 1795, five months after the application of the caustic, the same bougie was passed without meeting the smallest degree of resistance. In July, 1795,

O

he had a severe attack of cold, attended with
fever, and during the continuance of the indisposition, there was a degree of tenderness
along the membrane of the urethra; and
the bladder did not admit of being distended
to its usual size.; these symptoms however
all went off with the others, and in August
the same bougie passed into the bladder as
readily as before, and has continued to do so.

The bladder and urethra having taken
on a state of irritation, in consequence of
general indisposition, and recovering themselves without bringing back the contraction in the urethra, is a strong circumstance
in favour of the disposition for stricture being in this case entirely removed.

On January 22d, 1796, a bougie was
passed which was believed to be of the same
size with that formerly employed, and it was
found that it would not pass ; this led me to
conclude that the stricture had in a degree
returned; the caustic was therefore again
used, which, after remaining less than a
minute, went on to the bladder. Two days

after, upon comparing the bougie which passed formerly with that which had been now used, it was discovered that this last was larger; there was therefore no reason to believe that any thing had been lost, but that the passage had not before been enlarged so much as it ought to have been, although it admitted the bougies of the largest size in common use at that time, which in the course of a year's experience were found to be too small, and therefore these of a much larger size were employed, without recollecting that those formerly used were so much smaller. This patient from that time has passed the same sized bougie once a month, and in the year 1805 has had no return of the disease.

CASE II.

A gentleman between fifty and sixty years of age, who had been subject to a stricture for many years, and had been in the habit of using bougies, kept the parts by that means from contracting beyond a

O 2

certain extent; but as they were never
completely dilated, the contraction constantly returned. In February 1795, he
came from the country apparently free from
complaint, but found upon getting out of
the post-chaise that he could not make
water; which brought on great irritation
upon the bladder; and in this state he first
consulted me. After straining for some time,
he voided about half an ounce of urine,
which relieved him a little; but the desire
very soon returned, and he made the same
quantity with similar exertions. A small
bougie was passed into the bladder, and allowed to remain there till the desire to
make water came on; it was then withdrawn, and was followed by half a pint of
urine, which made him quite easy. The
reason why the bougie only gave temporary
relief, was then explained to him, and also
the advantages to be derived from the
caustic: with these he was so well satisfied
as to determine to give it a trial. He was
directed to remain quiet the next day; and

on the day following the caustic was applied to the stricture ; notwithstanding he was a good deal heated by the journey, and had some degree of general indisposition, his pulse being quick, his tongue white, and his sleep restless and disturbed, it brought on no irritation. The caustic was twice applied to this stricture, after which a common sized bougie passed through it ; but a second stricture was met with about an inch and half further back ; to this the caustic was applied four times, before the common sized bougie could go on to the bladder. The use of the bougie was not persevered in, and there has been no return of the stricture.

CASE III.

An officer from India, had for twelve years a stricture in the urethra, which brought on violent fits of irritation, and made him have recourse to bougies at different times through the whole of that period. The complaint however always returned, and he had given up all hopes of any permanent relief. But finding that some of his friends had received so much benefit from the use of the caustic, he wished to give it a trial.

In December, 1794, this mode of treatment was adopted. The caustic was applied three different times to the stricture before it was sufficiently destroyed, to allow a full sized bougie to be passed through it. In this case, as the complaint had been of very long standing, it was proposed that a bougie should be passed every day, and allowed to remain a few minutes in the passage, till the tenderness in the urethra from the use of the caustic should have gone off; this was done for ten or twelve days, and the bougie was then left off.

The bougie, for the first two or three days, brought on a good deal of irritation along the whole canal, which contracted with some force upon it ; and on withdrawing the bougie, it was found to have been tightly embraced by the urethra : this has happened in some degree in other cases, but not to the same extent ; the irritation however gradually went off. This gentleman went upon distant service, and no accounts have been since received ; when he left town he was free from complaint.

CASE IV.

A gentleman aged forty-six, suspected that he had caught a gonorrhœa, for which he applied to me for assistance; the symptoms did not exactly correspond with those more usually met with in gonorrhœa ; upon making a particular inquiry, they were found to be those of a stricture in the urethra. As he had been subject to irritation in the bladder, frequency of making water, and had for eighteen months been under the care of a surgeon for a gleet, which gradually disappeared, about a year

before the present attack ; there was reason
to believe that the stricture had been formed
for many years. On examining the urethra
by means of a common sized bougie, a
stricture was found there : to this the
caustic was twice applied, and removed it,
so as to allow the bougie to pass about an
inch and half further on, where it was
stopped by a second stricture ; this had the
caustic applied to it three times, and then a
full sized bougie found a free passage into
the bladder. The discharge and other
symptoms all went off, and the patient remained free from complaint.

In this case, as well as in many others,
there was a tenderness felt in that part of
the membrane of the urethra, where the
inflammation in gonorrhœa is commonly
situated. This symptom is the cause of many
cases of stricture being misunderstood ; but
it is a very common sympathetic effect of
irritation being produced on the stricture,
and subsides as soon as that irritation is
removed.

CASE V.

A gentleman who had been some years in China, upon his return to England, had connection with a women, and was supposed to have caught a gonorrhœa; but the symptoms were not removed by the usual means, and were afterwards discovered to arise from stricture. Upon having recourse to the bougie, the urethra was found to be extremely irritable, so much so that an abscess formed in perinæo, while he was under that course; this on leaving off the bougie got well; and by returning to it again, the stricture, which was about three inches from the orifice of the glans penis, was dilated: but after the use of the bougie had been continued for many months, it could not be retained in the canal without giving very unpleasant sensations. On attempting to pass the bougie on to the bladder, another stricture was met with at the bulb of the urethra, which allowed a small bougie to pass, but did not admit of the necessary increase for its dilatation. So very irritable was the canal, that the surgeon, after having proceeded thus far, rather chose to leave the second stricture, than run the risk of bringing on irritation by continuing the use of the bougie.

In this state the patient consulted me; the use of the caustic was proposed, both with a view to enlarge the second stricture, and make it less liable to return; it was explained to him at the same time that this stricture was the original disease, and that which had been dilated only a consequence of it. He said, he had no objection to try the caustic, but had great apprehensions that it would not succeed, from the uncommon degree of irritability of the membrane of the urethra, which his former surgeon, a man of eminence, declared to be greater than he had ever met with.

On the twenty-fifth of May, 1795, the

caustic was applied to the second stricture; the pain felt at the time was unattended by irritation, and was by no means so severe as he had formerly experienced in retaining in the passage a bougie, that had gone through the first stricture; it did not however go off for several hours after the caustic was withdrawn; a heat and uneasiness remaining in the canal during that period. On the twenty-seventh, the caustic was applied again; and while it was pressing against the stricture, the end of the bougie went through, which made it necessary to withdraw the caustic: there was a slight degree of pain in the passage all day, and a little blood was discharged; on the following day, when he made water, there was a tinge of blood upon his linen; but not the smallest degree of irritation. On the twenty-ninth a full sized bougie passed into the bladder without difficulty, gave no pain, and produced no irritation; it was allowed to remain a few minutes, and was then withdrawn. The next

day he passed the same bougie himself with
equal ease, and immediately withdrew it.
He was advised to do the same for seven
days, to keep the parts in that state till they
had perfectly recovered themselves.

Some time after this, he told me that he
was perfectly well, and felt now the truth
of the remarks which had been made to him;
for before the caustic was applied, he had
been subject to erections in his sleep, attended with uneasiness, and sensations about
the bladder, which he then supposed to be
natural, as he had been long accustomed to
them ; but these were now entirely removed
and he passed his water more quickly than
before, and without his usual degree of
straining towards the latter part of the time.

On the eleventh of July he caught a severe cold, which brought on an irritation
upon the bladder and urethra, and the stream
of urine was very much diminished ; this
alarmed him a good deal : but it proved to
be only a temporary complaint, for the same

sized bougie passed readily into the bladder, and these symptoms disappeared as soon as the effects of the cold were removed.

In this case the bladder had been so long under the necessity of using great force in expelling the urine, that it took some time to adapt its action to the enlarged state of the urethra. When the patient had the desire to make water, the bladder acted so powerfully, that the urethra immediately dilated, being unable to resist its action and restrain the urine; this put him to the inconvenience of voiding it at a very short warning; the water was by these means so quickly expelled, that the bladder from habit continued to act for some time after it was emptied, and this contraction upon itself produced a degree of uneasiness.

These symptoms in a few weeks went off.

C A S E VI.

A gentleman who had been many years in India, and whose constitution had suffered severely from the climate, returned to England, in 1793, in a very bad state of general health, and with a stricture in the urethra. In India he had an ague for four years, and had affections of his joints, for the removal of which mercury was very freely employed; but without effect, and brought on an irritable state of body, from which he had not recovered.

For the stricture in the urethra, on May 10th, 1795, the caustic was applied. After it had been used four times, a common sized bougie passed through it; but another stricture was discovered a little further back in the urethra, to which the caustic was applied three times before the bougie could proceed to the bladder. The passing of the bougie was attended with some difficulty, and brought on irritation;

the caustic was therefore applied a fifth time, after which the bougie passed readily. The bougie was now directed to be passed every day, for a short time, to prevent a return of the disease, and at the end of six days was left off. The use of the bougie had been attended with a slight degree of irritation, during the whole six days. Two days after leaving it off, the patient was caught in a shower of rain, the weather at that time being very variable, and liable to uncommon and sudden changes of temperature, and caught a violent cold, which brought on a severe attack of ague, exactly like what he had in India; an abscess now formed in the under part of the penis, on the corpus spongiosum urethræ, where it is covered by the scrotum. This showed that the ague was symptomatic of the irritation in the urethra, which brought on the abscess; and it is highly probable, that the ague he had in the East Indies was caused by the stricture, which kept up a constant irritation in the urethra. The ague returned very violently every other day, for eight days; the abscess now pointed just before the scrotum, and was opened by the point of a lancet; after this the ague went off, the inflammation subsided, and part of the urine came through the abscess, but by introducing the flexible gum catheter every time of making water, this was in a great measure prevented; and in a few days the external orifice healed up.

The stricture did not return; but it was thought right to use a full sized bougie, for several weeks, till the parts had entirely recovered themselves. It was afterwards necessary to continue the use of the bougie, introduced for a few inches, to prevent the urine lodging in that part where the abscess had communicated with the urethra; which happened whenever this precaution was not taken; this effect however gradually diminished, till it went entirely off.

In this case an abscess formed; but as it is the only instance that has been met with where such an event took place, and as the first symptoms came on eight days after the last application of the caustic, and only two after using the bougie, it is with more propriety to be attributed to the irritation of the bougie, than any violence from the caustic : particularly as it is a very common effect of the use of the bougie when applied to an irritable urethra.

CASE VII.

An officer in the navy, twenty-five years of age, in the year 1790, while stationed in the Mediterranean, where he had been for some years, had a discharge from the urethra, which he considered as a gleet in consequence of a gonorrhœa : this was removed in about three months, under a course of injections, and a regular mode of living ; and while he continued to live in that manner, he remained free from the discharge, and thought himself well. But in the year 1795, being thrown into situa-

P

tions that required exertions, which rendered his mode of life less regular, and impaired his general health, the discharge returned. As he supposed it to be the gleet returned, little attention was paid to it ; and when he consulted me in the end of August, it was only mentioned accidentally as a proof of general weakness. This symptom was considered by me to be the effect of a stricture ; and this opinion was confirmed by his making water more frequently than is usual for persons in health to do, and from his having erections in his sleep, and involuntary emissions whenever he eat suppers, or drank a glass or two of wine beyond his usual quantity ; which had been the case for the last year. On passing a bougie, it was stopped at the bulb of the urethra ; on allowing it to remain there for a few minutes, it went on with difficulty, attended with pain ; there was also an impression of stricture left on the bougie : the caustic was applied to this stricture three different times, at the usual intervals, and the passage then admitted a common sized bougie. Finding that in other cases the passing a bougie, under these circumstances, brought on irritation, the parts were left entirely to themselves.

CASE VIII.

A gentleman about forty years of age had a stricture in the urethra, brought on in the East Indies, in which the symptoms of irritation increased to so great a degree, that he returned to England for the recovery of his health. When he arrived in London, he had been eight years afflicted by this complaint, and frequently in that time subject to strangury, from spasmodic affections of the stricture. He had recourse to the bougie, and persevered in its use for nearly three years: during the latter part of this time he attempted little more than to preserve the passage in the state to which he had before been enabled to dilate it, which was only sufficient to admit a bougie about half the common size. In June, 1795, he was obliged to return to India, which made him think more seriously of his situation, and he was induced to try the caustic; it was applied twice to a stricture three inches from the glans, which it removed; but another was discovered a little further on; this second seemed to be in the membranous part of the urethra. The caustic, after it had been applied twice, appeared to have produced no effect; but after the third time, the water passed more freely, and a degree of irritation which had come upon the parts went entirely off. The fourth time the caustic went through, and a full sized bougie passed into the bladder; this was followed by an hemorrhage, that lasted the whole day in a slight degree; the parts were entirely free from irritation, although in making preparations for his voyage he was obliged to undergo considerable fatigue; this was attributed to the bleeding, which in other cases has produced a similar good effect. A bougie of a full size having passed readily into the bladder, he was advised to leave the parts for a few days entirely to themselves, as the bougie had been found in other cases to bring on irritation; he was afterwards to pass a bougie every day for a week, and let it remain a few minutes, to prevent the recurrence of the disease.

This precaution was considered as necessary, because the patient was going to a climate in which the disease is more liable to return.

CASE IX.

A gentleman, about twenty-two years of age, in his way to Bristol, consulted me in May, 1795, respecting a stricture in the urethra, and fistula in perinæo, to know how far they could be connected with complaints in his chest, which were supposed to be of a serious nature. Also to give an opinion upon the best mode of treating the stricture. In making the necessary inquiries,

it appeared that the use of the bougie had
been begun under the direction of another
surgeon, and every thing was going on very
favourably; the plan that had been taken
up was approved, and a steady perseverance
in it enforced. He set off next day for Bristol,
where he remained four months, and received
much benefit in his general health; he had
also dilated the urethra till it very freely
admitted the common sized bougie, which he
continued to use for a fortnight, to prevent
a return of the disease.

In passing through London in the latter
part of September, he called upon me to
say that he was perfectly well of the stricture. In the course of conversation, he was
admonished never to travel without bougies,
as the disease was liable to return, and it
was therefore necessary to be upon his
guard. He asked me to pass a bougie, and
ascertain the present state of the parts, as it
was nearly a month since he had passed
one; on doing so, it was stopped by the
stricture, which had contracted so much in

that time as not to admit a bougie of half the common size.

Under these circumstances the use of the caustic was recommended, which he readily agreed to try, and it was immediately applied. The application was repeated four times before the passage allowed a full sized bougie to go through the stricture; it was however much larger than any that had been passed before. The parts were left entirely to themselves. In this state he went into the country. It was found afterwards that the parts when left to themselves got into a state of contraction, which was taken off by the bougie being occasionally passed; he has therefore continued to do so, and in 1805 there was no return of the stricture.

CASE X.

A gentleman about thirty-five years old,
who was going upon foreign service, consulted me for an old gleet which was very
troublesome, and which he was desirous to
remove before he went abroad.   The cause,
upon examination, proved to be a stricture; and for the cure the caustic was employed.   The use of the caustic was begun
in September, 1795.   It was applied twice
to the first obstruction, after which the
bougie passed about an inch further on to
another obstruction; and when this second
had been twice touched by the caustic, the
bougie went on to the bladder; each application of the caustic was followed by a good
deal of blood.   The bougie that had been
armed with caustic and made use of upon
this occasion, after it had passed through
the stricture, appeared to be too small to
bring back the narrow part of the urethra
in this patient to the natural size;   it was

therefore proposed to arm a larger one, and repeat the application till the stricture should allow it a free passage. For this purpose, one, or probably two applications of the caustic were considered as all that could be necessary; we were however astonished to find that, after it had been applied three times in this way, nothing was apparently gained. This want of success led us to believe that a further continuance of its use would avail but little in increasing the width of the stricture; but the fourth application destroyed the remains of the obstruction, and a large bougie went on to the bladder. The caustic was once more applied, to make the bougie pass with greater freedom, and then the parts were left to themselves.

The use of the caustic in this case did not give the smallest uneasiness, beyond the local pain, which was neither violent nor of long continuance. This was in part attributed to the bleeding, which always relieves when it takes place.

CASE XI.

A gentleman, sixty-nine years of age, who had been many years in warm climates, had lived a regular life, and even in his youth had never suffered from venereal complaints ; in the spring of 1795, was attacked with a violent inflammation along the whole internal surface of the urethra, extending over the glans penis, and inside of the prepuce. This complaint came on a few hours after toying with a young woman, with whom he had no intercourse ; and therefore could not originate from a venereal cause.

These appearances led me to suspect a stricture in the urethra, and my inquiries were directed to that point ; but he declared that his water passed in a full stream, and not more frequently than is usual at that time of life ; which led me to treat it as an irritation and inflammation, brought on by unusual action in the parts. The inflammation subsided, but the discharge continued for several months; but as it was attended with no pain, very little trouble, and could not be of a venereal nature, hardly any notice was taken of it. At the end of four months a new symptom appeared, the parts in the perinæum had become swelled, and were extremely tender when pressed; upon examination a small abscess had formed there, and had come so near the skin, that it burst while my finger was applied to it. This swelling had not the appearance of a recent inflammation, and the parts surrounding the membranous portion of the urethra were hard and thickened, which could in no way be accounted for but as the effect of a stricture; permission was therefore requested to pass a bougie, which met with an obstruction a little further on than the middle of the canal. The abscess in perinæo, as well as the former symptoms, were now very readily explained; they were all brought on by the stricture. As soon as the presence of a stricture was ascer-

tained, the patient, who was a very intelli-
gent man, recollected many circumstances
in proof of this obstruction having continued for some years, which till now he
had attributed to other causes. The application of the caustic was proposed as the best
mode of treating it ; to this he readily ac-
ceded.

The use of the caustic was begun on the
seventh of September, at which time there
was a good deal of uneasiness in the perinæum ; this went off immediately after
the first application, and the parts became
less indurated than they had been before.
The second application of the caustic destroyed this stricture ; but a little further on
there was another, which had the caustic applied to it eight times, without any advance
being gained ; the caustic however gave
little or no pain, and the other symptoms
were upon the whole diminished ; this induced us to persevere, and after the twelfth
application the stricture was sufficiently destroyed to allow a common sized bougie to

pass through it; as soon as this object was gained, the parts were left to themselves.

This gentleman had no return of symptoms in the urethra till the month of June, 1805, when his bowels had from neglect become much loaded, and it was ten hours before an evacuation could be procured by medicine; while in this state of constipation, with ineffectual efforts to go to stool, a suppression of urine was brought on, which induced him to send for me; a small flexible gum catheter was passed, and nearly a quart of water drawn off; he afterwards passed his water without difficulty; but from exposure to cold during this attack, a violent inflammation came upon the diaphragm, which in 60 hours proved fatal.

On inspecting the body, the disease which occasioned his death was confined to the chest, but the prostate gland was found much enlarged; there was no return of stricture, but the two parts where they had been were readily detected, having a different appearance from the rest of the urethra, being rather narrower, and the membrane more compact in its texture; the surface was equally smooth with the rest of the canal.

The suppression arose from the enlargement of the prostate gland, and the confined state of the bowels.

CASE XII.

A gentleman, seventy years of age, in May, 1794, had a suspicious connection which brought on a discharge from the urethra; this was supposed to be venereal, and treated accordingly by his surgeon. Under this plan the symptoms went off in a fortnight, and he considered himself as cured. On repeating the connection, the same symptoms returned, which induced him to put himself under my care; the symptoms were suspected to be those of stricture, and my suspicions were confirmed by a bougie being unable to pass into the bladder. The case was now treated as a stricture, and the patient directed to take up the use of the bougie. Two strictures were met with, and in three months the passage was so much dilated as to allow a bougie of a common size to pass through both of them ; as the disposition for contraction is in this way not commonly removed, the use of the bougie was continued for a fortnight longer, to establish the cure.

In three months the disease returned ; and was treated as before, till the parts were dilated to the same extent as formerly. The patient now thought himself quite well ; but in less than two months had a relapse.

The mode of treatment by caustic was now explained, and it was proposed to make trial of it, as the benefit derived from the bougie was so short in its duration. In the beginning of the month of Sept. 1795, the caustic was used ; it was applied twice to the first stricture, and four times to the second ; by this means they were both removed ; after which the parts were left to themselves.

The caustic in this case gave no pain whatever; the sensation produced at the time of its application scarcely amounted to uneasiness. In twelve days it procured a passage for a larger sized bougie than could be admitted after three months had been constantly employed in dilating the parts.

CASE XIII.

A sailor, about forty years of age, who had been many years in warm climates, came into St. George's Hospital with a stricture in the urethra; which did not readily admit the smallest sized bougie to pass. The caustic was applied to it three different times, after this a common sized bougie could be passed into the bladder, but not without difficulty; this was used once a day, for two or three days together, a few minutes each time, but the bougie brought on a considerable degree of irritation, and was therefore left off. On the following day he had a total suppression of urine;

this symptom was relieved by opiate glysters, and he made water in small quantities, but not without a good deal of straining. After the experience acquired, of the effects of the caustic in relieving spasm, its application was proposed for the removal of the present symptoms. With this view the caustic was now applied, about twelve o'clock at noon; the irritation during the evening and night was very much relieved, and next day it was entirely removed. On the following day a large bougie passed very readily into the bladder. This was used two, or three times, for a minute or two, and was then left off; the man was allowed to remain in the hospital for a few weeks, and at the end of that period, having no return of his complaint, was discharged.

CASE XIV.

A gentleman, fifty years of age, had for three years been very much distressed by a difficulty in making water, for the removal

Q

of which he had recourse to the use of bougies ; at first he received considerable benefit from this practice, but afterwards became rather worse than before.

In the year 1796 he consulted me ; and upon examination it was found that there was a stricture three inches from the external orifice; this he said could not be, as he had no stoppage nearer than $5\frac{1}{2}$ inches, and another at $6\frac{1}{2}$ inches. He confessed, however, that once when he had passed a very small bougie through the last stricture, which he did with considerable difficulty, upon attempting to withdraw it, it was held fast, and could scarcely be withdrawn ; after it came out, the bougie was nearly cut through at three inches from the external orifice. It was explained to him that this arose from the sympathy between the strictures ; an irritation upon that next the bladder exciting an action in the stricture nearest the external orifice, so that it grasped the bougie, which it had never done before. The caustic was applied to this stricture at three inches, which readily gave way; the two others in succession were also destroyed by six applications of the caustic. He made water in a better stream than he had done for many years, had no spasm, and left me free from any complaint.

Some time after there was a return of spasm, and upon examining the urethra, it was capable of admitting a bougie three times larger than the one that had been used; so that the stricture had only been partially removed, and still required several applications of caustic of a larger size to destroy it.

CASE XV.

A gentleman, aged twenty-six, had a gonorrhœa in the year 1787, which lasted for a year, and was at last removed by the use of injections. From that period the urethra and bladder were more irritable than usual, and his water was voided at shorter intervals.

In February, 1789, symptoms came on which were suposed to arise from a recent infection; but as they were mild and went off in a short time, they were considered to be the consequences of an irritated state of the urethra.

In May, 1793, he had so much difficulty in making water, that some obstruction was suspected to have formed in the urethra, and a bougie was passed; a stricture was met with, which only admitted the smallest sized bougie to go on to the badder; but in six weeks the passage was dilated by bougies to its ordinary size.

In October, 1794, he went a journey which heated him very much, and had a connection the same night, for the first time for some months. The irritation from the connection brought on a strangury, attended by very violent symptoms, which lasted for several hours.

This return of the stricture made him again have recourse to bougies, to restore the urethra to its former state; they were left off the 10th of November, 1796, and only passed once a-week to prevent a return of the stricture.

Under these circumstances, upon examining the urethra the external orifice had a pouting appearance, and was very small, but was readily dilated, and admitted a bougie of a size larger than its apparent opening. The bougie passed on to the bladder, and was allowed to remain in the canal for a few minutes, to take an impression of any irregularity in the urethra ; upon being withdrawn, there was an indentation marking half the circumference of the bougie on the left side, to the depth of one-tenth of an inch, about $4\frac{1}{2}$ inches from the external orifice ; and the rest of the bougie to the point had the appearance of having been squeezed so much smaller.

It was evident from this examination, that there was a stricture at the distance of $4\frac{1}{2}$ inches. It was therefore concluded, from experience in other cases, that there must be another nearer the bladder, which had allowed itself to be relaxed in consequence of the other being dilated.

This was explained to the patient, and that this stricture was first to be removed, and afterwards we must act according to circumstances. The caustic was applied to this stricture, which was removed by two applications.

The bougie now passed with ease for $5\frac{1}{2}$ inches, where it met with a second stricture, which made an impression on the same side of the bougie, and to the same depth. This was removed by three applications of the caustic.

Another stricture was met with at $6\frac{1}{2}$ inches on the same side of the urethra; which required six applications to destroy it.

Six months after there was no return of the disease, but the discharge continued.

The curious circumstance in this case is, that there were three strictures, all formed on the same side of the urethra, and only extending over one half of the circumference. The pain from the caustic was inconsiderable.

Nine months from the application of the caustic, there was a return of the stricture. The patient had never been entirely free from a discharge, and a certain degree of uneasiness in these parts ; but this was so much less than he had before, that he did not take notice of it.

From this circumstance it was wished to ascertain whether the bougie that had been used was the full size of the canal, and it was found that a bougie much larger could pass readily down to the last stricture ; so that in this case the appearance of the orifice had made me believe the canal smaller than it really was. The stricture therefore required being destroyed by armed bougies of a larger size.

CASE XVI.

A. B. aged fifty eight, an out-door clerk to one of the large brewhouses in London, an habitual drinker of spirituous liquors, had been sixteen years troubled with a difficulty in passing his water, and in that period had many alarming attacks of suppression. For six years he was in the constant use of bougies, and in 1795 he passed the smallest size with difficulty.

At that time the caustic was used to three different strictures, which were all removed; but the number of applications necessary for that purpose amounted to fifty. The caustic gave less pain than in many other patients.

In 1797, he continued well, although no change had been made in his former habits of drinking, which are particularly hurtful in this disease.

CASE XVII.

An Austrian officer, forty-six years of age, came to England in the year 1796, and put himself under my care, for the relief of a difficulty in making water, under which he had laboured for many years.

The urethra was very small, and there was an obstruction $3\frac{1}{2}$ inches from the external orifice; there was another at $5\frac{1}{4}$; and the whole canal had an uncommon disposition for contraction. Recourse was had to the use of the caustic, which gave a good deal of local pain, but produced no irritation. Its effects upon the strictures were uncommonly slow, so much so as almost to make me despair of success; however, after one hundred and twelve applications, the bougie passed into the bladder.

During this long period, no irritation, suppression, or constitutional affection was produced; the only inconvenience was, that at two or three different times the urethra refused to let the bougie pass, but next day admitted it.

In this case the cuticular lining of the urethra came away upon the surface of the bougie, at different times, in small detached pieces. At one time the quantity was so great as in some measure to stop the canal. This was only met with near the time of the strictures being removed; and the same circumstance has occurred in other cases.

CASE XVIII.

A gentleman, forty years of age, had been troubled with strictures for fifteen years, during which period he had consulted the most eminent surgeons in London. He had used bougies under the direction of Mr. Pott, and afterwards had consulted Mr. Hunter. Upon examining the canal, and feeling the perinæum externally, Mr. Hunter said that the membranous part of the urethra was in a diseased state, was considerably thickened, and he could give him very little prospect of relief from the use of the bougie.

In the year 1796, he put himself under

my care. At that time he was very irritable, had considerable straining in making water, made it in small quantities at a time, and at short intervals. Upon examining the urethra, a stricture was met with at four inches from the external orifice; to this the caustic was applied; after six applications this stricture was destroyed, and the bougie passed on an inch and half further to a second stricture; this after twelve applications was also removed, but the bougie only passed a little way further on, and the end of the bougie had no regular impression made upon it. This was not satisfactory; but as the patient made water better, and all the other symptoms were a good deal relieved, there was sufficient encouragement to persevere in the use of the caustic. By doing so the bougie evidently passed further on, and the end of it had a flattened impression; in time an inch in length was gained, and the same length of the bougie was flattened and made rather smaller than the rest. He now found that he made water very well, and considered himself free from all his former symptoms of disease.

He was told there was still something particular in his case. The part beyond the stricture was narrowed in consequence of having been long diseased, but it was gradually becoming dilated; it was therefore necessary to persevere. When in this way we had gained an inch and half, the end of the bougie received a regular impression of a stricture, which explained the case, and shewed that the space between the stricture at five inches and a half, and another at seven inches, had been so much narrowed, and thickened, that externally the parts felt hard to the touch; it required the continued use of the caustic for a considerable time to make this space of the same width with the rest of the canal, after which the last stricture was destroyed.

It is curious that the caustic should be capable of producing this effect, as it cannot be supposed that the whole internal parts were destroyed. The effect of the caustic must have also disposed them to relax, and fall back into their natural state.

This is a case which explains the idea of a long stricture, but certainly is not, properly speaking, of that kind.

The caustic in this case was applied in all about sixty times, before the last stricture at the end of this narrowed part was destroyed.

CASE XIX.

A gentleman who had resided ten or eleven years at Bombay, returned to England with a stricture in the urethra, which had been coming on for several years before he left India. The surgeon, under whose direction he placed himself, conceived the idea of overcoming the stricture by pressure, and instead of the bougie, passed a catheter down to the stricture, and made

use of some force in pressing against it.
This mode of treatment brought on irritation, gave pain, and did not after some
time afford any prospect of a cure. Having
heard that the use of the caustic had proved
more successful, the gentleman put himself
under my care.

The stricture was situated near the bulb
of the urethra : there was, therefore, every
reason to suppose there was only one, to
which the caustic was applied in Nov. 1794.
After it had been twice used, a full sized
bougie passed through, but did not go into
the bladder. The prostate gland was now
suspected to be diseased ; but upon examination that was not the case, and this
second obstruction proved to be another
stricture, which it is highly probable was
the original. The caustic was applied to
this second stricture five times before a
middling sized bougie could be passed, and
this by no means with ease ; the urethra
was beginning to become irritable, and the
weather was intensely cold ; these were

circumstances peculiarly unfavourable to his constitution, which even in India had been affected by the cold season of that climate, and was much more so by the winter here. Having relieved the immediate symptoms, he was requested to remain quiet, and only to pass a bougie for a few minutes daily for some little time, till we should see what would be the effects of a change in the weather, upon the local as well as the constitutional irritability; and if the complaint was not removed under these circumstances, it would be necessary to return to the caustic.

Nothing was done for six months; in which time the symptoms, instead of being lessened, were a good deal increased; and the caustic was again resorted to. In returning to it, the second stricture only required to be removed; the first, which had been completely destroyed, not having returned. The first time the caustic was applied it gave little pain; but the second time the parts were all disposed to contract, and he was directed to take twenty drops of the tincture of opium, to diminish this degree of irritability, before it was again applied.   This medicine had the desired effect; for the parts were in a much more relaxed state, and a middle sized bougie was admitted into the bladder.   This, however, was not considered as sufficient, and the application of the caustic was continued for ten or twelve times; nor after all could a full sized bougie be passed, the canal at this part not being enlarged to the same width as the rest of the passage.

Finding that nothing more at present could be done, in August, 1795, he went to the sea, and found his general health much improved by bathing; but the strictures were disposed to contract, and every four or five days he found it necessary to pass a bougie down to the last stricture, but he did not get through it, and if this was neglected the other began to lose ground.   He went on in this way till January, 1796, when he came back to town and put himself again under my care; and as the weather was uncommonly mild, it was agreed to try the caustic, and see whether it now could be persevered in so as to destroy this last stricture, which had hitherto baffled all our efforts. The first applications brought on a degree of spasmodic action of the parts as before, but this was prevented by opiates; after ten or twelve applications without the smallest progress, the end of the unarmed bougie was impressed by the stricture on one side only. This being observed, the caustic was opposed exactly to that part; it was made larger, and after remaining about two minutes the stricture gave way, attended with a considerable hæmorrhage, and a great deal of pain; but wholly confined to the part, not extending along the canal to the glans penis, as it used to do: the stream of urine was found to be larger than before. A second application made in the same way effectually removed this obstruction; the bleeding and pain

R.

continued several days, after which a discharge came on, and they abated, and there was now a total absence of the irritation, which before had always been felt in those parts.

This however did not prove to be the last stricture, there was another three-fourths of an inch further on. This stricture had a larger caustic applied to it than is usually employed; after five applications little was gained, but no irritation was produced; the seventh effectually removed it, and a common sized bougie passed into the bladder. In destroying this last stricture, there was neither hæmorrhage nor irritation as in the others.

In this case the strictures were very difficult of removal, the caustic having been very often applied, and the time required was longer than in any case that had been hitherto met with. This perseverance was however in the end successful.

The three following Cases were communicated to me by Mr. Stephen Blackader, surgeon to the 99th regiment, quartered at Dublin.

DEAR SIR, Dublin, 23d April, 1795.

Your observations on the treatment of strictures in the urethra, have led me to make use of the caustic, in the case of a soldier under my care. The case appears to me so extraordinary, that it is sent inclosed ; and as you mean to write upon the subject, you may, if you please, give it a place in your publication.

CASE XX.

Isaac Earl, private soldier in the 99th regiment, thirty-three years of age, having caught cold upon duty, was reported to me with the following symptoms ; very frequent desire to make water, which he passed

R 2

in a stream like a thread ; and when he suppressed the desire, it came away involuntarily ; at night he had frequent emissions of the semen. He said that two years before he had a gonorrhœa, and from that period his urine had been voided with difficulty.

Upon passing a middle sized bougie, a stricture was found about three inches from the glans penis ; one of the smallest wax bougies passed through this, but was stopped by another stricture at the bulb of the urethra ; a small catgut bougie, the size of the first string of a violin, passed through the second stricture into the bladder. The catgut bougies were passed for a few days, and the symptoms became rather milder. At this time, in consequence of my leaving the regiment to come to London, the man was sent into the Dublin infirmary. On my return he had been discharged from the infirmary, and was in a much worse state than before. He now made water only by drops, and every ten minutes or quarter of an hour had an attack of spasm or violent straining come upon the bladder, attended with excruciating pain. When his shirt, or any thing touched the glans penis, some urine came away involuntarily. On passing a full sized bougie, a stricture was discovered about an inch from the glans ; this might have existed before, as on my first examination so large a bougie had not been passed. Profiting by your instructions, the caustic was applied to this stricture ; for five hours after the application of the caustic he had no desire to make water, and when the desire came on he made it more freely ; in the course of the night he only made water every hour. Next day a full sized bougie passed down to the second stricture, to which the caustic was applied two days successively; and so far was it from producing irritation, that he made water seldomer, with less straining, and slept better at night. The caustic was omitted one day, and the day after a middling sized bougie passed also through this stricture; but as it was not sufficiently removed, the caustic was again applied to it a third time; he made water only twice in the night. After touching the second stricture six times, a bougie of a moderate size passed through it; he now made water with more freedom, and had seldom occasion to void it during the night. The caustic was applied to the third stricture seven times, at intervals of two or three days; this gave more irritation than when applied to the forgoing strictures, sometimes producing pain in the testicles, with frequent inclination to make water for a day or two; but after the irritation subsided he always made water more freely, and less frequently. Still no bougie could be passed; it was therefore touched three times successively, which gave but little uneasiness, and afterwards a small bougie could be passed. Next day the same bougie did not pass, and the second stricture was increased; this led me again to apply the caustic to the second stricture, five times, and at the end of that period he made water much better, and a moderately large bougie passed into the bladder; so that the third stricture had been principally contracted from spasm, which was taken off by touching the second. In this state of the parts, the patient makes water tolerably freely, and says he is as well as ever he was in his life, nor can he be persuaded to remain longer under my care; although the stricture is certainly not sufficiently destroyed, to render that part of the urethra of the same width as the rest of the canal.

Believe me yours, &c.

S. BLACKADER.

Dear Sir, Dublin, 10th July, 1795.

In my last letter another case of stricture was mentioned to be under my care. As it is not so remarkable as the former, the following abstract will be sufficient.

CASE XXI.

Joseph Crawfurd, about twenty-nine years of age, contracted a gonorrhœa about a year ago, and has had the usual symptoms of stricture ever since. When he applied to me he had much pain and straining in making water; and a small bougie could with difficulty be passed. Having applied the caustic five times, a bougie about the common size could be passed. He now made water pretty freely, but yet not so well as might have been expected from the size of the bougie; and it often came away in two streams: this was supposed to proceed from a small projection in the stricture, which made an indentation in the side of the bougie about the breadth of a straw. My attempts to destroy this projection, by passing as large a caustic as the canal would admit of, eight or nine times, have not hitherto been attended with success. Yours,

S. BLACKADER.

DEAR SIR, Dublin, 12th Aug. 1795.

Inclosed is another interesting case of stricture, which has turned out still more to my satisfaction than Earl's; though from the following account which the man gave, led me to expect more disease than in the former case.

CASE XXII.

Robert Butler, private in the 99th regiment, applied to me on the 21st of July, for a difficulty in making water, which he passed drop by drop, with much pain and straining, and it often came away involuntarily, particularly when asleep. He told me he had the venereal disease, with a discharge and scalding in making water, about three years ago. He continued ill until he went into St. Bartholomew's Hospital about fifteen months after; at which time he had a swelling as large as a hen's egg in the perinæum, which burst, and the urine came through the orifice.   He rubbed mercurial ointment on the part, and the orifice healed; after which he first remarked the difficulty in making water. On passing a middle sized bougie, a stricture was met with about five or six inches from the glans penis.   On withdrawing this, and passing one of the smallest size, another stricture was dis- covered about an inch beyond the former. Next day the caustic was applied to the first stricture; and after six applications, a full sized bougie passed through it.   The second stricture was now touched with the caustic five times; it gradually gave way, and enabled a bougie of nearly the above- mentioned size to pass into the bladder. He now makes water pretty freely, though still frequently, about three or four times in the night; but it has almost ceased to come away involuntarily.   After the appli- cation of the caustic, he sometimes could not make water for three or four hours, and sometimes with difficulty till next morning; but the symptoms were never at all severe. It was generally passed every second day.

Yours, &c.

S. BLACKADER.

In a subsequent letter, dated in September, it is mentioned that he was perfectly well.

SECTION II.

CASES OF STRICTURE ATTENDED WITH AN
UNUSUAL DISCHARGE, WHICH WENT OFF
WHEN THE STRICTURE WAS REMOVED.

STRICTURES in some patients are attended
with a very great discharge of matter from
the urethra; and this symptom is often the
only one that gives the patient the least
uneasiness. These cases are commonly mistaken for gonorrhœa, or gleets, and this is
the more readily done, as the passage admits a small sized bougie to go into the
bladder; and passing bougies of that size
does not remove the discharge beyond the
time in which they are in use.

In those patients the stricture has not
contracted in so great a degree as materially
to impede the urine, but only to keep up a
constant irritation in the urethra, inducing
the formation of matter: that this is the

case is evident, for on the removal of the stricture the discharge in general ceases.

Cases of this kind have very frequently come under my care, and a number of instances could be adduced, but the following appear sufficient to convey all the information deserving of attention.

CASE I.

A gentleman aged twenty-five, in Jan. 1792, contracted a gonorrhœa, which was so violent, from the degree of inflammation, phimosis, chordee, and pain in making water, that he was not able to use an injection till the month of April; he then used, by the advice of his surgeon, a strong injection of calomel, sugar of lead, and rose-water; this, about the middle of May, removed the inflammatory symptoms, and lessened the discharge; but after coition, hard drinking, or hunting, it was liable to return in considerable quantity. He bathed, and took bark all the summer and autumn, but to no effect. In June, 1793, he had a very violent discharge, without one inflammatory symptom; for which he used a vitriolic injection, composed of sixteen grains of white vitriol, and six ounces of elder flower water, mixed up with a little gum arabic, which he injected every hour in the day, for three weeks; this stopped the discharge, except that when he committed any excess, it was liable to return. In May, 1794, the discharge became very great, without the least inflammation; the same vitriolic injection was used as before, and the discharge again diminished; he then took large doses of bark, and balsam of Tolu, copaiva, and Canada balsam; he also bathed all the summer, but the discharge never disappeared for more than a month at a time. While he was hunting in the October following, he leaped over a five-foot wall, into a gravel pit, which brought on a swelled testicle, inflammation of the spermatic chord, and a pain in the back, also a pain in the perinæum. The swelling of the testicle was removed by cold applications; but he did not venture to hunt till Jan. 1795. A small discharge now and then appearing, his surgeon introduced a bougie, and said he had a stricture; but after a course of bougies for three weeks, he told him he was perfectly well. The discharge returned in May, 1795. He came over to London, and put himself under the care of a surgeon, who gave him an injection, which stopped the discharge in six weeks; he was, however, subject to a return every two months, but the injection always stopped it again in a few days. In May, 1796, he had a copious discharge, without inflammation, which was treated as a gonorrhœa, till about the 12th of June, when, on passing a bougie, the surgeon found a stricture, and kept him under a constant course of bougies, wearing them for twelve or fifteen hours a day, till July 21st. The bougies were never introduced beyond six inches and a half down the urethra. July 21st, he had evident symptoms of a swelling in the same testicle which had been affected in 1794. He used constant applications of goulard, which allayed these symptoms in three days. He then returned to the use of the bougies, gradually increasing the length of its application, till he again retained it from twelve to fifteen hours a day, till the 12th of August; from that period he diminished the time of their remaining in the urethra till the 22d, when, though he had a considerable discharge, the surgeon said that he was perfectly well of the stricture; that he need not fear its return; and that bathing, with the use of the injection before employed, would remove the discharge in a very few weeks. On the 24th of August he went to the sea, and bathed every second day till the 21st of September, without benefit.   This induced him to return to London on Friday, Sept. 23d. and put himself under my care.

The use of the caustic was recommended, to which he readily agreed; and it was immediately applied, and repeated every other day, without giving any violent pain, or producing inflammation. On the second of October the first stricture was removed, and the caustic applied to another at $6\frac{1}{2}$ inches; this created unpleasant sensations about the bladder, so that it was necessary to quiet the parts by spirituous applications, and to give opiate medicines. Under this treatment he was well enough to bear another application of the caustic on the 5th, again on the 7th, and on the 9th, when the bougie went with ease into the bladder; on the 11th this was repeated, and the caustic passed through the stricture, after which it was left off. There was a good deal of bloody discharge for some days; on the 17th the discharge was less bloody, and less in quantity. A fortnight after, the discharge was nearly gone; a month from the last application of the caustic, the bougie passed with ease into the bladder. The discharge ceased; and from accounts, many years after his leaving town, there has been no return of discharge, or any other symptom.

S

CASE II.

A gentleman, thirty-two years of age, had a discharge of matter from the urethra for five years, which was believed to have its origin from a gonorrhœa. He had at the same time occasional difficulty in making water. All means that could be devised for stopping this discharge had been tried, and proved ineffectual. These were injections of various kinds, internal remedies, and the use of the bougie, also the baths in Italy, strongly recommended for that purpose, and sea-bathing.

After having done every thing that had been suggested to him, without receiving more than a temporary benefit, he began to reconcile himself to his situation ; but upon hearing of the effects of the caustic in removing strictures, and conceiving his symptoms might all arise from that cause, he consulted me upon this subject.

On passing a bougie, it was found that

the urethra admitted one of a very large size, which readily passed $6\frac{1}{2}$ inches, where a stricture had formed. This was destroyed by the caustic, but the symptoms were not removed. Another stricture at $7\frac{3}{4}$ inches stopped the progress of the bougie. This distance, exceeding what is usually met with, led me at first to suspect some disease independent of stricture; but as the penis was uncommonly long, the distance of the stricture was accounted for. Every time the caustic was applied to this last stricture the parts bled, but only in small quantities; after six applications the patient had an attack of strangury, which continued twelve hours, and was removed by repeated doses of opium, and keeping him warm in bed. When the strangury went off he was left quiet for a few days; the bougie was then passed, and went readily into the bladder, the discharge gradually ceased. The bougie was passed a week after, and again in a fortnight, when it was admitted very

S 2

readily, nor has there since been any return of the discharge.

CASE III.

A gentleman, twenty-five years of age, had a gonorrhœa followed by a gleet, which resisted all the means employed for his relief; these consisted in injections, the internal use of the balsams, sea-bathing, and wearing bougies.

After persisting in these means for three years without effect, he put himself under my care. A stricture at five inches was destroyed by the caustic; there was another at $6\frac{1}{2}$ inches; this had seven applications of the caustic made to it without producing any degree of irritation, although he rode on horseback every day, and even mounted his horse immediately after the application. This liberty was contrary to my advice, he therefore did it at his own risk. After the eighth application, he called upon me on horseback, to acquaint me that he could not make water. A bougie, could not be passed, and the caustic was applied; in five minutes he passed his water: he was induced in consequence of this alarm to give up horse exercise; after three more applications, the stricture was removed. He still had a great discharge, and went to the sea and bathed; he also took the balsam copaiva in large doses, but these means had no effect. In six weeks he went into the country, and pursued his usual exercises which were principally on horseback, and the discharge disappeared; nor has there been any return either of the discharge or stricture, as a year after his recovery, the same bougie passed with ease into the bladder.

In general, where the discharge from the stricture is great, it requires a month or six weeks after the use of the caustic has been discontinued, for the discharge entirely to disappear.

CASE IV.

An officer in the navy, thirty years of age, had a discharge from the urethra, straining after making water, and a frequency in voiding it, which continued for three or four years. In 1796 he put himself under my care. In the investigation of his complaints, two strictures were discovered, one at $5\frac{1}{2}$ inches, the other at $6\frac{1}{2}$ from the external orifice; these were readily removed by the caustic, and the frequency in making water, as also the straining after it, entirely ceased; but the discharge from the urethra continued. He went down to the sea, but after remaining there for three months, came back to town without any abatement of the discharge. It was therefore suspected that the stricture had not been completely removed, but the bougie passed readily into the bladder. A larger sized armed bougie was then passed through the stricture, but still the discharge continued.

The balsam copaiva had no effect; the bougie anointed with balsam copaiva and olive oil, and passed a few inches every day for ten minutes, did not remove it; and it still continues in a small degree.

SECTION III.

CASES OF STRICTURE WITH A THICKENING
IN THE CANAL, FORMING A SWELLING,
WHICH SUBSIDED WHEN THE STRICTURE
WAS REMOVED.

In some cases of stricture there is a thickening of the parts, forming a small tumour.
The stricture is commonly about four inches
from the external orifice. This tumour,
when it occurs in that particular part of
the canal, appears to arise from one of the
lacunæ of the urethra being close to the
stricture, the coats of which have been inflamed, and remain in a thickened state.

My reasons for adopting this opinion are,
that in four cases in which it has occurred,
the situation in the canal has been the
same, and in a part of the urethra where a
lacuna is naturally situated. The tumour
in all of them was on the lower side of the

urethra.   Similar swellings also occur in
consequence of the use of injections in cases
of gonorrhœa, in warm climates, in the
same part of the canal ; and gradually subside when the inflammatory symptoms go
off.

It appears from the following cases, that
this swelling, from whatever cause it arises,
subsides after the stricture is destroyed by
the caustic. Such swellings, therefore, instead of being an objection to the use of the
caustic, are reasons for employing it.

These tumours may arise from a thickening of the parts simply; for a tumour of
this kind in the perinæum, which was suspected to be a small stone lodged there,
was entirely destroyed by the use of the
caustic.

CASE I.

A gentleman, fifty-seven years of age,
who had resided chiefly in the West Indies
since the year 1764, during which time he

enjoyed a very good state of health, returned to England in May, 1792; he caught a
severe cold on his arrival, and continued
feverish and unwell for six months; from
that time till August, 1795, he had very
good health; he was then seized with a
violent pain in his side whenever he made
water, which he voided frequently in small
quantities, and the effort was attended with
great pain. The urine was extremely thick,
and had a white sediment, which induced
his surgeon to pronounce the complaint to
be in the kidneys : he gave him the Canada
balsam, which afforded relief, but when he
drank more wine than common the symptoms returned. This happened repeatedly
in the course of the year.

In June, 1796, he visited a friend at
Portsmouth; while there, he found occasionally his water did not come in a full
stream, but dribbled on his shirt after he
thought he had done. On his return to
town, the 18th of the month, he had
recourse to his former medicine, and got so

much better, that he set off for the North
of England on the 25th of July. He was
perfectly well during his journey. On the
3d of August he dined with a friend, in the
evening felt extremely unwell, and his
water was very thick ; he had recourse to
the balsam, but received no benefit from it.
On the 12th, he went to an assembly ; while
there, he found his bowels very much out of
order, and as he was returning home at
twelve o'clock, felt an inclination to make
water, and just as he had done, was seized
with a violent spasm, which gave him so
much pain that he was hardly able to stand.
He took some warm negus and went to bed.
At three o'clock he awoke in agony, and
every time he attempted to make water the
spasms returned, and nothing came but
blood and mucus : relief was procured by
taking opium in large doses. The water
came from him all night involuntarily,
which obliged him to change his linen
thirteen times. He remained in this state
till the 1st of September, when he found his

health so much impaired, from pain and
low diet, that he began to apprehend if he
did not attempt moving homewards, he
should soon be too much reduced to under-
take so long a journey.   He therefore set
off for London ;   while travelling, he found
himself no worse for the motion of the
carriage.

He arrived in London, September 14th,
and the next day consulted me.

At that time, the external orifice of the
penis was so small, that with difficulty it
admitted the point of the smallest sized
bougie that is made.   The caustic was therefore applied to the orifice, and after two or
three applications, an armed bougie passed
down to the first stricture, which was only
an inch from the external orifice ;   when
applied there it gave great pain, which
lasted near an hour ;   the spasms and other
symptoms were not diminished, and required the constant use of opium to relieve
them ;   there was a second stricture at the
distance of three inches;   before these two

were destroyed, the caustic was applied forty-six times. The bougie now passed four inches, where there was a tumour formed, of the size of a common pea, which could be felt externally ; to this the caustic was applied ; it gave less pain at this part, so that it could be suffered to remain a much longer time. In twenty-six applications this was destroyed. At $6\frac{1}{2}$ inches there was a third stricture, which yielded to two applications, and the bougie went on to the bladder; a flexible catheter passed with equal ease ; its use was then left off, as the patient was free from all his former symptoms. Ten days afterwards the same bougie passed without difficulty, and he went into the country. This gentleman occasionally passed a bougie, once a month, or once a fortnight, according to circumstances, and has had no return of the stricture in the year 1805.

CASE II.

A gentleman, aged about thirty-five, had for several years a difficulty in making water, and had been very often seized with a complete stoppage of urine. He had given bougies several trials, and suffered all the inconveniences they produce; he had even been confined for six months at a time to give them every advantage; but was unable at last to pass one larger than a knitting needle, and that did not go on to the bladder.

Under these circumstances he put himself under my care, in March, 1796. There was a stricture about two inches from the orifice; this was with very great difficulty removed, requiring ten or twelve applications of the caustic; a second was met about four inches, and at this part there was a tumour which could be felt externally, the size of a large pea. After getting through this, which required a great many applications, the canal at this part could not for a long while be enlarged beyond a certain size, but by increasing the diameter of the caustic, which was allowed in one application entirely to dissolve there, the tumour began to diminish in size; and in three months from his being first under my care, during which time the caustic was applied to it forty times, it was almost entirely gone. During this time he had several attacks of inflammation of the throat; these were suspected by some of his medical friends to be venereal. By my request he did not use mercury, and they went off without any particular means being used for that purpose.

A bougie now passed into the bladder, and the parts were left to themselves; but a week after, on attempting to pass a bougie, a stricture was met with at six inches, which from its connection with the other, had been relaxed, but afterwards contracted again. The caustic was applied to this stricture several different times, and when the bougie got beyond it, there was the feel of a hard substance, which made me suspect a small calculus concretion was lodged behind it, keeping up a degree of irritation in the canal; this however was not the case.

As soon as a bougie went freely into the bladder, a flexible gum catheter was tried, but without success. By persevering with the caustic two or three times more the catheter passed, and in a future trial the patient could introduce it himself, which he was recommended to practise, with the view of promoting absorption in the thickened parts by its pressure while lying in the canal.

The passing a flexible gum catheter, and leaving it in the bladder, at first view appears a more harsh application, and more liable to irritate than a bougie; it may therefore be objected, that while the mild application of a bougie is condemned in particular cases, a harder substance is recommended; but the advantage of the catheter is, that the bladder can be emptied by it whenever there is the slightest irritation. This takes off irritation, and leaves the parts in an easy state, which is not the case with a bougie. It will be found in several of these Cases, that experience is in favour of the catheter; the same urethra which could not bear a bougie for half an hour, will allow the catheter to remain for many hours without the smallest inconvenience.

The gentleman who is the subject of this Case has had no return of his complaints from the time he left me, and the disposition to ulceration in the throat has been entirely removed; so that it is highly probable the former attacks were brought on by the action of the caustic on the stricture, irritating the constitution, and inducing that complaint. Another instance of stricture has occurred, where a similar affection of the throat came on while the caustic was used; it returned several different times; but as it was attributed to the effects of the caustic, it gave no alarm, and

T

always went away under the most simple modes of treatment.

CASE III.

An officer, forty years of age, in the year 1793, while serving on the Continent under the Duke of York, contracted a gonorrhœa, for which the surgeon whom he consulted gave him an injection of corrosive sublimate. Its strength by mistake was much beyond what it ought to have been; and the immediate effect was a very severe irritation about the middle of the canal; nor was it probable that the injection passed beyond that part, for it was immediately thrown out again, and the pain was such as to forbid a repetition. He was seized with a strangury, which after some hours went off, and he gradually recovered from the inflammation that had taken place in the urethra.

From that time he had been unable to

pass his urine otherwise than in a very small stream, often attended with difficulty, and always more frequently than before.

These symptoms distressing him very much, and having in vain had recourse to the use of the bougie, which had only relieved the temporary suppression of urine, he put himself under my care in the year 1796. At this time, the external orifice was so extremely small, that a bougie large enough to carry caustic could not be introduced. The caustic was therefore applied to the external orifice; this was done twice before it could pass, and then went on three inches to the second stricture. In applying the caustic to this stricture, it only sometimes could be got down to it, at others the bougie stuck upon the orifice, which was oblique, the external opening not being exactly in the direction of the canal, so that after entering it, the first direction it took was downwards, and then horizontally along the urethra. After five or six applications to the orifice, this was got the better of, and

T 2

with a little management, the bougie was directed to the stricture at three inches.

This stricture gave way to four or five applications of the caustic ; another was met with at four inches ; when feeling this stricture with the finger and thumb through the substance of the penis, there was a knob or lump distinctly felt where the bougie stopt. The caustic was applied to this stricture ; it gave a good deal of pain, and the uneasiness it produced remained some hours ; if he went out or took any exercise it brought on a strangury, which was relieved by passing a very small catgut bougie through the stricture ; this occurred seven or eight times, and was generally the consequence of exercise or exposure to cold ; it was unaccompanied by any kind of sympathetic irritation, as ague, headache, loss of appetite, or affection of the bowels. To this stricture the armed bougie was applied above twenty times before it passed through it, and there was reason to hope that no obstruction existed beyond it; but one was met with at $6\frac{1}{2}$ inches. This, however, was not attended with the same difficulty, for five or six applications procured a passage into the bladder.

The urethra was very unusually small in its natural state. He was therefore directed, after the canal was made pervious, to pass a flexible gum catheter, nearly of its full size, every day for a fortnight, to prevent the parts as much as possible from renewing their disposition to contraction, and he continued free from complaint above a year after being under my care.

He left off the use of the catheter, and two years after caught cold, and lost the use of his lower extremities, so as to be obliged to use crutches. This brought on a return of difficulty in making water, which induced him to return to London, and put himself under my care, in 1802; the caustic was again used, and seventy or eighty applications proved necessary to get into the bladder, but the bougie was now much larger than that formerly used. He was advised to pass

a catheter every other day, and was in-
structed in the mode of doing it. The affection of the nerves of the loins render this
case not only unfavourable, but an exception
to all common rules.

In 1805 the catheter passed with the same
readiness as in 1803.

CASE IV.

A gentleman, forty-seven years old, consulted me on account of strictures in the
urethra of many years continuance. The
following is the history of his complaints.

At the age of sixteen he contracted a
gonorrhœa, which was difficult of cure,
and it was nearly six months before it was
removed ; when only seventeen he perceived
his stream of urine evidently diminished, but
had no difficulty in passing it ; when he was
twenty-two the stream was rather smaller,
and occasionally there was straining for a
short time before it could be made to flow.
This symptom alarmed him, and induced

him at the age of twenty-five, to have recourse to the use of the bougie. At first he applied to it, with the hope of obtaining a cure; but after repeated trials, found no permanent effect was to be expected; it was, however, necessary from time to time to have recourse to it, whenever the difficulty in making water brought on irritation upon the bladder.

After using the bougie occasionally for twenty-two years, he consulted me on the propriety of using the caustic. He was of a very irritable habit, liable to a violent degree of inflammation from slight causes, and had been, in every sense of the word, a free liver. These circumstances, however unfavourable in themselves, were not particularly so to the use of the caustic.

On the 10th of May, 1797, on examining the canal, by passing a bougie, it was found that one of a small size could only be passed one inch and a half. To this obstruction the caustic was applied; and after three applications, once every other day, the bougie went through it, but was again stopped at 4 inches. To this second stricture the caustic was applied, in the same manner, seventeen times, without producing much effect upon it; but by feeling the urethra externally this was readily accounted for, as there was a hard tumour at that part, the size of a small pea; the parts had become so tender, that the caustic was not used for fourteen days; it was then applied three times, and omitted for nineteen days; after which it was used eight times, and the bougie passed through the stricture. To effect this required twenty-eight applications. The urethra was so tender where the tumour had been, that it was fourteen days before it could bear the bougie passing over that part.

Another stricture was found at the distance of six inches, which yielded to three applications; and a fourth at seven inches, which also gave way, after the caustic had been thrice applied to it.

He now made water with less effort than he had done for many years, and less frequently; but the caustic was several times applied, with a view of removing entirely the strictures, and making them less liable to return, as the urethra, either naturally, or from long being habituated to a contracted state, was of a small size. The caustic was applied in all about fifty times.

CASE V.

A gentleman, forty-six years of age, who had resided twenty years in India, for the last fifteen years had been subject to an irregular ague, caught in a hilly part of India, where strangers are liable to fevers. This disease continued upon him for several years, but, on leaving that district, went off. He had at the same time frequency in making water, attended with straining; this was attributed to an ill-treated gonor-rhœa, and it was supposed would soon go off, but continued in a greater or less degree from that time.

Five years after he returned to the same

place, and was again attacked by the aguish complaint, which proved more violent than it had been before, and the difficulty in making water became extremely severe; he had frequent suppressions of urine, which were relieved by warm baths, passing bougies, and various other means. His health gradually declined. For the last three years he made water every half hour, for twenty-four hours before the fever came on, and during its continuance; but next day only once in twelve hours, after which the frequency returned as before.

In the year 1796, he was ordered to leave India, as the only mode of preserving his life. He arrived in England in 1797, and consulted a physician for the feverish complaints he had so long laboured under, and which he believed to be his only disease, as the medical persons who attended him in India had no suspicion of there being any other. The physician asked him how often he made water; he said he was obliged to do it ten or twelve times a night. This led to the idea of his complaint being in the urethra, and the fever only a symptom arising from the effects of that irritation on the constitution. Upon this idea it was thought right to ascertain the state of the urethra. On examination a stricture was found $4\frac{1}{2}$ inches from the external orifice; to this the caustic was applied; and it is curious, that after the second application, he had less feverish indisposition; and by the time the first stricture was destroyed, it was almost entirely gone; and his bowels, which had been in a disordered state for two years, had become regular without the assistance of medicine. He made water less frequently, with less straining, and began to improve in his general health. Another stricture was found to stop the bougie at $5\frac{1}{4}$ inches; this was also destroyed without bringing on any symptoms but local pain; a third stricture was discovered at $6\frac{1}{2}$ inches, and beyond this there was a tumour about the size of a large pea, which could be readily laid hold of between the finger and thumb, when the parts in the perinæum were relaxed. The feel was so distinct, that there was little doubt of its being a small calculus lodged behind the stricture; it proved, however, to be only one of those tumours from thickening of the parts, for as the stricture gave way it diminished, and at last was not to be distinguished. This stricture required twenty-six applications to destroy it; after which the bougie went into the bladder, but in passing over that part gave great pain. Before this stricture was entirely destroyed, the applications of the caustic brought on an attack of fever, and a want of power to pass the urine for six hours. Nor did this irritated state of the general system subside till the stricture was entirely removed, which was not till a fortnight after.

The caustic was applied in all about fifty times.

SECTION IV.

CASES OF STRICTURE WITH FISTULÆ IN PE-
RINÆO, WHICH HEALED WHEN THE STRIC-
TURE WAS REMOVED.

STRICTURES in the urethra, when of long
continuance, attended with great difficulty
in passing the urine, very frequently produce
an abscess behind the stricture, formed by
the pressure of the urine against that part of
the urethra ; when this abscess breaks externally, the urine comes through the orifice,
and continues to do so, forming what is
termed a fistula in perinæo.

In some cases of stricture, abscesses form
in perinæo, which have no communication
with the urethra, and arise from irritation
having been produced, either from the use
of a bougie, or any other cause.

Such abscesses most commonly occur in
patients who have irritable urethras affected

by slight strictures, and require no other
treatment than opening the abscess as soon
as matter is distinctly to be felt, and afterwards passing a bougie once every 24 hours,
and immediately withdrawing it, as leaving
the bougie in the urethra might bring on
irritation ; this is to be repeated two or three
times. Several cases of this kind have come
under my observation, and are here taken
notice of, to distinguish between the two
kinds of abscess.

Abscesses in consequence of irritation not
only form in the perinæum, but sometimes
within the pelvis ; these either open in the
groin, or at the root of the penis. The
matter forms on the outside of the coats of
the bladder, producing inflammation, and
bringing on pain, when the bladder contracts
in expelling the urine. An Officer who had
the fever at Gibraltar in the year 1804,
while labouring under that disease had great
difficulty in making water, and a large
abscess formed in the lower belly, which
broke in the groin, but could not for many

months afterwards be made to heal; it was considered as the termination of the fever, but upon enquiry there was great pain in throwing out the last drops of urine, which pain extended to the groin, and there was difficulty in voiding the water. On examination, a stricture was found in the urethra, the removal of which relieved all these symptoms, so that the fever had aggravated all the symptoms of the stricture, and by doing so had been the predisposing cause of the abscess.

When a fistula in perinæo takes place in consequence of stricture, it cannot be permanently healed up while the obstruction remains in the urethra, and prevents the urine from passing readily in its natural course.

This is a self-evident proposition, which is very generally understood; the only treatment of such fistulæ is therefore the dilatation, or the destruction of the stricture. The old practice of laying open these sinuses, which is still followed by some surgeons, will be found not at all necessary, and when done, in no respect forwarding the cure.

The following Cases are given in proof of this doctrine; they at the same time shew, that where fistulæ in perinæo have been formed, the parts behind the stricture are so much thickened, and are rendered so indolent, that the common bougie is unable to dilate them; and the lower surface of the urethra, in consequence of inflammation and ulceration, where the fistulous orifices have their origin, is rendered so irregular, that a bougie cannot readily pass over it. If this is not understood, the surgeon may be led to mistake the case, and suppose that there are other obstructions which prevent the bougie from passing on. The flexible gum catheter is therefore, in such instances, the only instrument by which the real state of the canal can be ascertained; since, when introduced with a stilet of metal which is bent to the curve of the urethra, the point of the instrument is always directed upwards, and avoids any irregularity on the lower surface which might obstruct it.

CASE I.

A. B. aged forty-four, had, in the year 1775, an obstruction to the passage of his urine, which was so considerable as to make him apply for medical assistance. He was directed to use the bougie, and when he began that course, one of the smallest size only could be passed; it was however, in the course of some months, increased to a larger size, so as to allow his urine to pass with tolerable ease, and then it was left off. After some time the obstruction returned, and the same mode of relief was resorted to, but the passage did not admit of being dilated beyond the middle sized bougie. In the year 1785, during one of the returns of the obstruction, the scrotum became swelled, but subsided again when the obstruction was removed. The patient found

U

however, that he could not bring the canal to the same size as before, gradually losing ground in his endeavours to dilate it by the bougie, his stream of urine being smaller, and the desire to make water more frequent. In July, 1794, an abscess formed in perinæo, attended with a considerable swelling of the scrotum; the abscess broke, and part of the urine passed through the external orifice, which gave him immediate relief; a fresh inflammation some time after came on, attended with much pain; this also abated upon its breaking and discharging the matter and urine externally. A repetition of this process brought on an irritable state of the parts, and he became unfit for any exertion, the least exercise bringing on pain and irritation. The scrotum was, from the repeated inflammations, become much enlarged and thickened. In these circumstances he put himself under my care in the month of July, 1795. It was explained to him, that the only mode of relieving his present symptoms was to bring the canal to its natural size, which could not be done by the bougie; and therefore the use of the caustic became necessary. A large bougie met with an obstruction not much more than two inches from the external orifice; to this the caustic was applied; and on the next trial the bougie passed down about three inches, to a second obstruction. The caustic was applied here three times, after which the bougie of a full size went on about four inches, to a third obstruction. The symptoms were now very much abated; the irritation to make water was less violent, and considerably less frequent, not recurring more than twice in the night, whereas before it had come upon him every hour. The caustic was applied to this third stricture seven times before the bougie went into the bladder, and as soon as this was effected, the water ceased to pass through the fistula; the scrotum became gradually less, till it was nearly reduced to its natural size; and he did not void his urine oftener than is commonly done in health. It was thought right, from the length of time the disease had continued, to use the bougie for a few minutes every day to establish the cure; but the bougie gave pain, and the second time of being used brought on irritation, followed by a disposition for inflammation in the perinæum; it was therefore left off, and the caustic again applied till the full sized bougie passed readily; and then the parts were left to themselves.

Three months after the caustic had been used, a common sized bougie passed into the bladder: in other respects he felt himself perfectly well.

CASE II.

A. B. a bricklayer, about forty years of age, came into St. George's Hospital in August, 1795, with a stricture in the urethra, several fistulous orifices in the perinæum, and one upon the under surface of the penis, before the scrotum ; through these openings the urine passed, hardly-any being voided by the natural orifice.

He gave the following history of his complaints : eighteen years before, he had fallen from the top of a chimney, and pitched upon the ridge of the house, with his legs astride; by which means the scrotum and perinæum were much injured. These parts recovered themselves without proceeding to suppuration.

Ever since that time he had fouud a difficulty in passing his urine, and twelve weeks before he came to the Hospital, after having undergone considerable fatigue, an abscess formed in perinæo, which burst, and discharged blood and urine. Three weeks after another abscess formed, which opened externally before the scrotum. This also gave a passage to the urine, and when the urine insinuated itself into these sinuses, the pain was excrutiating.

When he came into the hospital, he made water every ten minutes through the fistulæ, had a considerable degree of straining in the bladder, and tenesmus in the rectum. The external skin of the scrotum and its neighbourhood, was excoriated by the urine.

On passing a bougie, it met with no difficulty till it reached nearly to the bulb of the urethra, and there it stopped. The caustic was applied to this stricture, after which he had less irritation in the bladder; this was repeated, and the stricture gave way, allowing the bougie to go an inch further, where it was again obstructed; to this second stricture the caustic was five times used, and a full sized bougie was passed into the bladder; but before this was effected the symptoms were very much abated.

The number of fistulous orifices, and the readiness with which the urine got into them, made it necessary to introduce into the bladder a flexible gum catheter, which was retained in the urethra, and the urine thus prevented from getting into the fistulæ. It could not however be retained above a day or two, without giving uneasiness; it was therefore, from necessity, occasionally removed. At the end of eight weeks the fistula near the anus and those in perinæo were healed, that only before the scrotum continued open.

This stricture, brought on by an accident, and of eighteen years continuance, was entirely removed in fourteen days, by means of the caustic.

CASE III.

A gentleman aged twenty-three, in the beginning of the year 1769, was attacked with a violent gonorrhœa, attended with heat of urine and violent chordee, which continued without abatement for twelve weeks. At the end of about six months the stream of urine lessened, and as there was reason to suspect the formation of stricture in the urethra, a bougie was introduced, and he was desired to let it remain for some time; but from the great irritation it occasioned, he could not bear it more than a few minutes. On withdrawing it, the urine flowed more freely but not with less pain. From this time the bougie was passed once every twenty-four hours, for some months, when a suppression of urine took place, and not a drop could flow till the passage was forced by a bougie; he was now obliged to pass one every time he made water.

About the year 1774 he was recommended to apply to Mr. Hales, who, on passing a bougie, assured him he would effect a cure, and gave him some bougies for that purpose; these he used for a considerable time, without any benefit.

In the year 1778 the stricture became more contracted, and the painful symptoms increasing, attended with a tenesmus, he applied to Mr. Hunter; who after examining the prostate gland, declared his cure to be in his own power. This assertion induced him to put himself under Mr. Hunter's care, who made use of the lunar caustic, passed through a canula, to a stricture at $6\frac{1}{2}$ inches from the external orifice; but no material benefit being obtained after applying it twenty-one times, he gave it up, and recommended the use of the bougie as before. About the year 1784, the passage was so much contracted, as not to admit the smallest bougie, and no urine flowed for more than forty-eight hours, notwithstanding the warm bath and opium were made use of. Of tincture of opium, one hundred and twenty drops were given in twenty-four hours. When nearly all hopes were at an end, a small catgut bougie passed into the aperture, and the urine followed; after this a great discharge of brown coloured mucus issued from the bladder with the urine, attended with an aching pain and frequent solicitations to make water. The mucus was equal in quantity with the urine, and gave it a pungent volatile smell. The bougie could now pass as before; the mucus gradually diminished in quantity, and in about ten days disappeared. This symptom has attended the going off of every paroxysm of the complaint.

About the year 1789 he applied to Mr. Pott, who recommended him to be satisfied with passing the bougie, and told him that he never knew any relief obtained by the use of the caustic.

The complaint increasing, and the total suppressions of urine becoming frequent, about 1791 he desired his case might be sent to a surgeon in London, who after due consideration, sent him some bougies, armed by having nearly an inch of their points covered with powdered lunar caustic, which he desired might be passed through a canula (sent for that purpose) into the stricture: this was done without much benefit. In April, 1795, he was again attacked by a suppression of urine, attended with a violent strangury, symptomatic fever, loss of appetite, and continual nausea, by which he was confined to his bed for three weeks : this was followed by a swelling of the left

testicle, and a considerable enlargement of
the epididimus. These symptoms abated
in the usual way, by a great discharge of
mucus from the urethra and bladder, and
also by a discharge of a considerable quantity of opake, white, gritty matter. In
June, 1795, he was attacked with a most
violent pain in his back, which confined
him almost constantly to his bed for three
months; for this symptom he was advised
the use of the warm bath, electricity, bark,
&c. but without effect. In January, 1796,
he was attacked with a swelling near the
rectum, occasioned by the urine escaping
into the cellular membrane every time he
made water; this swelling increased, with
a violent smarting pain, and by degrees it
extended along the perinæum as far as the
scrotum; at the end of a fortnight it burst
and discharged near twelve ounces of pus,
having an urinous fetid smell : he was reduced by this attack to such a state of debility
as to faint on being taken out of bed. The
bursting of the tumour left an opening,

through which, every time he made water, some part of the urine escaped, with a violent smarting pain. As soon as his strength was sufficiently restored to bear the motion of a carriage, he came to London, which was in the beginning of May, 1796, and he immediately applied to me.

As during the complaint, bougies had been passed more than twenty thousand times, he had long been of opinion, that no permanent relief was to be expected, but from the substance being destroyed, either by the knife or the caustic. At this time the general symptoms were, a continued gleet, pain in making water, and, for some time after, frequent and copious discharges of matter, chordee, and every sensation that attends a fresh-contracted virulent gonorrhoea.

Upon examining the urethra, by passing a bougie as large as the external orifice would admit, a stricture was met with at five inches, and the patient was told that the first thing to be done was to remove that

obstruction. He told me that none of his former surgeons had found any stricture there,
nor had they thought it necessary to attempt any thing at this part : that circumstance alone, was considered as the cause
of their failure; for he must recollect perfectly, that after the caustic or bougie in
former trials had been used for any number
of times, a contraction always came on at
this part, and prevented him from persevering in their use ; and therefore, although
the stricture was slight, it was necessary it
should be removed. He assented to the
truth of my remark, and readily submitted
to my conducting the cure in the way best
adapted for that purpose.

The caustic was applied to the stricture at
five inches, which after four or five applications was removed. The bougie now
passed down to the original stricture ; to
this the caustic was used for several weeks.
The pain in the application was severe, and
he was obliged to pass a small bougie at
the time of making water as before. The

fistula became very troublesome. These symptoms however gradually abated, and the pain from the caustic, after some time, hardly deserved that name; by the middle of July the use of the small bougie became unnecessary, and the call to make water was less frequent; only three times in the night

On the 25th the fistula was healed up, and the constant uneasiness in perinæo removed. The caustic was used in September every day for three weeks, and apparently with advantage, but the smallest bougie did not go into the bladder. Sept. 24th, the fistula broke out, in consequence of the formation of a fresh abscess; on the 30th, a silver sound passed into the bladder, and after it got beyond the part to which the caustic was applied, met no difficulty. The caustic when applied every day, gave more pain; so that after a few applications it was only used on the alternate days, and then again for a few times every day. October 17th, the end of the bougie was more distinctly marked by the stricture. By

Christmas the silver instrument was more readily got into the bladder; the irregularities behind the stricture preventing so weak an instrument as the bougie to pass over them. He now made water very well, and all his former symptoms were removed. He went into the country, and was to pass, once every two or three days, the silver sound into the bladder, to keep the parts in their present state. Six months after he left town he continued free from complaint.

After that time he omitted passing the silver sound, and his symptoms gradually returned, with a considerable increase of the diseased thickness of the parts in the perinæum. He returned to town in the year 1799, but the disease was not within the power of relief, the ulceration having extended to the neck of the bladder; and he returned into the country, and died some months after.

CASE IV.

A gentleman, thirty years of age, had a stricture, and in consequence of it, a fistula in perinæo, which made him miserable, and induced him to take the opinion of several surgeons separately, and afterwards in consultation, upon the means of healing up the fistulous orifice in the perinæum.

The means proposed were to lay open the parts to the bottom, remove the diseased urethra, and then heal up the wound. This operation was in itself so severe, that he preferred a trial of the use of the caustic to the stricture; for whatever had been his dread of a caustic, it was overcome by a still greater horror for the knife. He therefore consulted me before he would submit to this operation.

After hearing all the particulars of his case, it was stated that there appear no reason why he might not get well without any thing being done to the external parts, as

all that was wanted for his recovery consisted in enlarging the natural canal, which,
by removing the obstruction the urine met
with in coming forward, would allow the
parts behind to recover themselves, and in
a very short time they might all heal up.
That the caustic was certainly the most effectual means of removing the stricture,
and therefore its use was recommended in
this particular case. He wished a consultation
respecting the danger. To this there was no
objection; but there was no desire on my
part to remove from myself the responsibility
respecting the effects of the caustic. His fears
for the knife induced him to trust himself
entirely to my care. Upon examination, it
proved that he had two strictures, which
were both removed by eight applications of
the caustic. He then felt himself much
easier, made water less frequently, and a few
drops only passed through the fistula, but
still a bougie did not go into the bladder.
This was conceived to arise from the irregularity in the urethra, where the orifices

X

leading to the fistula had their origin, behind the stricture. A flexible gum catheter with a stilet was therefore passed to throw the point forwards, and avoid these irregularities. This went with ease into the bladder. The fistula healed up, and in a few weeks the parts had so much recovered themselves, that the surface was smooth enough to allow a large bougie to pass into the bladder.

A year after the passage continued in the same state, although he was liable to occasional irritations in it, in consequence of the parts remaining weak; these always went off without any remedy being applied, and in the year 1805 he had no return of the complaint.

CASE V.

A gentleman, forty-six years of age, had a stricture, which was not known till it produced a swelling in perinæo, in Oct. 1793, at which time the use of the bougie was begun.

The abscess afterwards burst, forming a fistula in perinæo. He was extremely irritable, and no progress could be made by that instrument, without every mode of palliating its effects being adopted, such as warm baths, opium, ether, and the caustic alkali taken internally, which soothed the irritation of the bladder. His skin was so irritable, that mercurial ointment inflamed it, if twice used to the same part. The lunar caustic was applied to the orifice of the fistula, and the effects were severe, beyond any thing usually met with.

By the application of the bougie, the internal use of the caustic alkali, and great management, the passage was dilated, and the fistula healed up, but neither a bougie nor a catheter could be passed into the bladder; after a few months, the perinæum swelled again, and opened anew. In this state, March 30, 1796, he consulted me; the caustic was applied to a stricture at the distance of $5\frac{1}{2}$ inches, it gave no pain, and brought on no irritation; the second time this stricture

X 2

gave way; another stricture $1\frac{1}{4}$ further on, was touched twice, and the bougie went into the bladder. This gave more pain and lasted longer. On April 2d, an armed bougie a size larger was applied; it halted at the first stricture, but went through and was applied to the second.

April 10th, the bougie went into the bladder. April 15th, a larger bougie passed through the first stricture with difficulty; it brought on irritation, and the fistula opened; this soon went off. Afterwards the caustic was applied to the last stricture, without irritation. May 10th, a catheter went into the bladder (which it had never done before).

The use of the caustic was continued till the 20th of May, when a flexible gum catheter as large as a full sized bougie passed, but the bougie itself could not the reach the bladder.

After this the parts were left to themselves, but the symptoms were not found to abate. In June, a sound was passed to examine the bladder ; no stone was found, but something hard in the perinæum. The flexible gum catheter of the largest size was passed every night at bed-time, and left in all night ; it produced no irritation, nor did it give pain : in July the patient passed it himself, the hardness in the perinæum was almost wholly gone, and the urine did not come at all by the fistula, which was nearly healed ; unless when he was very costive, or there was irritation in the bowels.

Finding some part of the hardness remain, which the use of the catheter had not subdued, in December the caustic was again used about twenty times, when this projecting part was much diminished, without producing irritation. The passage was now freer at that part, the hardness much subdued, and the thickness in the scrotum entirely gone.

In May following the use of the caustic was again taken up, with a view of removing the hardness entirely ; it was applied about twelve times, after which the parts appeared to be brought as much into a natural state as could be effected by the use of the caustic.

The canal admitted with ease any sized instrument, but there was a turn necessary to get past the irregularities where the orifice of the fistula had been formed in the urethra.

In this case, the thickening and induration at the stricture next the bladder was so great, as to give the feel, in several examinations, of a hard substance ; and led me to suspect that a stone was lodged there. This callous part was reduced by the application of caustic, in a greater degree than could have been imagined possible, without doing harm, in parts totally hid from the eye. This could not have been attempted without receiving so correct an impression of the parts on the end of the soft bougie, as to ascertain the progress made, with the same accuracy as if they had been exposed to view. In this case there had been no return of any of the symptoms in the year 1805.

CASE VI.

A gentleman, aged fifty-six, who had been repeatedly attacked by gonorrhœas, in the month of July, 1788, being then in England, had a swelling between the fundament and scrotum, which after great inflammation and much pain broke. As it communicated with the urethra, the urine passed through the opening; but after a voyage to the East Indies, the fistula healed in Feb. 1791.

In the month of August he first observed that there was a disorder in the urethra, and from the discharge of matter thought it was a gonorrhœa, and used medicines for the cure; but this process caused much uneasiness and pain. As the discharge continued, it was supposed to be a gleet, and for a considerable time was treated as such. As he did not find any relief, but a difficulty and pain in passing the urine, with a frequent desire to discharge it, he at last concluded there was a stone in the bladder; he was, however, assured that he had not any positive symptom of that disorder. On the 19th of January, 1796, he sailed for England. On coming round the Cape of Good Hope, the weather being very cold, he found a slight suppression of urine every night after being in bed. This continued until his arrival in England, on the 3d of August, 1796, and was much the same until the end of September, when, having caught a cold from exposure to rain, a total suppression of urine came on in the night, and afterwards frequently returned. On the 15th of December, 1796, he applied to a medical gentleman near London, who gave him boluses composed of mercury and opium, till the 10th of February, 1797. Not perceiving any prospect of relief from this medicine, he applied to a surgeon in London, informing him of the suppression of urine, and that he conceived it to be produced in consequence of strictures in the urethra. The surgeon desired the urine might be saved for his inspection;

after seeing it, he told him it did not arise from a stricture in the urethra, but from a contracted bladder, which he said he would cure in about three weeks. He injected the bladder with warm water for four months; at this time, the patient finding the complaint much worse, and that his general health was declining very fast, this treatment was left off. The same surgeon now took it up as a stricture, and finding an obstruction, applied a bougie armed with caustic; it was kept at the stricture for six minutes; this, as might be expected, brought on violent inflammation. The patient, alarmed at this practice, did not persevere in it; the pain lasted ten days, and then went off.

In June, 1797, he put himself under my care. On examining the canal, there was an obstruction at six inches; and from the impression it made on the end of the bougie, the orifice of the stricture was very small; but as the patient informed me it had at several times been considerably dilated by bougies, but always contracted again, the caustic was applied, which gave little or no pain, and was attended by no inflammation ; after the second application, the aperture of the stricture was evidently enlarged ; after the third application he had a paroxysm of fever, followed by a moisture on the skin ; some hours after this went off there was another more severe (the shivering fit was without the feel of coldness); a profuse sweat terminated the attack. He was told that it was probable this stricture was now destroyed, as these attacks very often occurred when that happened. This proved to be the case ; for at the next trial the bougie went through the stricture to another, three quarters of an inch further on. It is a curious fact, that the severe application of the caustic for six minutes, before he came under my care, which gave so much pain, and produced so much inflammation, was unattended by any constitutional irritation ; and an application, which produced neither the one nor the other, but which destroyed a stricture, should produce a paroxysm of fever.

Every application to this stricture was attended in the evening with a suppression, requiring the use of the catheter to remove it; ten or twelve applications however destroyed it; and the bougie went on into the bladder, although there had been a fistula in perinæo. He now lost the spasm and suppression, but the parts remained uneasy, and the caustic was applied several times before the bougie passed with facility, after which the uneasiness went of.

This gentleman had, for twelve years, a feverish attack at night, principally every fortnight, which entirely went off when the stricture was removed. After the removal of the strictures in the urethra, a spasm came upon the bladder, in the middle of the night, attended with suppression, for several times, generally only every other night, and then went off.

———————

This gentlemen had no return of the complaint in his bladder, and died of a dropsy in the year 1803.

SECTION V.

CASES OF STRICTURE WITH UNCOMMON IR-
RITATIONS, WHICH WENT OFF ON THE
REMOVAL OF THE STRICTURE.

IN many cases of stricture, irritation takes
place in the urethra when thrown into
strong action, as in the coitus. This produces pain, and brings on spasm. An effect
not very dissimilar is in some instances produced by passing a bougie over the parts
immediately after a stricture has been removed, the tender surface is irritated, and
the effects extend to the bladder; these
however go off, and are not afterwards met
with.

In the first case, the spasm is removed by
the caustic, and in the other, it is an accidental violence which goes off of itself, as will
appear from the following Cases.

There is in the minds of many surgeons,

and almost all patients, such a dread of inflammation on the bladder, that when any
symptom of irritation attacks that viscus,
all means of preventing or removing inflammation are immediately had recourse
to, and the ready abatement of the symptoms under their treatment, although they
would have subsided of themselves, is attributed to the means made use of, which en-
courages the practitioners to pursue the
same plan in similar cases.

CASE I.

*Of Stricture with Spasm at the time of making
water.*

A gentleman, about thirty years of age,
had a stricture which was not very troublesome, but which rendered the stream of
urine small and interrupted; it required the
finger to be applied to the perinæum to
throw out the last drops ; after two applications of the caustic the unarmed bougie

passed on to the bladder; after this was withdrawn, as the patient was anxious not to lose any time, a larger armed bougie was applied to the stricture to enlarge the passage.

After this, he never remained quiet but walked about for several hours. This imprudent conduct brought on pain, local and general irritation, which lasted three days; the pain in making water then became less severe, a discharge came on, and the symptoms gradually abated; in eleven days the discharge was almost the only symptom that remained; this was removed by balsam copaiva. A bougie was now passed into the bladder to ascertain the size of the canal, which was considered of a sufficient size, and therefore nothing more was done. The passing of the bougie however brought on a discharge again, which lasted for ten days, and went off. A year after, an opportunity occured of passing the same bougie into the bladder.

CASE II.

Stricture in which the parts were so irritable that the Caustic brought on spasm and fainting.

A gentleman, thirty-six years of age, who had been many years in India, and had for a great part of that time been affected by the symptoms of stricture; in the year 1796 put himself under my care, and had the caustic applied. After it had been used several times to a stricture $6\frac{1}{4}$ inches from the orifice, the end of the bougie went through the stricture, the parts bled freely, and the pain was very severe; at the next application the bleeding returned again, and some hours after he had a spasm come on after making water, and nearly fainted. He passed the night tolerably well, but next morning, in making water, while upon the close-stool, the pain was so severe that in two minutes he fainted away; he was much relieved by a glyster of warm water, and had no return of the fainting. The caustic was applied several times more to this stricture, and almost always attended by hæmorrhage, and more or less of the feel of faintness and languor. He had been subject to complaints in his stomach for many years, and this violent effect probably arose from sympathy with the stomach, which in him was uncommonly irritable.

When this stricture was destroyed, three-quarters of an inch further on there was another, but the caustic when applied to it did not give the same pain, and the sensation was confined to the part. The caustic was used sixteen times to this last stricture before it was destroyed, and the last three times the caustic was made as large as the bougie would admit of, after which a full sized bougie passed freely into the bladder.

CASE III.

Of Stricture in which a Spasm prevented the emission of the Semen.

A gentleman, about thirty years of age, had an irritation in the urethra at the time of having connection with women, and at that time the semen was not propelled forwards. This gave him a great deal of uneasiness, and induced him to apply to me for assistance. He was told that there was no cause which could produce such an effect but a stricture; and on examining the urethra, one was found about $5\frac{1}{2}$ inches; this was removed by two applications of the caustic: another at $6\frac{1}{2}$ required seven or eight applications; and the last two or three times the caustic was used there was a good deal of bleeding.

The symptoms went away as soon as the stricture was removed. The gentleman went to sea, and remained on board of ship

Y

for three or four months; after which he returned to town, when an opportunity occurred of examining the canal, which was in exactly the same state, the stricture having in no degree returned.

CASE IV.

Stricture with Spasms at the time of making water, so as to prevent its flowing, and also obstructing the Semen.

A gentleman, aged thirty, about seven years since had a venereal gonorrhœa; he immediately used an injection, and in about a week (as he had no disagreeable sensations, and no discharge) he concluded himself well, and therefore left off the injection; in about three days, however, the running returned with considerable violence: he then applied to a physician, who ordered him to drink whey in great quantities, and to take gum arabic and nitre. The scalding and running rather increased under this treatment; he therefore, in about six weeks, applied to a surgeon, who began by giving mercurial pills and gentle purges; but not finding these to answer, gave balsam copaiva, elixir of vitriol, and an injection.

At the end of a month, he found a difficulty in making water, upon which the surgeon passed a bougie of about 4 inches in length, which met with some obstruction; he advised him to continue the bougie in the urethra the whole of that day, and repeat it for about four or five hours the next day; and in about three or four days he directed him to wear the bougie the whole day. After wearing it for a month, the surgeon said the stricture must certainly be removed, and the bougie was left off. Bathing was afterwards directed for the cure of the discharge, which still continued as bad in colour, and as much in quantity, as ever.

In a week the running and scalding became so disagreeable, that he determined

Y 2

to apply to another surgeon: this gentleman advised taking larger doses of copaiva
and elixir of vitriol than before, but this was
of no service; he afterwards took hemlock
pills, but with no effect. He attempted sea-
bathing, but this disagreeing with him he
left it of. The running and scalding, after
he had been some little time at the sea,
seemed rather to abate. He had during
this period frequent connection with women. After he had been at the sea about
six months, he felt more disagreeable sensations in the urethra than usual, and the
running so much increased that he concluded himself again infected, and made
use of an injection of sugar of lead and
rose-water; this was of so little service
that he determined to go to London. He
was then put under a course of bougies; he
began by using one five minutes at a time,
and increased it. After wearing the bougie twice, one of the testicles gave pain in
the morning, and before night it swelled
considerably; the swelling and pain did not

leave him for more than a month. He made water freely during that month; but after the swelling had almost subsided, and he was sufficiently well to go out, he found at times a good deal of difficulty in making water. He passed a bougie when this happened, and then the urine came forward very well: the bougie was at some times a good deal more obstructed than at others. Once he was a great deal alarmed at not being able to pass it at all. He was ordered to go to bed, and to take a decoction of marshmallows; he made water tolerably well before morning. It was now supposed that the complaint in his urethra proceeded from spasm. A bougie was passed repeatedly to ascertain this point, of which he at length thought there was no doubt. It was now wished to have Mr. Hunter's opinion. Mr. Hunter passed a bougie, and after it was withdrawn, said that there were three strictures in the urethra, but from the account concluded they were spasmodic. Mr. Hunter recommended, therefore, that he should always be provided with bougies, for the purpose of passing them when he had any difficulty in making water; he also advised the patient to take the extract of hemlock. The running still continued the same in quantity and colour: he took the hemlock, and entirely left off wine. Scarce a day passed without his being obliged to make use of the bougie, to enable him to make water. He perceived at times, that different parts of the urethra obstructed the bougie; at others a moderate sized bougie went into the bladder with scarce any obstruction. While he remained in London he had frequent nocturnal emissions, which commonly awoke him; the semen was always discharged.

After he had been some time in the country, he was much alarmed by having been awakened by such an irritation, without any emission. He had connection with a woman, and took means to ascertain exactly whether this would constantly be the case, and found that the same thing happened five or six times afterwards. The seventh time he had connection with a woman, in the same manner, the semen came forward, but in very small quantity. He now made use of exercise on horseback (which he had before left off) ; but did not find any alteration. The symptoms at this time were exactly these: a discharge from the urethra, similar to that from a gonorrhœa, attended with some drops of blood, which generally followed the urine; a small degree of uneasiness in one of the testicles; the semen seldom coming forward in the action of the coitus, and then in small quantities; a necessity of making use of the bougie, to relieve a suppression of urine, sometimes once, sometimes oftener, in the course of the twenty-four hours. Notwithstanding these circumstances, he continued in his general health as well as he had been before he had the complaint. In about eight months he returned to the use of wine, which made no alteration whatever in the complaint for the worse; it continued without any variation till about the 7th of October, 1795. He had been in the country shooting the whole of September, and felt one morning when he was out a constant desire to make water, with a good deal of uneasiness in the bladder, which obliged him to return home and go to bed; he took an opiate draught, and had bladders of warm water applied to the perinæum.

He felt a good deal of pain in the bladder after making water, and also in the back and kidneys; the whole of this time, the water came in a full stream. He continued in a good deal of pain for about ten days, after which it abated.

A surgeon passed a bougie, and told him that he had one permanent stricture in the urethra, which was the cause of his complaints; he advised, as his testicle had been swelled before, that he should use the warm bath at the same time with the bougies; that he should pass the bougie, not into the bladder, but a little beyond the stricture;

the pain in the bladder and kidneys gradually subsided.

He then required the occasional use of the bougie (which he had not done while the pain continued) in order to make water. He now took exercise as usual, determining to put off the passing a bougie for the present. He did not commence wearing the bougie till May, and did not go into the warm bath. He increased the time of wearing it to about two hours in the morning, and the same at night. He continued this plan till January; the semen now almost always came forwards, but not in the usual quantity. He had connection with a woman, and in about four days had a discharge attended with a good deal of irritation in the bladder.

Under these circumstances he put himself under my care. Upon examining the urethra, a stricture was found at about five inches.

The caustic was applied while there was a very great discharge, much irritation and tenderness. The pain of the caustic did not increase the irritation, or bring on affection of the testes, or any other unpleasant symptom. The discharge diminished considerably, even under the use of the caustic. After applying the caustic twice to the first stricture, and five times to one at six inches, the bougie went into the bladder, and afterwards a bougie the full size of the canal passed without difficulty, but gave a great deal of pain, and brought on a paroxysm of fever, which went off; next day the discharge increased ; but disappeared in a few days.

The semen now came forward in the full quantity, and all the former irritations subsided; nor did they return during the period of his remaining in London, which was for several months after his recovery.

SECTION VI.

CASES OF STRICTURE ATTENDED WITH UN-COMMON CONSTITUTIONAL AFFECTIONS, WHICH DISAPPEARED ON THE REMOVAL OF THE STRICTURE.

STRICTURES in many patients affect the stomach, and through the medium of the stomach the whole system, so as to derange the general health; this cannot be known in any other way, than by the return of health when the stricture is removed.

In other instances strictures bring on both constitutional and local complaints, which are not suspected to be in any way connected with them.

The inference which it is natural to draw from these observations is, that wherever there is a stricture in the urethra, and also other complaints of an ambiguous nature, it is a necessary step towards the investigation of these complaints, to remove the stricture, so as to ascertain in what degree it is connected with them.

CASE I.

Stricture attended with Complaints in the Stomach and Eruptions on the Skin.

A gentleman, thirty years of age, had an eruption on his skin, attended with discoloration of the cuticle, that spread over different parts of his body, particularly his breast and arms. He had a complaint in his stomach which distressed him exceedingly, frequently producing sickness and great uneasiness. Added to these distresses, he had a gleet, and frequency in making water.

Every medical assistance had been given for the complaints in the stomach and skin without much benefit, and it was for these only that he consulted me. Upon a more accurate investigation, it proved that he had a stricture; and from the intimate connection between that complaint and the stomach, it appeared probable that the stricture kept up such a degree of irritation in the general system, as to prevent the other symptoms from being removed. Upon this ground it was proposed first to remove the stricture; this was done by five or six applications of the caustic, and afterwards the stomach was found to be less irritable, and small doses of corrosive sublimate now removed the complaint in the skin, which had before resisted the effects of mercury in that form, as well as in several others.

The stricture has not returned, nor any of the other symptoms, although it is now more than ten years since it was removed.

CASE II.

Stricture with Irritable Stomach.

A gentleman, aged-forty six, had a stricture for twenty years, brought on while in India. For the last twelve years of that period, he was made very miserable by an irritable state of the stomach, which was sometimes more violent than at others. He had occasionally suppressions of urine; but almost always upon going to bed, as soon as laid down, he had a pain and heat in the stomach, with restlessness, a dry tongue, quick pulse, and general uneasiness; these symptoms continued till three or four o'clock in the morning, when they began to abate. His stricture admitted a small bougie, and could be dilated by that instrument to a certain degree; but any attempt to exceed these limits brought on irritation, and the canal at that part contracted as much as before the bougie had been used. Under these circumstances he was told by the most eminent surgeons he consulted, that the complaint could not be remedied; he must therefore bear with it, and palliate the more severe symptoms when they occurred,

In October, 1796, he put himself under my care. On examining the urethra, a stricture was found about $4\frac{1}{2}$ inches from the external orifice, which was removed by three applications of the caustic; when the bougie went through it brought on a severe paroxysm of fever, with an extremely profuse perspiration. Another stricture was met with at $5\frac{1}{2}$; this required six applications, which gave a good deal of pain but produced no irritation in the stomach; when the stricture was destroyed, another very severe paroxysm of fever came on, and was succeeded by a second equally violent. The caustic was now applied to a third stricture at $6\frac{1}{2}$; it was repeated twenty-two times before the bougie went through; this was followed in a few hours by an attack of irritation in the bladder, and a strangury that lasted four hours; these went off, and a violent paroxysm of fever, which was followed by a second, terminated the effects of the irritation. The complaints in the stomach now went off. The caustic was not applied for fourteen days; but it was found necessary to use it four times more before the bougie passed with ease to the bladder. He passed the common bougie for two months, a few minutes every day, to give him every security against a return.

The curious circumstance in this case was, that in ten days after the last stricture was destroyed, he was able on going to bed to go to sleep (the usual irritation having been removed) which he had not been able to do for twelve years.

He has found it necessary to pass a bougie once or twice a week without letting it remain in the urethra, and under this treatment there has been no return of stricture in nine years.

The wife of this gentleman has several children, but had none for some years before the stricture was removed, since that time she has had two.

CASE III.

Stricture with Fever and Delirium.

A gentleman, twenty-five years of age, in the year 1761 had an attack of strangury ; as this was the consequence of gonorrhœa, mercurial injections were recommended to him, and he went into the country. From that time he never made water freely, and finding himself get worse in that respect, in 1773 he came to London, when it was ascertained that there was a stricture, but a bougie could not be passed. He was obliged to return into the country in a state of almost constant distress, his urine passing involuntarily, attended with violent attacks of irritation.   In June, 1785, he had a rigor, and very severe attack of fever, excruciating pain in making water, and discharge of mucus and blood from the bladder ; this attack lasted a fortnight, after which he found himself easier, his urine did not pass involuntarily, nor had he so much pain ;

Z

but he soon relapsed into a worse state than before. After dragging on a miserable existence for ten years, by the advice of Dr. Darwin he resolved to try the caustic, and came to London in the beginning of May, 1796. At the time of his arrival he made water with excruciating torture, the straining brought on the piles in a great degree, and considerable inflammation in perinæo; his water came away mostly involuntarily, he had frequent attacks of delirium, little or no appetite, with nausea and vomiting. In this state the caustic was passed; it gave no pain, but was followed by a rigor, and the other complaints were aggravated, which made it necessary to wait for a week; and from the general distress under which he laboured, it was suspected there was a stone in the bladder, particularly as a great deal of mucus was at intervals thrown off from the bladder. The caustic was again applied; it gave less pain, and was followed by less irritation: there were two strictures. The caustic was applied in all twelve times, and a tolerably large bougie passed into the bladder. All the symptoms now subsided, he made water in a full stream, and only once or twice in the night; the tenesmus went away, and the bladder appeared to have perfectly recovered itself.

CASE IV.

Stricture with Nervous Fever.

A gentleman applied to me for assistance, in Feb. 1796; his complaints were nervous affections, restlessness, quick small pulse, uneasy and disturbed sleep, with heat in the skin, symptoms which were considered to constitute nervous fever. He had at times uneasiness in the bottom of the belly, and straining to make water, and his urine was loaded with mucus, which also came off after the urine had ceased to flow. He made water commonly once in the course of the night, but had no apparent

Z 2

difficulty in voiding it, nor did he believe that the stream was smaller than is natural. He had been ill for several years in India with the same feverish indisposition, attended with affections of the bladder, and a discharge of mucus after making water; but these local symptoms had always been referred to the constitutional complaints, and when he came to England, not suspecting any local disease, he put himself under the care of a physician, who declared that all the symptoms were effects of the fever, and treated them as such. They did not yield to the prescribed medicines; and upon stating his complaints to some of his friends, they told him that they had similar affections arising from stricture in the urethra, and thought it probable that his symptoms might arise from the same cause. Upon this idea he was led to consult me.

He had never passed a bougie; it was therefore necessary to ascertain by that instrument the state of the urethra. In doing so an obstruction was met with about $5\frac{1}{2}$ inches from the external orifice, which led me to conclude there was another nearer the bladder. The caustic was applied to this stricture; it gave pain, but brought on no irritation : this was repeated, and the bougie went through the stricture, but did not go on above an inch further, having met with another obstruction ; this allowed a small bougie to go through it, which led me to conceive that its destruction would be attended with little difficulty ; and his never having used a bougie, was a probable cause for the stricture being in a more natural state, therefore more readily to be acted on by the caustic. All these opinions proved erroneous, for it required six applications; after three of them there was a good deal of blood and faintness, but this went off; and he told me after the sixth application, that he felt himself uncommonly well, his general irritation had left him, his spirits were good, and he was more himself than he had been for a considerable time. After receiving this account, the bougie was passed to ascertain our progress, and it went into the bladder, but it required above six more applications before a common sized bougie could be admitted to pass; it was about the 20th of March, 1796, when it was left off. In June the same sized bougie passed with ease, and he has had no return of his stricture. His feverish symptoms left him along with those of the stricture, they therefore probably arose from the same cause.

CHAPTER V.

CASES OF STRICTURE WHICH BROUGHT ON A DISEASED STATE OF THE NEIGHBOURING PARTS.

WHERE two diseases are present in the same patient, in parts connected with each other, and employed in performing the same functions, it is difficult to ascertain what are the appropriate symptoms of either of them. These can be only determined by removing one of the diseases, and attending to the symptoms that still continue, which must belong to the remaining disease.

From this view of the subject, the instances contained in the present Chapter, would appear to shew that strictures are sometimes secondary complaints, as little alleviation of the patient's sufferings is gained by their removal; in this light they were considered in the former edition, but a more extensive experience has made it evident, that in all of them the stricture is the original complaint ; but too frequently when they have been established, something more is necessary than the removal of the stricture for their cure.

SECTION I.

CASES OF STRICTURE PRODUCING A SPAS-
MODIC CONTRACTION OF THE ORIFICE OF
THE BLADDER.

IT has been ascertained that when there is a
stricture beyond the bulb, and the patient is
unable to make water, the spasm is not at
the neck of the bladder, but at the stricture;
since a bougie passed down to the stricture,
and allowed to remain there, is capable of
taking off the spasm, and the water readily
flows from the bladder. This is so generally
true, that it entirely overturns the received
opinion of a spasm at the neck of the bladder
being a common occurrence; but the two
following cases are sufficient evidence, that
it sometimes happens, and is a symptom of
stricture, brought on by the injudicious use
of the bougie; at the same time this circumstance happening so seldom, becomes a
proof that the orifice of the bladder is in

itself less irritable than it was natural to expect.

CASE I.

A gentleman from the West Indies, 36 years of age, of a very irritable habit of body, had laboured under a stricture for 16 years. He had tried the use of the common bougie at different times, but was unable to encrease the size beyond that of a large crow's quill, and when it was left in the urethra for an hour, a very unpleasant irritation was brought upon the bladder, there was a difficulty in withdrawing the bougie, and when it was examined there was an appearance impressed upon the last half inch of it unlike any thing met with in other cases. The point of the bougie was turned upwards, and a transverse groove formed on the under surface, a quarter of an inch from the point, going only half round it, $\frac{1}{10}$ of an inch wide. The opposite surface of the bougie was smooth, but had a depression of an oval form upon it, extending $\frac{1}{4}$ of an inch further from the point, and the bougie at this last part was flattened and rendered broader: this impression was made by a spasmodic contraction of the neck of the bladder, and gives a better idea of the mode in which it shuts the orifice than can in any other way be acquired; it proves that the lower lip is the innermost, and acts with greatest force, is only about $\frac{1}{10}$ of an inch broad, and presses against the upper one, which is a rounded surface; when the bladder therefore shuts with force upon a soft substance, it makes a transverse groove below, but none above, and the upper surface of the substance pressed is rendered concave.

Having ascertained by measuring the bougie, that this impression was made by the neck of the bladder, the bougie was not allowed to remain above a minute or two in the bladder at any one time.

In this case the caustic was used, but the patient was at the time in so irritable a state that it could not be persevered in.

CASE II.

A gentleman consulted me respecting an unusual appearance on the bougie which he had passed into the bladder. that had given his mind nò small alarm ; finding it exactly similar to that which has been described, it was explained to him that this impression was the consequence of the bougie having been too long retained in the bladder, which had produced a contraction of the orifice on the point; he said it had never happened but when the bougie was retained two hours, and his alarm arose from the apprehension that the bougie might be cut through, and the point retained ; this indeed was so nearly the case, that his alarm was by no means without foundation. Having satisfied him of the nature of the impression, he was advised not to allow any instrument to remain in the bladder.

SECTION II.

CASES OF STRICTURE PRODUCING ENLARGEMENT OF THE PROSTATE GLAND.

BESIDES the diseased enlargement of the prostate gland, which arises out of the changes the gland is liable to undergo in old age, there is another of a very different kind, and of a much less serious nature, which is attendant upon strictures.

It happens, as it would be natural to expect, that when the urine passes through a stricture in the urethra with great difficulty, the parts that lie between the obstruction and the cavity of the bladder, are kept in an irritated, and often an inflamed state, by the pressure of the urine against them, in the necessary efforts that are made for its expulsion; this is often found to be the case, and if the parts are examined by passing a finger up the rectum, a fulness is felt which will lead to an opinion, that the disease is in the prostate gland, rendering it enlarged, whereas the disease is, in reality, a stricture in the urethra, producing a tumifaction in the parts beyond it, by disturbing their functions; but as soon as the stricture is removed, they fall back again into their natural state. Nothing is so common as this mistake in medical practitioners, and whenever it is made, it fills with distress the mind of the patient, who considers his disease incurable. Whenever an affection of this gland is mentioned to me as a primary disease, or one of a serious nature, under 60 years of age, my request is not to be uneasy on that account, as when the stricture is removed, it will be found that the gland will recover itself. It will not be going beyond the truth when it is declared, that in many hundred instances, in which the case has been stated as a disease of the prostate gland connected with stricture, under 50 years of age, the case stated in this Section is the only one in which any symptoms of its enlargement remained after the stricture was removed, and these only in a very slight degree. Beyond 50 years of age all the instances in which the enlargement of the gland continued, have been three.

Strictures when allowed to continue beyond 50 years of age, produce another effect upon the prostate gland, which is exciting inflammation in its substance, and forming abcesses in it, which break, sometimes into the urethra, at others into the bladder. Cases of this kind are stated in the second volume, when treating of the diseased state of the bladder, in consequence of stricture.

The following history will explain the manner in which a stricture irritates the neck of the bladder, as well as the bad consequences that attend the two diseases being present at the same time.

A gentleman sixty-six years of age was attacked with the symptoms of a low remitting fever, for which the assistance of a physician was called; in the symptoms were not very violent, but did not abate, and at the end of 16 days had undergone little change; at this time there was a total stoppage of water, and upon enquiry being made, it was found that he had laboured under a stricture for 30 years, had lived very freely, and for the last ten years had neglected passing bougies; his making water very badly for the latter part of that time, had been obvious to his acquaintances, but an unwillingness to confess it had prevented him from applying for advice, as no absolute necessity had arisen for so doing. In this state he caught cold, and there is every reason to believe that the fever was only symptomatic of the state of the stricture, and the consequent irritation on the bladder. My assistance was desired on account of the stoppage of urine. When called to the patient, he expressed great dread at anything being done, and was in so low a state that nothing could be attempted but to palliate the symptoms. On passing a small catgut bougie, it went with difficulty through a stricture at 4½ inches from the external orifice down to one at 6 inches, in which the point was caught, and on letting it remain there he made water, but did not afterwards pass any till the same process was repeated; and when asleep a good deal came away involuntarily. In this way the bladder was prevented from being much distended, although never emptied; but no bougie could be got into the bladder. This mode of treatment in five days had gained nothing upon the stricture; his strength gradually diminished, he became commatose, passed his water involuntarily in his sleep, and in seven days from the time of my being called in he died.

Upon examining the parts after death, there were three strictures in the urethra, one at 4½ inches, a second at 6 inches, and a third at 7. These were not attended with any thickening or hardness of the urethra at these parts, and in the dead body they were so relaxed as to admit readily a crow's quill, although in the living body they would not receive the smallest sized catgut bougie. The

A a

prostate gland was enlarged, and projected
½ an inch into the urethra, so that no bougie
could pass beyond it, as the point would
always be caught at that part. The bladder
contained two pints of urine; its internal membrane was unusually vascular, but no coagulable lymph was thrown out upon it in consequence of inflammation.

In this case there were three strictures
which had not, as it appeared, undergone any
great change, or become materially worse
for the last ten years ; but by impeding the
urine had made it press upon the prostate
gland, which had inflamed, and became the
cause of the stoppage of urine; it had also
brought on irritation upon the strictures, so
as to prevent a bougie from passing through
them, and ascertaining the diseased enlargement of the gland, which was in reality the
disease of which he died.

That this was the case, is in some measure
ascertained by two cases of partial suppression in patients of 70 years of age, that
were not relieved by small bougies which

went down to the neck of the bladder ; but when the repetition of the bougie had taken off the spasm from the strictures, and a small sized flexible gum catheter, which had its point curved, could be passed into the bladder and draw off the water, nothing more was necessary than this operation, twice a day, to relieve the bladder, and make the swelling of the prostate gland subside.

These facts have led me to conclude, that strictures in themselves after 60 years of age, when they have not previously brought on any violent symptoms, become no longer a dangerous complaint, otherwise than by producing an enlargement of the prostate gland, and on that account alone ought to be removed; since the use of the bougie, under such circumstances, becomes very dangerous in unskilful hands, always striking against the gland, and in many instances irritating the membrane of the urethra which covers it, and producing very serious consequences.

CASE I.

A gentleman, forty-six years of age, had all the common symptoms of stricture which have been so frequently described; for these he consulted me.

Upon examining the urethra two strictures were met with, and were both removed by the use of the caustic; the bougie passed readily through the strictures, but stopped at the prostate gland, and could not go on to the bladder. A flexible gum catheter with a stilet a good deal curved, readily passed; the bougie was again tried, bent at the end, and with a slight stoppage at the prostate gland, it passed over it. These circumstances were explained to the patient, and sea–bathing and quietness were recommended, to see how far the removal of the stricture would in time dispose the gland to subside. He went to the sea, and returned to me six months after.

The symptoms of irritation were much diminished, and the bougie now without any
halt passed into the bladder ; so that the
diseased enlargement of the prostate gland
had evidently subsided since the stricture
was removed.

CASE II.

A gentleman, aged fifty-one, in May,
1779, was exposed to the heat in India, during the time of the year when the hot winds
prevail most, in a situation where they are
remarkably violent, and when from particular circumstances he felt much anxiety of
mind.   This brought on a severe fit of suppression of urine, for which the usual applications were made ; these relieved him so
as to enable him to pass his urine drop by
drop ; there was much spasm at the neck of
the bladder, which continued with very little
abatement for about two years ; the complaint then seemed to abate gradually, but

during the whole continuance of the symptoms he found most relief in cold weather. From the year 1781 the symptoms became more favourable, and he was able to make water in a small stream till 1785, when he left India.   On his passage home they gradually diminished, and as soon as he came into cold latitudes he seemed to be perfectly well. He could not ascribe these complaints to any venereal disorder ; but within the three last years finding a return of the irritation (though very different from what he had formerly) with a difficulty in making water, he conceived there might be a stricture in the urethra ; as ever since his return to Europe, he had been at times liable to slight returns of the strangury, which opiates relieved, and he found himslf better in winter than in summer.

In 1796 he put himself under my care ; and upon examining the urethra, there was a stricture at six inches.

The caustic was applied to this, and three applications destroyed it : there was another at seven inches, which gave way after four applications; the bougie now passed through it, but did not go into the bladder; an attempt was made with the catheter, but it would not pass, although he made water very well, and experienced much relief from the strictures being destroyed.

The prostate gland in this case was enlarged, and prevented, by its size or irregular form, the catheter from going into the bladder.

This is the only case, either of stricture or enlarged prostate gland, in which it has been mentioned to me that the symptoms were aggravated by warm weather, and relieved by cold; it is in general the reverse.

CASE III.

A gentleman, sixty-eight years of age, had been troubled for a year and half with a frequency of making water, a discharge of mucus from the bladder, and pain and irritation in the region of that viscus. After having tried the effects of internal medicines without relief, he consulted me upon the subject of his complaints.

Upon examining the urethra there was a stricture about six inches, which was removed by the caustic after five applications, and the bougie when much bent went into the bladder; but his complaints were not at all relieved, so that the stricture was not the only complaint.

He caught cold some weeks after the stricture was removed, the weather at the time being uncommonly severe, and a strangury came on, which required the use of the catheter, nor could it pass unless the instrument was very much curved; in any other form it stopped at the prostate gland; this swelling of that gland did not subside entirely for several months, although it diminished sufficiently to allow of his passing his urine with some degree of difficulty.

CASE IV.

A gentleman, sixty-four years of age, consulted me on account of a stricture which he had laboured under for fifteen years. The symptoms he said were an occasional leakage from the bladder, by which he meant an involuntary passing of the urine; an inability to pass a bougie into the bladder unless it was curved, and was composed of materials which preserved that curve; that the part it stopped at was about eight inches, and the attempts to get beyond the obstruction brought on hæmorrhage; that if a plaster bougie (one made of linen), was passed, it brought on great irritation, and was with difficulty withdrawn; but an elastic gum bougie came out with tolerable ease. In the morning he was unable to pass a bougie more than a few inches into the urethra, but in the evening it went on to the bladder; and for the last fifteen years he had occasionally passed one of elastic gum, curved for that purpose, which being used two or three times, relieved the involuntary flowing of the urine.

From this account, considering his age, that the symptoms had been only occasional, that there had been no great increase, that a curved bougie passed better than a straight one, that there was only an involuntary discharge of urine and no suppression, there appeared sufficient evidence to conclude that the stricture was not the cause of the present symptoms ; but begged he would allow me to examine the canal, to ascertain the real state of it. To this he objected ; saying that it would bring on irritation, and for several days he should be unable to pass his bougie ; but upon declaring myself unable to give any opinion, without such examination, and if he was desirous of having it, he must submit to such temporary irritation, with some difficulty he assented. As the present disease was not believed to be stricture, no attempt was made to pass a bougie, but a full sized flexible gum catheter with a curved stilet, passed without pain or difficulty into the bladder, although four times larger than the bougie he had used, and drew off the urine, and in the act of withdrawing it was not grasped by the urethra. The disease was therefore an enlargement of the point of the prostate gland, which this instrument, from its shape, readily passed over, and therefore produced no irritation ; the bougies formerly used, on account of the stricture, had probably kept it from contracting, but when passed under the present circumstance irritated the gland, and brought on a contraction along the whole canal.

It was stated to the patient, that when he caught cold the gland enlarged, and in that state he had an involuntary passing of the urine; when that happened in future, all that was necessary to be done was occasionally passing the catheter till that subsided ; that the use of the bougie only kept the parts at the neck of the bladder in a state of irritation, and should therefore be left off.

CASE V.

A gentleman, aged sixty-five, had used bougies on account of a stricture for many years, but for the last year the symptoms were much increased, attended with great irritation in the bladder, making water fifty times in the twenty-four hours. Finding no relief under the most eminent physicians and surgeons in London, he resolved, although extremely irritable, to try the caustic. In Aug. 1796 it was applied to two strictures seven times before they admitted a large bougie to pass into the bladder; and after it had done so, the symptoms were little if at all relieved. This led to a suspicion of the prostate gland; but as the bougie passed with tolerable ease into the bladder, it gave reason to believe that gland was not much enlarged. On passing a catheter into the bladder, it drew off three times the quantity of water he usually made; and he was able to keep in the catheter three hours without making water, although he never could retain a bougie half an hour. The disease for the last year was therefore principally in the gland. This plan was now adopted. The water was drawn off once in twenty-four hours. In a very few days the quantity of mucus in the urine was diminished, and he passed it less frequently; there was less straining to go to stool, and he felt himself every way better. He attempted passing the catheter so often as to prevent the bladder from acting, but the intervals rather diminished, the first time $1\frac{3}{4}$ hour, second $1\frac{1}{4}$, so that the irritation appeared to be in the coats of the bladder; the uva ursi in powder was administered, but did nothing. The caustic alkali was afterwards given, but its use was interrupted by the bowels being affected. He found, however, that drawing off his water three times a day diminished the irritation, which therefore he continued to do. Oct. 17, he found himself in every respect better by using the catheter three times a day, there was less mucus from the bladder, and that less tenacious.

In March, 1797, he had periodical returns of discharge and irritation in the bladder, and was nearly, in respect to uneasiness, in the same state as when he first consulted me, the disease producing the irritation being evidently in the bladder. He had however this advantage, that he could now always empty it by passing the catheter, and in that way could draw off the mucus as fast as it was formed, which in a degree relieved the bladder, and prevented more serious attacks from the disease.

SECTION III.

CASES OF STRICTURE PRODUCING AN IRRI-
TABLE STATE OF THE BLADDER.

CASES of irritable bladder too frequently
occur from stricture, at least many instances
of it have come under my observation.
The following Cases will be sufficient to
shew the symptoms which this disease and
state of the bladder produces. In the former
Edition this was considered as a disease in-
dependant of stricture, but a more enlarged
experience has convinced me that the stricture is the cause of the disease in the bladder, and that when the bladder has become
diseased, it is in some instances so violently
affected, as to be unable to recover itself even
after the cause is removed. It is however
reasonable to believe, that if the stricture is
allowed to increase, or even to remain, it

must render the irritation in the bladder more violent, and its consequences of a more serious nature. But when the membrane of the bladder has been long diseased, the removal of the stricture aggravates its symptoms, by allowing the contraction of its cavity to be more complete, and the irritated internal membrane to be more compressed, which is attended with the most excruciating pain.

CASE I.

A gentleman, thirty years of age, of a very irritable body and mind, had a discharge, frequency in making water, pain in the region of the bladder, and a considerable quantity of viscid matter deposited from his urine.

A stricture was met in the urethra, to which these symptoms were attributed; he therefore applied to me to have it removed. One at $5\frac{1}{2}$ inches was destroyed by the caustic, and another at six inches, after by the caustic, and another at six inches, after which the bougie went readily into the bladder. The symptoms, particularly the frequency in making water, and the quantity of viscid matter thrown out with the urine, were by no means diminished. Stone was now suspected, but upon sounding the bladder, none was felt; as the end of the sound passed over the inner surface of the bladder, it came against the rugæ of the inner membrane of that viscus, and when these were touched the patient expressed much pain. This disease of the bladder appeared sufficient to account for the symptoms.

A year after the stricture was removed, the bougie was passed to ascertain whether there was a return; but it passed with the same ease as before. No medicines that had been tried, the principal of which were the uva ursi, and the mephitic alkaline water, quieted the irritation in the bladder; it was however in that period much relieved.

B b

CASE II.

A gentleman, aged thirty, had a frequency in making water, particularly in the forenoon, which continued through the day, but went off entirely on going to bed, and he did not make water till he got up in the morning. He had also a gleet, as it was termed, in consequence of gonorrhœa, which had continued upon him for two years.

From the frequency in making water, and the discharge, a stricture was suspected, and the urethra examined by passing a bougie; a stricture was met with at five inches; this was removed by the caustic; another was found at $6\frac{1}{2}$ inches, which was also destroyed, and the bougie passed with ease into the bladder. The parts were now left to themselves, and the symptoms continued without any abatement. At the end of a month, the bougie was passed to ascertain whether the stricture had been entirely removed, and it passed with great ease. The circumstance of the bladder being at ease during the whole night, made me suspect stone, which by its motion gave uneasiness, but none when at rest. On sounding the bladder, nothing hard was felt. The disease appears therefore to be an irritated state of the membrane of the bladder, brought on by the stricture.

In this case there was little sediment in the urine. By the use of the mephitic alkaline water this patient almost entirely got the better of his complaints.

CASE III.

A gentleman, twenty-six years of age, had for three years a frequency of making water, and his urine, when allowed to stand, deposited a sediment, which at times adhered to the bottom of the vessel, at others, was in the form of mucus. He had frequent attacks of irritation, attended with pain in the region of the bladder, and the desire to make water incessant; these went off and returned at very irregular intervals.

Distressed by these symptoms he put himself under my care. When the urethra was examined, it was evident that the affection of the bladder was connected with stricture, as the bougie at $5\frac{1}{2}$ inches met with an obstruction.. It was therefore proposed that the stricture should be removed. For this purpose the caustic was employed. One stricture was destroyed after four applications, but another was met with an inch and half further on; this required twelve applications of the caustic before the bougie went into the bladder. When this was accomplished, the use of the caustic was left off.

He felt himself better, the frequency of making water was less, his general health was improved, but still he was by no means well; the urine deposited the same sediment, although in less quantity, and he made water oftener than persons in health. In a few weeks his complaints got worse, and he consulted me again upon a supposition that the stricture had returned. The bougie was found to pass with great ease. It was therefore proposed to sound the bladder; the sound passed readily, and nothing hard could be felt. The complaints were therefore the effects of an irritable bladder, brought on by the stricture, which had not subsided, although the cause had been removed. This is not unfrequently the case, and the bladder requires some months to recover itself.

In this case the irritation in the bladder is the same in the night as in the day, or nearly so.

SECTION IV.

CASES OF STRICTURE IN WHICH CALCULOUS
CONCRETIONS WERE MET WITH IN THE
URETHRA AND BLADDER.

CALCULOUS concretions are more frequently
met with in the bladder and urethra of patients who have stricture, than is generally
believed. It will appear from the following
Cases, that in many instances the presence
of the stone can in no other way be ascertained than by the use of the caustic ; since,
in some of them the stone had been formed
for years, and although every other mode
of investigation had been adopted, this was
not discovered, till by the use of the caustic
the nature of the case was explained. It
is curious, that in M. Daran's work* only

* Observ. Chirurg. sur les Maladies de l'Uréthre,
traitées suivant une nouvelle Méthode. Par Jaques
Daran. Nouvelle edition. Paris; 1748.

three cases are mentioned in which calculous concretions were discovered. In two, the stone was in the perinæum; in one, it was in the bladder.

Calculous concretions when in the urethra keep up a continual irritation, which can only be relieved by their being voided, or removed by an operation.

A stone in the bladder not only causes an irritation in that viscus, but also produces a contraction in the urethra, forming stricture. As these are two symptoms of the same disease in different parts, it is natural to suppose that the removal of the stricture would diminish the uneasiness in the bladder; but the fact is otherwise; it often increases it; this may take place by the bladder being enabled to empty itself more completely, and to contract upon the hard stone. This is an effect that could not have been expected *a priori*; it is therefore right to mention it particularly, that this circumstance, when it occurs, may not mislead the surgeon, or be considered by the patient as the consequence of any irritating effect of the caustic.

CASE I.

Stricture and Stone in the Urethra.

A gentleman, twenty-four years of age, consulted me for a complaint in his bladder, of which he gave the following account. When he was seven or eight years of age, he had at times pain in the region of the bladder, and his urine was very high coloured ; to these symptoms he paid little attention, but recollects that they were sometimes so severe as to make him stop in the middle of his walks, and sit down for some minutes, till their severity abated : under these circumstances, when ten years old, he passed two triangular stones, each side of the triangle exceeding one–eighth of an inch in length ; these gave a great deal of pain in coming through the urethra; but after their expulsion the former symptoms entirely disappeared, and he continued free from complaint for three years. The same symptoms however recurred at thirteen years of age, and have continued ever since. The attack came on most commonly after emptying the bladder; it began by heat in the urethra, extending to the glans penis; and when it reached that part it was most severe, and gradually subsided. These attacks lasted sometimes four hours, at others a much shorter time; they brought on sickness at the stomach, and general uneasiness over the whole body; they were less frequent in cold weather; the longest intervals were five months; but in summer they often returned in a fortnight.

For the last three years they have been more frequent, the intervals rarely exceeding ten or twelve days; and for three months past, the attacks have come on with more or less violence every day, which induced him in July, 1795, to apply for relief.

At this time his urine passed in a small stream, and never in any very considerable quantity, which led me to suspect a stricture; and upon examining with a bougie, a stricture was met with. This, however, allowed a small sized bougie to go into the bladder; it could not therefore be supposed that all the symptoms arose from that cause, and it was suspected that there must be a stone in the bladder. To determine that point, a small bougie was passed, and after lying some time in the urethra, a very small silver sound was admitted with difficulty into the bladder, but no stone was found. This induced me to believe there might be a calculus behind the stricture, too small to obstruct the passage, but too large to pass the stricture; and that this, whenever it was thrown into a particular situation, brought on those fits of irritation, which could not be attributed to the stricture alone.

From this view of the case, it was proposed to destroy the stricture by the caustic; for which purpose it was applied five times, and a full sized bougie passed through; but during this period, which was ten days, there had not been the smallest abatement of the symptoms.

This discouraged the patient; but it was found, when this stricture was destroyed, that there was another a little further back towards the bladder, which sufficiently accounted for the continuance of the symptoms. The caustic was now applied to the second stricture; this was done eight times before the stricture would admit a tolerably large bougie; and in passing it the last time the caustic struck upon something hard, so as to be felt by the patient, and very distinctly communicated to the hand that was passing it. There was now no doubt of the presence of a small stone behind the stricture, which led me to persevere with the caustic, to give as much room as possible for voiding the stone. The patient had now for the first time a remission of the symptoms for a week; the caustic was applied twice more, and a full sized bougie went on to the bladder; the patient voided considerable quantities of coarse crystallized sand, which he had not done before, and felt the small calculus giving pain, by moving in the passage from irregularities on its surface; this went off, it was therefore supposed the calculus was voided in making water, without his knowledge. The large bougie was passed for a few minutes every day, to keep the urethra from being again contracted; and in this state he went into the country.

The symptoms were entirely removed, and there has been no return since that time, now above eight years.

CASE II.

Stricture and Stone in the Urethra.

A gentleman, sixty-three years of age, had been ten years subject to the symptoms of stricture, and obliged occasionally to have recourse to the use of the bougie. For the two last years he could not make water at all, without first passing a small bougie through the stricture, and leaving it in during the whole time of voiding it. In the North of England where he resided, his complaint was supposed to be a diseased prostate gland.

In this state he came to London in June, 1796, and put himself under my care. Upon examination his case proved to be stricture. The caustic was applied three times to a stricture $5\frac{1}{2}$ inches from the orifice of the urethra, which it destroyed; it was then applied to a second at $6\frac{1}{2}$ inches; after the third application the unarmed bougie went through it, and the end of the bougie had a depression upon one side, evidently made by a rounded body; on feeling the parts externally, there was a small hard substance distinctly felt in that part of the canal.

The patient was told that the cause of his not making water without the bougie being kept in the urethra, as also the sensation he had often expressed of something falling into the stricture, could now be explained; for there was a small calculus imbedded in the urethra behind the stricture, which was forced, by the action of the bladder on the urine, against the orifice, so as to stop it up altogether. The size of the caustic was now increased, and applied to this part, so as to make room for the stone to pass.

After about seven applications of this large armed bougie, the end of the caustic went through, and passed over the stone, which made an impression upon the side of the bougie; this shewed there was no part of the stricture on that side of the urethra left, but that the caustic came directly on the stone.

It was proposed at our next interview to pass a silver instrument beyond the calculus, and disengage it from the hollow which it had made for itself behind the stricture: but that very night he voided it naturally, and also a smaller one which lay behind it, and found himself immediately after able to make water perfectly well.

The largest stone in its shape was pointed

at one end, and obtuse at the other, five-eights of an inch in length, and the thickest part three-eights of an inch broad; its figure was that of a flattened cone. It lay in the urethra with the apex directed to the external orifice.

The other was smaller and roundish, two-eighths of an inch in one direction, and one-eighth and a half in the other. They were dark coloured, and very compact in their texture.

The patient since that time, has continued perfectly well, a period of nine years.

Several cases similar to the above, in which the symptoms were less violent, have since come under my observation.

The circumstances in the two following, are deserving of attention.

CASE III.

Of spasmodic Stricture with Calculus in the Urethra.

The patient was eighty years of age; the symptoms which first came on, were a difficulty in making water, and great frequency in voiding it; these were treated as the effects of inflammation in the bladder, but not yielding to the means made use of, my assistance was required. Upon passing a small sized bougie, it was prevented from going further than 7 inches. At so advanced an age, there was little reason to expect that stricture was the disease, and next day a small sized bougie was again passed and went into the bladder; the patient however experienced no relief, and in the evening had a total suppression; this was relieved by passing a small flexible gum catheter and drawing off the water; in withdrawing the instrument a stone was distinctly felt in the urethra. Attempts were made to dislodge it by breaking it in the eyes of the catheter, but without success. Next day the silver instrument mentioned in the last case was used, which brought the stone out of the place where it had imbedded itself, into the canal of the urethra about an inch nearer the external orifice, and in the night while making water it was voided into the chamber pot. From this time, which was in the spring, he continued very well till the next year about the same period, when he voided a small calculus, and did the same the year after. He was advised to have a bougie occasionally passed, that the passage might always be sufficiently free to let any sand or gravel readily come away as soon as it was formed.

CASE IV.

Of Spasmodic Stricture and Calculus in the Urethra.

A gentleman who had been many years in India, upon his return found himself affected with the symptoms of stricture in the urethra, and applied to me for relief, and they were removed by the caustic. Four years after, an attack of irritation came upon the bladder, which was naturally believed to be a return of the same disease. To ascertain how far that was the case, a bougie was passed, but did not go further than five inches, the whole urethra being in an inflamed state; on the next trial two days after, it passed 7 inches, and on withdrawing it there was a gritty sand adhering to the point, which explained the cause of the irritation. By passing the bougie regularly every other day for four or five times, the urethra was relaxed and the irritation lessened, so that the calculus was gradually forced on, and extracted from the external orifice, where it lodged. This attack was in the spring of the year, and in the following spring an attack of the same kind came on, which was relieved in the same way, and a small irregular calculus was voided. In both these cases the attack was in the spring, which leads to the belief that in this country calculi are more liable to be generated in that period of the year, and if this should prove to be generally true, it will be of great importance in practice, since it points out the most proper time for taking the preventives of that dreadful disease, and makes it less necessary to continue them through the whole year.

CASE V.

Stricture and Stone in the Urethra.

A gentleman, fifty-eight years of age, in the year 1760, lived in the East Indies, and had a diminution of the stream of urine, requ'ring an unusual length of time to empty the bladder ; he remained in India till 1771, and in the course of the last ten years had four or five times a total suppression; this was not brought on by irregular living, for he was always moderate respecting wine, and the climate made catching cold a very improbable circumstance. It happened in consequence of retaining his water, from being in company with ladies, beyond the usual time; the symptoms became very severe; they were relieved by the warm bath, bleedings even to fainting, and the use of the silver catheter (bougies at that time not being in use in India) ; during this period the stream at all times was as small as a thread.

In 1771 he came to England, and put himself under the care of Daran's agent in London for selling his bougies, and in the course of five months, constantly persevering in their use, and retaining them four hours at a time in the passage, it was dilated so as to admit a bougie the size of the common flexible gum catheter. He found himself free from complaint, and retained his water the usual time of persons in health. In this state he left them off; but he found in a few months that his complaint had begun to return, and was obliged to recur to the bougie, and by means of its use kept himself very well till 1785; but during these fourteen years he was obliged four or five different times to put himself under the care of the same person, to restore the parts from the contracted state they had acquired; and after each course of bougies the intervals became shorter and shorter.

In 1785 the bougie began to fail him; he could not now retain it in the passage above an hour, sometimes not half an hour, nor could he increase its size as he had done before. Under these circumstances he consulted a surgeon of eminence, who was induced to believe there was some complaint in the bladder, and with a view to ascertain this, passed a small silver sound

into the bladder; this proved to be a very
severe operation, and from the difficulty
attending it, the surgeon was unable to
make a satisfactory examination, and proposed that it should be repeated; this however the patient could not submit to, as
he conceived the presence of a stone in
the bladder would be followed by symptoms which would sufficiently explain themselves.

Discouraged by this practice, he returned into the country, giving up all hopes
from medical assistance. He made water
every hour, could pass a very small bougie
into the bladder, and when he wanted to
make water, a bougie introduced a little
way assisted it in flowing. He made water
as frequently in the night as in the day.
He remained in this state, sometimes worse
but never better, and in 1795 had a very
severe attack of strangury, which lasted
several days, and very nearly carried him
off.

In October, 1795, by the intreaties of

his friends, he came again to London for advice; the bougie was tried, but the irritation brought on by passing it fourteen times sufficiently proved that nothing could be effected that way. December 10th, Mr. Heaviside, who attended the patient, proposed the use of the caustic, and desired my opinion respecting it. Recourse was had to the caustic. It was applied to a stricture at the distance of three inches, which was got the better of by four applications; one a little further on required six; a third, about $6\frac{1}{2}$ inches, required eight, and when the caustic passed beyond it, a longitudinal groove was formed in the side of the bougie. A fourth stricture was met with, and this after two applications allowed a small flexible gum catheter to go into the bladder, through which the urine passed so as to empty it: this had never been the case for ten years, the bladder always remaining half full, only throwing off the superfluous quantity. It now remained quiet till it had been filled to the usual standard, which required three hours, and then a desire to void the urine came on. Two more applications of the caustic admitted a common sized flexible catheter to pass into the bladder, which was allowed to remain there, to interrupt the habit the bladder had got into of not contracting so as completely to empty itself. From December the 10th to January 27th, a period of forty-eight days, the caustic was applied in all twenty-two times. When its use was begun, he made water with great straining, and after he had done, some mucus came away, which had been supposed to be semen. After the first stricture was destroyed, there was less straining; and after the second, less mucus; and the intervals sometimes exceeded an hour. While the caustic was applied to the two last strictures, after every application there was a rigor attended with fainting and great depression; this did not happen after the use of the caustic was left off, and the flexible catheter had passed into the bladder. His appetite gradually mended, his bowels became more regular, and he recovered strength. On February 15th he dined out of his own room for the first time.

His urethra, which for ten years could not bear a bougie half an hour at a time, after the use of the caustic, bore, without any uneasiness, the flexible gum catheter, which is a harder instrument, not only for hours, but for a fortnight, producing no sensation or irritation, although it kept up a discharge similar to that which attends the use of the bougie.

The bladder was free from the discharge of mucus, and other symptoms of irritation, but there was always a pain in expelling the last drops of urine.

April 3d, he used the decoction of uva ursi, and continued it for a fortnight, to lessen the irritation in the bladder, but did not reap the smallest advantage. He now took compound lime water, four ounces twice a day, and after two days took it in the same dose three times a day.

The lime water apparently did nothing. He then took the caustic alkali, thirty drops twice a day. April 20th, the catheter did not pass so readily, and the caustic was once more applied, without bringing on any irritation, which allowed the catheter to pass with ease.

He now went to Greenwich; and it was thought some advantage might be gained by making the passage still wider. With this view, May 5th, the caustic was again applied upon a bougie larger than one which had stopped at the stricture. After remaining there some little time, this bougie went on to the bladder, which shewed that a spasm had stopped the other, and that the caustic removed the spasm. This however did not give relief. June 20th, the passage again contracted, and the caustic was again applied, which grated against something just before it entered the bladder; this led me to suspect a stone near the neck of the bladder, and upon passing a solid silver sound, the stone was distinctly felt.

It was now explained to the patient that a small stone lodged in the urethra accounted for all his symptoms, the stone never leaving the orifice of the bladder in an easy state. An operation was the only mode by which he could be relieved, but it was left to himself to decide whether his present sufferings were such as to exceed the risk attending it in his weak state.

He was to take a fortnight to turn this in his mind. Before that period elapsed an inflammation took place in the perinæum, the parts swelled to a considerable size, the scrotum became enlarged, and the urine got into the cellular membrane. An operation now was not a matter of choice, but of necessity. On July 4th an opening was made in the perinæum, and a stone extracted about an inch long, pointed at one end, which lay in the neck of the bladder, and rounded at the other, which lay towards the stricture. One side of the stone was grooved by the action of the caustic, and stained of a black colour.

After the operation a flexible gum catheter was left in the bladder, he made water less frequently, and had little pain.

Things appeared to be going on favourably, but he was very low. On the fourth day he slept for five hours, which had not happened for ten years; on the fifth, fever came on, and on the sixth he died.

CASE VI.

Stricture and Stone in the Urethra.

William Albany, a labouring man, fifty years of age, was admitted into St. George's Hospital, on the 6th of January, 1796, on account of a stoppage of his urine, and was put under my care. Twenty years before, he had a difficulty in making water, which had been relieved by medicines, and in a little time he thought himself well. He continued so till July, 1795, when the same complaint returned, an abscess formed in perinæo, which burst, and gave vent to the urine; but it also was voided per anum. In this state he went into the Winchester Infirmary, and remained there without deriving much benefit, which was the reason of his being sent, by a very indulgent master, to St. George's Hospital.

At this time the parts in the perinæum were so much thickened by disease, that nothing could be learned from any examination, and the urine came wholly by the anus and perinæum, at very short intervals, the bladder being in an irritable state. On passing a bougie there was a stricture in the urethra, which was destroyed by the caustic. A second was met with, which was also destroyed; after this the bougie passed on readily, but instead of going into the bladder, went into the rectum; the flexible gum catheter did the same, and the wind from the bowels passed through it. All endeavours by different trials to get into the bladder were vain; but when a solid instrument much curved was used, it came against something hard, which explained the case to be stricture, with a calculus lodged between it and the bladder. It was proposed to the man to have it removed, to which he very readily submitted, as life in the present state was insupportable. The operation was performed on the 8th of February, 1796; a staff was passed down to the stone in the perinæum as a direction for the knife, and the stone was readily removed without cutting into the bladder; but that viscus was afterwards examined by a sound. This was easily done, as the cyst inclosing the stone had a very large opening of communication with the bladder, and a smaller one with the rectum. The stone was perfectly spherical, and its surface covered with innumerable spiculated crystals, very sharp and strong. As soon as the stone was removed, a flexible gum catheter was introduced from the orifice of the glans penis into the bladder, and left there.

On the fourth day after the operation he had symptoms of fever, and the catheter gave so much uneasiness, that it was thought right to remove it; on the fifth he was better, and was ordered porter and nourishing food; the wind from the bowels all passing through the wound instead of the anus, gave it a foul sloughy appearance.

On the ninth day the orifice in the rectum was healed up, and the wound put on a better appearance; on the thirteenth day he walked about three hundred yards, and got cold, had a very severe rigor, and on the tenth day the scrotum swelled, and an abscess, which had formed in the deeper seated parts, burst. He now got a little better; but on the fortieth day an abscess formed in the buttock, which broke and discharged a great deal of matter.

The hospital was now found to disagree with him, and he was sensibly declining in his health. He was removed from the hospital, and got so much better as to be able to be removed into the country.

On the 20th of June he could walk about with a stick, and retain his urine two hours, a great part of it coming the right way, and he appeared out of danger from the effects of the disease and operation ; but two or three days after, by exposing himself to cold in the evening, he was seized with a severe fever, attended with vomiting of bile, voided a large worm and a quantity of blood by the anus, and on the 30th died; having lived near five months after the operation.

CASE VII.

Stricture and Stone in the Bladder.

John York, aged sixty-six, had for several years a complaint in the bladder, and for the last eighteen months great frequency in making water, attended with pain, difficulty, and a discharge of viscid mucus.

In this state he came to London, from an idea that his complaints arose from stricture, and that the use of the caustic might relieve them. He was admitted into St.

George's Hospital in May, 1797. A bougie was passed, which met with an obstruction about $5\frac{1}{2}$ inches from the orifice, and the use of the caustic was begun ; but the air of the Hospital disagreed so much with him, coming immediately from the country, that he lost his appetite entirely, and in six days was obliged to go out. The use of the caustic was however continued, and this stricture, by several different applications of the caustic, was removed : another stricture was met with about $6\frac{1}{2}$ inches, which was also destroyed in the same way. The caustic altogether was applied twenty times. His symptoms were not however removed with the strictures, which led me to suspect a calculus in the bladder; for it is remarkable, that in all the cases of stricture and stone which have come under my care, the removal of the strictures has rather aggravated the symptoms of irritation in the bladder. The bladder was sounded, and a stone very distinctly felt, which fully explained the continuance of the symptoms. As he was

D d

very infirm, and could not live in an hospital, no operation was proposed; he was sent back into the country, to take up the internal use of the caustic alkali, with a view of palliating his distresses which he was not in a state to have removed.

CASE VIII.

Stricture and Stone in the Bladder.

A gentleman aged sixty-one, had a stricture and irritable bladder, for which he had been under the care of different physicians, and had gone through courses of bougies; but still his complaints remained the same. He had been sounded for a stone, but none was found. The complaint was considered as a complication of stricture, diseased prostate gland, and irritable bladder.

The symptoms were frequency in making water, pain after it was voided, discharge of a glairy fluid from the bladder, and frequent paroxysms of fever and irritation, which made his life miserable.

Under these circumstances he consulted me in September, 1796, and a stricture was discovered at 6½ inches from the orifice of the urethra. He was told that the stricture must be removed, before it could be ascertained what were his other complaints.

For this purpose recourse was had to the caustic; four applications entirely removed this stricture, and allowed a bougie of a full size readily to pass into the bladder; the symptoms were not however at all diminished.

It was explained to the patient, that the stricture having been removed, and the bougie with ease entering the bladder, proved that the prostate gland made no part of the disease, since any enlargement of that gland would have stopped the end of the bougie, and prevented it from going into the bladder; there must therefore be some disease in the bladder. For these reasons it was necessary to sound him again, as that operation could have been but very imperfectly performed, while the urethra was in a contracted state, as the instrument must have been grasped by the stricture, so as to render it impossible to examine the bladder. To this he assented. The sound passed with great ease, and a stone was distinctly felt ; which was removed by the common operation for the stone, assisted by Mr. Cline, and the patient got well in five weeks, and returned to the country. The stone was large, oblong, and very hard.

The caustic, in this case, by removing the stricture, enabled me to examine the bladder, and ascertain the nature of the disease, which before had been attempted in vain.

CASE IX.

Stricture and Stone in the Bladder.

In August, 1795, a boy was under my care in St. George's Hospital, only six years old, with a stricture in the urethra of three years standing. Upon examining the parts, two obstructions were discovered, one on this side of the bulb of the urethra, which admitted a very small bougie; another at the bulb, which was impervious to the bougie, but gave passage to the urine in drops, and in very small quantities at a time. The parents of the child said, that the disease was the stone; that the surgeon had sounded him a year and a half ago, and felt a stone in the bladder.

The strictures were destroyed by the caustic; the symptoms of an irritable bladder still remained, but his parents took him away from the hospital before the state of the bladder was examined. The symptoms

increased so much that his life was des-
paired of; and in this state he was again
received into the hospital, but died before
any thing could be attempted for his relief.

Upon examining the parts after death,
the cavity of the bladder was found entirely
filled up by two large stones, which, after
they had become dry, weighed six drams.

From the history of the case, there can
be no doubt of stone being the original
disease; and, from their hardness and size,
they most probably had been for some years
in the bladder before they arrived at that
state.

Another case of stricture occurred to me
in St. George's Hospital four years ago,
where there was also stone; the stricture
was dilated by the bougie, an irritable state
of bladder came on, and the patient died.
It was then discovered that a large stone
was the cause of the irritation and of the
patient's death.

CASE X.

Stricture and Stones in the Urethra and Bladder.

A gentleman, who had for many years found an obstruction to his urine, at the age of seventy-six came to London to apply for relief. At this time his urine passed from him involuntarily, and in consequence of coming a journey of fifty-three miles in an open carriage, and in rainy weather, he caught cold, and immediately on his arrival had a rigor and swelling in the perinæum; this in two days increased to a considerable size, and had an evident fluctuation in it; as the urine had found its way through into the perinæum, it was immediately let out with the point of a lancet, and the swelling subsided. Upon passing a bougie along the urethra, it readily went five inches, and there met with an obstruction; to this the caustic was applied; it gave no pain, but rather a warm and pleasant sensation; it was applied three different times, but the abscess in perinæo, at his age, and a long continued state of disease, brought on symptoms of irritation, of which he died.

On examining the parts, the bladder was found contracted to a small cavity, its internal membrane in a very unnatural state, soft, spongy, and extremely vascular, it contained a large stone nearly round, with a crystallized irregular surface. Just before the neck of the bladder, extending nearly to the bulb, was a cavity formed in the membranous part of the urethra, which contained twenty stones. This cavity appeared to be formed directly behind a stricture, in the usual situation, seven inches from the external orifice.

About two inches further on, towards the external orifice, there was another stricture, and directly behind it a small oval black stone, weighing five grains when dry, there being a dilatation of the canal in that part. This proved that it had acquired a considerable increase of size in this situation; there were also three smaller stones in the same situation, about the size of shot.

The twenty stones contained in the urethra, behind the last stricture, were faced and smooth, so that they must have had considerable motion on each other.

From this fact it appears that the original disease had been the stone; that a small stone had got into the urethra, but had been unable to pass along it, from its having irritated the membrane that lines that canal, and produced a stricture. This stone had been followed by others, and the space became enlarged to contain them, till at last the whole number amounted to twenty, and their sides had been made smooth by rubbing against each other. In this state the patient had gone on with less distress than in many other cases of stone; for all these stones, as fast as they formed in the bladder, got readily into this bag, and the urine passed over them, though not with ease, without a total stoppage.

One stone, however, continued in the bladder, having become too large to pass out, and remained increasing to its present size, and from the irregularity of its surface, kept up a constant irritation. One of the small stones which escaped from the bladder, had got beyond the original stricture, and was arrested in the situation of the second stricture, where it remained dilating the canal as it enlarged. There were also three other very small ones, which proves that lesser calculi were escaping all this time. The strictures in this instance were in the usual situations, five and seven inches from the orifice, and behind each of them were calculi, also one large one in the bladder ; it must be therefore allowed to be more probable, that the calculi were the causes of the strictures, than the reverse.

If in this case recourse had been had to the caustic at a more early period, the disease might have been ascertained to be the stone : but in no other way could that have been done, as a bougie, in parts so much irritated, could never have dilated the canal so as to admit a solid instrument to strike against the stone, and discover the nature of the disease.

CASE XI.

Stricture and Stone adhering to the Bladder.

Benjamin Pooley, aged twenty-six, a gentleman's servant, in the month of February, 1795, had a gonorrhœa, for the relief of which he applied to an unskilful person, who gave him an injection ; a few hours after using it he was seized with a violent pain in the region of the bladder, and had a total suppression of urine. This last complaint was so distressing that he was obliged to go into the warm bath, which took off the suppression. The irritation on the bladder was not relieved by passing the urine, but continued very severe, and there was a discharge from the bladder like the white of an egg, which followed the urine in considerable quantity. The urine was generally turbid, and upon standing deposited a sediment. He also passed it with pain, particularly the last drops. These symptoms continued for a year without abatement, although a variety of medicines had been used for their relief.

In Feb. 1796, he came into St. George's Hospital, and was under my care. Upon examining the urethra, there was a stricture about $5\frac{1}{2}$ inches from the external orifice; this was removed by the caustic, and there was another about six inches, which was also removed. When the bougie passed into the bladder, it brought on a considerable hæmorrhage.

The symptoms in the bladder were rendered milder by the removal of the strictures, but by no means cured; the pain in making water continued, and the frequency was very great, but it passed with less difficulty and less straining. These symptoms were relieved by the use of the common bougie, which was continued for three months.

Finding himself much better, he left the hospital. After he returned to his master his urine began to come away involuntarily, and without pain. This increased upon him, till at last he was unfit to remain in service, and returned to the hospital in January, 1797.

An instrument passed readily into the bladder, but met with something hard at the entrance of that viscus; it seemed to be a stone in the neck of the bladder, as the instrument in passing on got beyond it.

This circumstance explained the want of retention of the urine, as the neck of the bladder was kept open by the stone, and the sphincter vesicæ prevented from doing its office.

This was explained to the patient, and he was told that nothing but an operation could afford him relief.

He readily submitted to have the stone removed, and the operation was performed on the 28th of January, 1797.

When the forceps were introduced into the bladder, they readily laid hold of the stone, but as soon as it was brought to the orifice of the bladder the forceps slipped off; this happened several times. My finger was passed into the bladder, and while the abdominal muscles were pressed down by an assistant, it could distinctly touch the stone; but when that pressure was removed, the stone withdrew out of my reach; it receded with the anterior part of the bladder to which it adhered. After bringing away portions of it by many different trials, at last, with the assistance of a strong pair of polypus forceps, the nucleus was extracted. The operation lasted nearly half an hour, and the quantity of fragments altogether brought away, when dry, weighed nearly an ounce; and upon examining the bladder with the finger, no remains of stone could be felt.

The patient was put to bed. He had the

symptoms of inflammation, to be expected from so severe and tedious an operation, and part of the skin of the penis and scrotum sloughed off; but at the end of three weeks he began to recover, the sloughs were all separated, and the surface put on a healing appearance. His appetite was good; he drank a bottle of wine and a pot of porter, and was able to sit up for a few hours every day; his sleep tolerably good. While he continued in this state, he was disturbed by a patient in a delirium in the same ward; he lost his sleep, and was attacked by a diarrhœa: about the twenty-eighth day after the operation his health was evidently declining from the air of the hospital. He was therefore moved into private lodgings on the thirty-second day. He bore the moving very well in a chair, was refreshed, and felt himself better. The wound, which had never shewn any disposition to heal, but had its sides covered with coagulating lymph, incrusted with calculous matter, now put on a more healthy appearance. On the thirty-fifth day from the operation he appeared tolerably well, and in good spirits; but all at once complained of being low, and died in half an hour.

Upon examining the body, the immediate cause of death appeared to be a deep seated abscess on the inside of the pelvis on the right side, probably the consequence of the weak state consequent to the operation.

The contents of the abdomen were free from disease, and the bladder externally was in a natural state; but on being laid open, it exhibited a very uncommon appearance. At the fundus it was entirely free from disease; but towards the neck the internal membrane all round for a space of $3\frac{1}{2}$ inches, extending to the prostate gland, was covered with a layer of coagulating lymph, the surface of which was very irregular, the projections in some places three-quarters of an inch long: the whole of this new substance was incrusted with calculous matter, in a soft state, with which the stone had been connected. The cavity of the bladder at this part must have been nearly filled up by the stone, and the coats too much consolidated by previous inflammation to admit of being dilated.*

It appears from the history of this case that the injection employed for the cure of the gonorrhœa, had brought on inflammation upon that part of the internal membrane of the bladder with which it came in contact, and an exsudation of coagulating lymph was thrown out over that surface. This corresponds with the result of an experiment made by Mr. Hunter, in which the vagina and uterus were inflamed by an injection of corrosive sublimate, and a similar exsudation of coagulating lymph was found upon the internal surface.† This new-formed substance, which possessed in a very small degree the principle of life, admitted the calculous matter to adhere to

* See Pl. III. † See Hunter on the Blood, Inflammation, and Gun-shot Wounds, page 242. Pl. VIII.

E e

its surface, and form a stone of a very loose texture, which became suspended by these attachments to the bladder, just within its cavity, immediately beyond the prostate gland.

There is a calculus in the bladder of a horse, in the collection of Dr. Marshall, which adheres in the same manner, and it is easy to trace the portions of coagulating lymph from the surface of the bladder into the substance of the stone.

This case explained to me, how a stone can have a firm attachment to the coats of the bladder. Of the fact there are so many instances upon record, that it was impossible to doubt that it sometimes happens; but no mode of accounting for it, made use of, appeared to me at all satisfactory. Mr. Le Dran denies the possibility of stone adhering to a living surface, yet he supposes that fleshy excrescences lodge themselves in the cavities of the stone; it appears however that excrescences under such circumstances would be absorbed.* It was not known, when he wrote, that violent inflammation

* The following is the account given of the adhesion of stones to the bladder by the celebrated Le Dran.

" I am thoroughly sensible of the impossibility that " an animated body, which subsists by a circulation of " fluids, and another body which owes its bulk en- " tirely to an apposition of matter, should become one " and the same by any kind of adherence, let it be ever " so strong."——" That there are stones which ad- " here, I make no doubt, because I have seen instances " of them: but these adhesions are not of that nature to " prevent the extraction of a stone, provided it can be " laid hold of with the forceps. In 1730, I cut a lady, " and extracted a stone that weighed 7¼ ounces, one " side of it was uneven, likewise 3 inches long, and " 2¼ broad, and was in a manner entirely incrusted " upon that part of the bladder that is connected to the " intestinum rectum. This incrustation was occasioned " by the inequalities of the stone, which had produced " an excoriation of that part of the bladder upon which " they pressed; and in consequence thereof, a number " of fleshy or fungous excrescences arose from this ulcer, " and had lodged themselves in these cavities of the " stone!"

Operations in Surgery of Mons. Le Dran, translated by Gataker in 1749, p. 206.

E e 2

upon the internal surface of the bladder produces an exsudation of coagulating lymph, and not ulceration; the knowledge of this fact removes completely every difficulty, since this effect of inflammation interposes between the stone and the bladder a substance that receives blood vessels from the bladder, with which it adheres; but these do not extend through its substance, so that the opposite surface is hardly possessed of any active powers, and readily admits of incrustation. Another instance of this is given in the following case.

CASE XII.

Stricture and Tumour in the Bladder with a small adherent Calculus.

A gentleman, aged sixty-nine, had for two years occasional complaints in the bladder, which were supposed to be gouty. In the spring of 1796, he made bloody water, which continued a short time and then went off. It returned again in the spring of 1797, attended with great pain in making water, which was voided very frequently. The pain increased, and the water was more bloody, so as to give the alarm of a serious complaint forming in the bladder; and from the frequency of making water a stricture was suspected to have formed in the urethra. On this account he consulted me on the 17th of June. He stated, that he made water every half hour, that he had great pain at the time, but more particularly after it was voided; the pain was a burning heat in the glans penis. He had less of this if the water was voided lying, and least when he lay on the left side. These were stated to be symptoms of disease in the bladder, and not of stricture; if therefore he had a stricture, it was a secondary complaint, in consequence of the disease in the bladder.

Upon examining the urethra by a bougie, it passed readily five inches, but no further;

it was therefore concluded that there were at least two strictures. The urethra was very tender, yet the pain occasioned by passing the bougie soon went off.

It was proposed to remove the strictures, although it was not believed their removal would at all relieve the symptoms; it was, however, a necessary step towards gaining some knowledge of the state of the bladder, which till that was accomplished could not be examined.

This was agreed to; and the caustic was applied to this stricture, which was removed by two applications; there was another at six inches, which was also removed by two applications, and the bougie went into the bladder, but in doing so gave considerable pain.

The original complaints were daily increasing, the urine contained nearly as much blood as water, and the quantity voided at each time was scarcely an ounce. This led me to suspect that the bladder did not wholly empty itself at each time; with a view to ascertain this, a flexible gum catheter was passed into the bladder, but little more than an ounce of water was drawn off. The end of the instrument in passing into the bladder, rubbed upon something rough, and in coming out the opening or eye of the catheter caught hold of and brought away a small irregular portion of a calculus This rendered it certain that calculous concretion formed a part of the disease in the bladder; and as the stone, from what came away in the catheter, and two or three small portions which had at different times been voided since the strictures were destroyed was of a soft kind, it was thought probable that its irregular surface irritated the bladder, and brought on the present distressing symptoms.

In this state, with a diseased bladder and declining health, little or no appetite, and a great degree of constitutional irritation, which was termed fever, proposing an operation appeared too hazardous, it was therefore recommended to try the different

solvents; the caustic alkali disagreed with his
stomach; the lime-water answered better;
but the abatement of the symptoms in the
bladder was small, and his health more and
more reduced; the alkaline mephitic water in small doses agreed with the stomach,
but in larger quantities brought on a purg-
ing. He now felt within himself a convic-
tion that medicines could not afford him
relief, and that he was very rapidly sink-
ing; if therefore there was any chance
from an operation, he wished to undergo it.
Sir James Earle was called in consultation,
and the patient was sounded for the first
time. The instrument rubbed upon a soft
stone: this was felt both by Sir James Earle
and myself, but only in one direction, as if it
had been confined in a particular part of
the bladder. The pain and distress brought
on by sounding the bladder was so great,
that it required a week to recover from the
effects of it; and at this time his appetite
was so bad, and he was reduced so low,
that there was a doubt of his being able to

go through the operation ; and the day
previous to that fixed on for that purpose, he
had sickness and a fit of lowness, that did
not go off for the greater part of the day.

The operation was however performed,
at the patient's earnest request, on the 10th
of August. When the forceps were introduced, they rubbed against the stone, and
laid hold of it, but it gave way to the pressure of the blades ; and upon withdrawing
them, there was a small quantity of stony
matter, and some soft pulpy substance,
brought away. Upon introducing my
finger, a soft irregular excrescence was
felt, but nothing like stone ; Sir James Earle
felt the same ; the bladder was examined
by the sound, and there being no more stone,
the patient was put to bed.

The knowledge acquired from the preceding case prepared my mind, and enabled me at once to comprehend the nature of the disease, without distressing the
patient, or prolonging the operation by a
further investigation.

The quantity of stony matter extracted, when separated from the other substance, and dried, did not weigh more than thirty grains.

The operation, after its immediate effects went off, relieved him from the excruciating pain he suffered; his water became of the natural colour, without the least tinge of blood; and when it passed, although at times it gave pain, at others it did not.

On the eighth day after the operation he was able to be moved into the next room, and lay for several hours upon the couch; every thing appeared to be going on well, but he was unable to take medicines, except opiates and laxatives. Bark and all bitters were unpleasant to his palate, and took away the little appetite he had; they were therefore left off.

Every means to promote his appetite proved ineffectual; he could fancy nothing but a few grapes, and these affected his bowels, so that his nourishment consisted of broths, jelly, and small quantities of wine. He was daily moved into the next room; his urine never became tinged with blood; but on the twentieth day after the operation, from want of being able to take sufficient support, he died.

Upon inspecting the parts after death, a tumour of the steatomatous kind had formed in the coats of the bladder, where the right ureter entered it; this had increased in size to the thickness of $1\frac{1}{2}$ inches, two inches in length, and the same in breadth; the surface towards the cavity of the bladder was concave, and in a state of ulceration; the lower end of the tumour projected a little from the internal membrane of the bladder, was covered by a layer of coagulating lymph, and the calculous matter had concreted upon this part. There was also a layer of coagulating lymph laid over the membrane of the bladder from this end of the tumour to the prostate gland, about an inch and a half in length, the external surface of which was incrusted with calculous matter; the other surface was attached to the lining of the bladder, but could be separated from it without any injury to the membrane, except dividing small blood vessels. This surface was of a red colour and very vascular. So that in this case, as in the preceding, no part of the membrane of the bladder had any calculous matter adhering to it; but where the inner coat was covered by a substance possessed in a less degree of the principle of life, there the incrustations took place.

The tumour had obliterated the orifice of the right ureter in the bladder; the pelvis of the kidney and the ureter were very much enlarged, and contained above half a pint of matter. As the stomach sympathizes in a great degree with almost every affection of the kidney, the diseased state of that organ accounted for the stomach being so much affected, and never recovering itself.

The disease being on the right side of the bladder, and the right ureter impervious, accounted for the pain being less in making water when lying on the left side; as the urine entered the bladder on that side, it was not liable in passing out through the penis to come upon the ulcerated surface of the tumour.

SECTION V.

CASES OF STRICTURE IN WHICH THE PRINCIPAL SYMPTOMS HAVE BEEN IN THE KIDNEY.

THAT strictures in the urethra produce pain in the kidney whenever the bladder has been much distended, is a fact of frequent occurrence, and can be readily explained; but that one of the kidneys should be the seat of all the uneasiness is scarcely to be credited; it is therefore considered to be of sufficient importance to become the subject of a separate section.

CASE I.

A gentleman forty years of age had laboured under a complaint in his left side for a year and a half, which was so extremely violent as to make his life miserable; various remedies had been tried to relieve it, but no benefit had been derived from their use.

Opium gave temporary ease, and the dose necessary for that purpose was very great. In this state he consulted me in the year 1803. to know if there could be any connection between this disease and the urethra. He stated that the fits of pain were brought on by the effort in making water; that it required five grains of extract of opium to make them bearable, and in the course of the day he took 50 grains. Upon examining the urethra a stricture was discovered, and it was stated to him that the removal of this obstruction, by diminishing the effort in making water, would lessen the violence of his pain, but there was no ground to expect that it could remove the disease, which was probably either a stone or other fixed complaint in the kidney itself. It was thought adviseable to destroy the stricture by caustic, and during the process the pain became less, and before it was entirely removed, the use of opium was intirely left off, and as soon as the urethra was restored to its natural dimensions, the symptoms in the kidney had gone intirely away.

Since my attention was called to this case, others less strongly marked have come under my observation of a similar kind. In these cases the orifice of the ureter belonging to the affected kidney, is probably so open as to admit of regurgitation of the urine, so that in every effort to make water when attended with difficulty, the urine is pressed back into the pelvis of the kidney with sufficient force to occasion distress to the patient. The same thing sometimes happens to the internal membrane of the bladder; in one instance of stricture, the only symptom was a violent pain of a very distressing kind in the region of the bladder at the time of making water, which was not felt in the same degree after the stricture had been removed.

SECTION VI.

CASES OF STRICTURE WHICH APPEARED TO PRODUCE HYDROCELE SINCE THE HYDRO-CELE WAS CURED BY THE REMOVAL OF THE STRICTURE.

THAT there is a peculiar sympathy between the actions of the urethra and testicle, when either of these parts is diseased, no practitioner who has had any experience in the treatment of gonorrhœa can be ignorant of, since a swelling of the testicle is a common symptom in that disease. Many other applications to the urethra, which produce irritation, bring on a swelling in one of the testicles; this frequently happens from the use of the bougie.

As an irritation of a certain degree of violence produces a swelled testicle, so one of a slighter degree sometimes brings on and keeps up an uneasy and enlarged state

F f

of these glands, which subsides when that
irritation is removed. A well marked case
of this kind has lately been under my care.
A gentleman whose testicles had become
unusually large, and remained in an uneasy
state for many months, although different
modes of treatment had been adopted, put
himself under my care. In stating all the
circumstances of his complaints, he mentioned his not making water freely, which
led me to suspect a stricture; this suspicion
proved to be well founded; and made me
suggest the idea, that the uneasy state of the
testicles depended on the stricture, and that
nothing should be done till the stricture was
removed. This was no sooner effected than
the testicles became perceptibly smaller,
and lost in a great degree the uneasy sensations to which they had been accustomed.

This sympathetic connection between the
state of the urethra and the testicles, is
still more extensive, as the following Cases
shew, that in some instances hydroceles are
cured by strictures in the urethra being

removed, which makes it natural to suppose, that if no stricture had been formed, these patients would not have had the hydrocele.

It is not to be understood, that wherever strictures and hydrocele occur in the same patient, the hydrocele is a consequent disease; as in many cases the two complaints are independent of one another. That they are ever connected is a new idea; and without hazarding any opinion respecting the frequency of such a connection, the following cases are stated to establish that it does sometimes occur.

CASE I.

A gentleman, aged forty-nine, while resident in one of the Windward Islands in the West Indies, in the year 1778, was seized with a strangury, for which opening medicines, glysters, and the warm bath were used; but without effect; the warm bath was repeated, and blood was taken from the arm, and at the end of nine hours the spasm went off, and he was relieved.

From that time he had difficulty in passing his urine; in 1782, he discovered a swelling in the left testicle, which proved to be a hydrocele. In the end of 1796, he arrived in London, at which time the hydrocele was four inches long and eleven in circumference. He had a difficulty in passing his urine, attended with a discharge of matter from the urethra, and an involuntary discharge of urine, which had for the last seven years been very distressing.

In Dec. 1796, he put himself under my care, and had the operation for the radical cure of the hydrocele performed by means of an injection of equal parts of Port wine and water. The inflammation came on in twenty-four hours, and had entirely subsided in fourteen days; but the swelling remained without abatement. As the stricture was to be removed by the caustic, it was proposed to suspend all treatment of the hydrocele till that was accomplished, and if it did not subside in that time, to repeat the operation.

The urethra was examined the 10th of January, 1797, and it was found that this canal, near the external orifice, was preternaturally contracted, so that the bougie did not pass above an inch before it met with an obstruction; the caustic was applied to this, and to others in succession. About the 16th of February the bougie could pass five inches, and the symptoms of the stricture began to abate: there was less of the urine discharged involuntarily. The hydrocele was now perceived to diminish. The use of the caustic was persevered in, and on the 16th of March the urine flowed with less straining. The hydrocele had now diminished one-third of its size. By the 16th of April it was lessened one half. The stricture at six inches gave way to the caustic very slowly; but according to the progress of the cure the hydrocele became smaller; and on the 16th of May it was entirely gone. On the 14th of June a bougie passed into the bladder, and afterwards a flexible catheter nearly the size of the urethra.

The caustic had been applied seventy-eight times. The operation for the hydrocele was performed December 27th, the inflammation was entirely gone January 10th, and the hydrocele was then the same size as before the operation, nor did it sensibly diminish for a month; and did not subside entirely till near five months after the operation; but the progress of its diminution kept pace with the removal of the stricture.

CASE II.

An officer, nineteen years of age, who was going to America to join his regiment, consulted me for a hydrocele, which he was desirous of having removed before he went abroad. It was of a small size, and he attributed a gleet which he had at the same time to this affection of the testis.

The gleet, on examination, proved to be the consequence of a stricture. As soon as this was ascertained, he was told that the stricture was the more serious of the two complaints, would require the longest time to be removed, and when it should be cured, the hydrocele might possibly get well. It was therefore proposed to take up the stricture first, and leave the treatment of the hydrocele till after the stricture should be destroyed.

The caustic was applied to the stricture; this was repeated ten or twelve times, and the obstruction in this way was removed. As soon as the cure was completed, it was found that the hydrocele had disappeared. This was very flattering, but was not to be relied on, as it appeared probable that the hydrocele might return. He was, therefore, to let me see him a few weeks before he left England, (which was not to be for some months,) that we might ascertain whether it was disposed to return. He called upon me three months after, and there had been no return of the hydrocele; so that the removal of the stricture disposed the absorbents of the testis to carry off the

water from the cavity of the tunica vagi-
nalis.

CASE III.

A gentleman, aged fifty, who has laboured under the symptoms of stricture for
many years, had the urethra so much obstructed in the early part of the year 1796,
that the water passed with extreme difficulty, accompanied with symptoms of great
irritation. At this time a hydrocele came
on, which the patient conceived to be the
water forced by the straining into the
scrotum.

. In May, 1796, he put himself under my
care for the strictures. One $3\frac{1}{2}$ inches from
the external orifice, was destroyed by the
caustic. The hydrocele was at this time
so large and tense, that it was proposed
to him, when he should have leisure in
the autumn, to have it removed by an operation, as it was becoming very troublesome ; in the mean time the use of the

caustic was continued. In this, however, our progress was very slow, as he lived at Wapping, and was engaged in a business which made his calling upon me very precarious. The symptoms of the stricture have, however, been much abated, and its aperture a good deal enlarged ; although it is not even now completely destroyed, notwithstanding the caustic has been applied to it above forty times. But the remarkable circumstance is, that the hydrocele is not one half the size it was in May, 1796, is flaccid, and is lessening perceptibly every month; when the stricture is entirely destroyed, it will probably be completely removed.

It is now in my power to state that this was really the case, and since that time other instances of the same kind have fallen under my observation.

CHAPTER VI.

THE APPEARANCE WHICH THE URETHRA
PUTS ON AFTER STRICTURES HAVE BEEN
REMOVED BY CAUSTIC.

In considering the effects of the caustic
upon strictures, the first question that occurs is, in what state are the parts left after
the stricture has been destroyed ? From the
urethra allowing a bougie to pass smoothly
along it, after the effects of the caustic, there
was every reason to believe that the surface
at that part was made smooth, and upon a
plain with the rest of the canal; but as in
some cases this part remains tender for a
considerable time, and from this greater
degree of sensibility the patient can tell
when the bougie is passing over it, an idea
has been raised in the minds of some people
that this spot, while it remains tender
must be in the state of an ulcer, and that

any discharge which continues to flow from the canal must come from that part.

In the following case an opportunity occurred of inspecting the parts to which the caustic had been applied.

A gentleman had a stricture for many years, which produced a fistula in perinæo; the symptoms at last became so severe as to bring on strangury and irritation, which obliged him to come to England. Upon catching cold he was subject to violent attacks in his stomach, which were considered as gout.

Upon his arrival in England, his symptoms were great irritation in the region of the bladder (supposed to be from stone) attended with frequency in making water. On passing a bougie a stricture was met with 9½ inches from the orifice; this decided the complaint to be strictures, and till these were removed no opinion could be given respecting the bladder. It was inconvenient for him to stay in town, and the surgeon who attended him in the country was, under my direction, to use the caustic; its use was begun Oct. 31, 1796. Three strictures were met with, one at $3\frac{1}{2}$, one at 5, and one at 6 inches; the caustic was applied nine times before the bougie went into the bladder, and then with difficulty. An ague came on, which was very severe, and on this account the caustic was left off the 18th of November. Some professional business brought him to London in December, and the complete removal of the stricture was put off till his return into the country. While he was in London he caught cold; had for several days aguish symptoms, which were followed by one of his usual attacks, supposed to be the gout in the stomach. This was so violent as to make the attendance of a physician necessary; the pain in the stomach increased, constant vomiting came on, and in a few days he died.

From inspection of the body, it was observed that the cause of death was peritoneal inflammation; the internal membrane of the stomach not being inflamed. This attack then appears to have been the consequence of an inflammation of the bladder, from exposure to cold; its internal membrane was much inflamed, and the stomach and bowels had been only sympathetically affected.

The state of the urethra was examined.

The space where the first stricture had been was scarcely discernible, and the membrane was nearly in the same state as the rest of the canal; its connection with the surrounding parts having the natural appearance.

The space where the second stricture had been situated had also put on the natural appearance, but the membrane had a closer attachment to the surrounding parts.

At six inches from the external orifice there was an irregularity on the lower surface, in the situation of the third stricture, the internal membrane having been removed for the space of a quarter of an inch, and a new membrane formed in its place, but there was an irregular ridge at the end of that space, which had not been destroyed, and must still have occasionally obstructed the passage of the bougie towards the bladder.

From the dissection in this case, the real state of the parts after the use of the caustic is ascertained; there is a membrane formed similar to the natural lining of the canal, no granulations project beyond the surface, and no appearance of ulceration remains.

From what takes place after injuries committed on the inner membrane of the mouth, which is in most respects similar to that which lines the urethra, no doubt was entertained of the membrane of the urethra being readily renewed after the effects of the caustic; but before this case was examined there was no proof that it was so.

Frequent opportunities have since occurred of examining the state of the urethra after death in patients who had strictures removed by the caustic, and the appearance in all of them was a smooth surface, similar to that described.

CHAPTER VII.

UNCOMMON EFFECTS OF THE CAUSTIC IN THE TREATMENT OF STRICTURES.

MANY and dreadful are the effects which have been supposed to be produced by the caustic, when applied to the internal membrane of the urethra; sufficient evidence has been adduced, in the different parts of this work, to prove that this is by no means the case.

As the disease differs in its symptoms, and the degree in which these symptoms distress the patient, so the effects of the caustic are also found to vary in different patients; in many, it produces little or no sensation; in others, the pain is acute, and of some continuance. Besides the simple pain that is felt, there are other less common symptoms brought on in particular cases, which will form the subject of the present Chapter.

These symptoms are swelling in the perinæum, hæmorrhage, occasional strangury, and ague; but they are in general the consequence of some imprudence on the part of the patient. They are such as may alarm the surgeon, and hurry him into the use of means for their removal which are not necessary, or may ultimately do harm, unless he is made acquainted with the cause from which they arise, and is informed that they readily subside under the most simple mode of treatment. With a view to communicate this information, the cases in which these different symptoms have occurred, are here brought together.

SECTION I.

SWELLING IN THE PERINÆUM.

IT is not sufficient for the cure of stricture that the canal be made wide enough to give a free passage for the urine; if any projecting parts are left, the stricture is liable to return; the use of the caustic is therefore to be persevered in till these are destroyed. In removing that part of the stricture nearest to the sides of the urethra, it sometimes happens that a swelling of considerable size takes place in perinæo.

The following are the only instances met with in which this symptom has occurred. The swelling is totally different from that brought on by the irritation which sometimes arises from a bougie remaining too long in the passage, and which terminates in the formation of abscess; it is entirely

G g

produced by the blood extravasated in the cellular membrane, which is readily absorbed. The inflammation brought on in such cases is very slight, and readily subsides.

CASE I.

A gentleman, aged about forty, in February, 1796, put himself under my care for a stricture; he was of a very irritable habit, and had, in consequence of a hurt received some years before, very uncommon symptoms of constitutional indisposition.

The caustic was applied to a stricture about three inches from the external orifice, which gave way to the second application ; a little further on there was another stricture, which yielded to two applications of the caustic. There was a third, which required five applications ; and a fourth, exactly seven inches distant from the orifice, which after six applications admitted a bougie to pass into the bladder, but not of a sufficient size; the applications were therefore repeated six times more: on the last of these the bougie went through; this was followed by a considerable degree of a peculiar kind of pain, that communicated with the rectum and ran down the thigh. This lasted for a few minutes; he made water by drops, and a swelling came on in the course of a few hours in the perinæum. Spirits of wine and camphor were applied, but the swelling continued the same for four days. In a few days more it entirely subsided, after which a full sized bougie passed into the bladder.

This swelling must have been an extravasation of blood, otherwise it could not have come on so soon, nor have so readily gone off.

The bougie that now passed was uncommonly large; and the gentleman called upon me six months after to say that it passed equally well.

CASE II.

A gentleman, thirty-five years of age, had a complaint supposed to be a gonor-rhœa : the symptoms were a discharge, inflammation upon the glans penis, and swelling of the body of the penis. These symptoms had continued for months, at-tended by frequent irritation to make water

Under these circumstances a stricture was discovered, and the use of the caustic begun in March, 1796 : the stricture was three inches from the external orifice.

Two applications of the caustic destroy-ed this stricture, and all the symptoms abated. A second stricture was discovered at six inches; this also soon yielded. Ano-ther, at seven inches, gave way to the third application of the caustic; this happened at eleven in the forenoon. He now felt an uncommon sensation of a very distressing kind, and in half an hour nearly fainted; was in great pain all day, had a rigor in the evening, with swelling in the perinæum; passed a very restless night, had great pain in making water, which came away in a small stream, and was voided every two hours. Next morning he had head-ach, sickness, and retching without vomiting. This he was subject to on many occasions, and considered it as bilious; passed a good deal of bile by stool. The fulness in the parts now diminished; and he made water only once in the night. The next day he was less languid; in four days all these symptoms went off, the water flowed in a good stream, and the parts were in a better state than before the application of the caustic.

A fulness remained in the perinæum; but what was singular, the parts laterally, on each side of the penis where it projects on the os pubis, were much swelled and puffed. In this state he went into the country for four days; on his return, the parts in perinæo had subsided, but not those on each side of the penis; a bougie was now passed, but did not go into the bladder. It was not thought right, in the present sate of the parts, to proceed with the caustic. He went therefore into the country. He returned about the end of April; the caustic was once applied, gave much pain, and brought on a tendency to fainting; but the next time it was applied, the bougie went into the bladder.

The pain and slight chordee did not go off for a fortnight. He was, however, after that time perfectly free from both. All the symptoms except the discharge now went off; but that continued, though in a less degree.

In 1797, there was no return of stricture; but the discharge had not entirely ceased.

In 1804 the bougie passed without any difficulty.

SECTION II.

HÆMORRHAGE.

ONE of the effects of the caustic in some particular cases, is very profuse hæmorrhage. This symptom, as will appear from the following cases, has several times come under my notice. In every one of them, where the parts were left entirely to themselves, the bleeding gradually diminished, till it ceased without producing any unpleasant consequences. This symptom has never occurred with violence but where the stricture was completely destroyed. It has, however, alarmed many surgeons, as well as their patients; and has indeed been considered as one of the strongest objections to the use of the caustic; so much so as to deter many practitioners from employing it.

The great dread that has been entertained of such bleedings, is not on account of the absolute loss of blood, but lest it should pass into the bladder and coagulate there. This, it will appear, does not necessarily happen; but as such an event is possible, and the consequences that would arise from it are not generally known, the following observations are introduced, taken from a paper published in the eighty-sixth volume of the Philosophical Transactions.

As every change the blood undergoes must appear an object of importance to those who study the economy of animals, the present observations on the change produced on it by being mixed with the urine, will not be considered as wholly undeserving of notice.

My attention was called to this subject from considering the following case, which came under my care.

A gentleman, seventy-one years of age, in the spring, 1795, found that in making water, the urine had the appearance of blood, and congealed into a solid mass as soon as received into the vessel. This complaint appeared to have arisen from the rupture of a vessel in one of the kidneys, for he had a pain in his loins, but none in the region of the bladder. He seemed to void no water, for the whole quantity which was expelled at any one time, amounting to about four ouuces, formed itself into a coagulum; next day he voided bloody water, which did not coagulate. This continued for three or four days, and then went entirely off.

In the spring, 1796, he had a return of the same complaint. It came on in the evening of the 3d of April; on the 4th it was very violent; and in the afternoon there was a total suppression. A catheter was passed six or seven times; but the oval holes near the end of the instrument were always filled with coagulated blood, and no urine could be drawn off. On the 5th, a larger catheter was passed, with small round holes, less likely to have the coagulum entangled in them, but no urine came away

In the evening it was introduced again, having its cavity completely lined with a flexible gum catheter, which was withdrawn as soon as the instrument was carried to the fundus of the bladder; and in this way four ounces of a bloody fluid were drawn off, which on exposure coagulated.

On the morning of the 6th, a pint of bloody urine was drawn off. This operation was repeated three times in the twenty-four hours, and the same quantity was brought away each time.

On the 7th, the urine drawn off was less tinged with blood; and when it was allowed to stand, the upper part became tolerably clear. There was little change in the circumstances for six days; but on the 13th the urine drawn off was of a darker red colour, and in smaller quantity. On the 16th the colour was more of a light brown, and after standing some time, a whitish powder was deposited; the urine drawn off in the morning upon getting up, was nearly of the natural appearance, but that brought away in the course of the day had a deeper tinge, and more of the white sediment. It is also to be remarked, that the sediment evidently passed off only with the last part of the urine. On the 19th, the urine was tolerably clear, and the white sediment more completely separated, and in greater quantity. In the course of the night, while lying in his bed, the patient voided naturally, in many different attempts, four ounces of water, but could not make any when up. The urine now continued clear from any tinge, but no more passed without the catheter being introduced, till the 28th, when he again made some water naturally, but could not completely empty the bladder; on the 29th, the quantity which required being drawn off was less; and by the 5th of May he made water as usual, at which time the sediment began to diminish, and gradually disappeared.

From the symptoms which have been stated, it appears that part of the blood which passed into the bladder from the kidney had remained there, and formed a coagulum, which coagulum gave a bloody tinge to the urine, and caused an inability to void it without assistance, till the coagulum was dissolved.

With a view to ascertain how far this had been the case, and discover what changes the blood undergoes when placed in such circumstances, the following experiments were instituted. They were performed by Mr. Charles Grover, a very ingenious surgeon, at that time house surgeon in St. George's Hospital.

Experiment 1. Four ounces of blood were drawn from the arm into a phial containing four ounces of fresh urine, and the phial was kept in the temperature of the human body; in fifteen minutes the whole mixture formed an uniform firm coagulum, and appeared wholly composed of blood.

This experiment was made to ascertain the probable time the blood would take to coagulate in the bladder.

Experiment 11. Six ounces of blood were

drawn from the arm into six ounces of fresh urine; in fifteen minutes the whole mass became one solid coagulum. In seven hours, six drams of clear fluid were separated from it; this was poured off, and the same quantity of fresh urine was added; after standing nine hours it was poured off; some red globules were mixed with it, but sunk to the bottom undissolved. The coagulum had fresh urine added to it three times a day, the former urine being previously poured off, and allowed to stand some hours for examination.

For the first five days the coagulum appeared to undergo little change, except becoming smaller in size, and the urine poured off from it was tolerably clear, but on standing deposited a dark cloudy sediment.

On the sixth day, the urine, when poured off from the coagulum, was of a dark red colour, and deposited a greater quantity of a dark coloured sediment, but on standing became tolerably clear.

On the ninth day, the coagulum was

reduced to the size of the original quantity of blood drawn from the arm.

On the thirteenth day, the size of the coagulum was a good deal reduced ; the urine poured off from it was still more tinged with the red globules ; but when allowed to stand, the upper part became clear, and free from the red tinge, and the sediment had the appearance of a whitish powder. From this time the quantity of white sediment increased, and the size of the coagulum diminished. In its decrease from this period the loss was from its external surface, and nearly equally all round ; what remained appearing like the nucleus of the original coagulum. On the twenty-fifth day, it was of the size of a large cherry, and on the twenty-ninth it entirely disappeared. Some red globules were very distinctly seen in the sediment along with the white powder.

To see how far the changes the blood had undergone in this experiment depended on the peculiar properties of the urine, the following experiment was made, with blood and common water.

_ *Experiment* III. Six ounces of blood were drawn from the arm into six ounces of water. In a quarter of an hour the whole became one solid coagulum. In twelve hours, six ounces of a clear water, of a bright red colour, were separated, nor did it on standing deposite any sediment.

This coagulum had fresh water added to it twice a day, and what was poured off was allowed to stand for examination.

The coagulum on the second day began to break ; on the fifth had a putrid smell ; and in eighteen days was almost entirely dissolved.

The water which was poured off was of a bright red colour from the beginning to the end of the experiment, in consequence of the red globules being dissolved ; it had a very offensive smell, but never deposited any white sediment ; the coagulating lymph dissolved from putrefaction.

As it is evident, from the result of the

last experiment, that the coagulum remaining so long undissolved in the second experiment depended upon its being mixed with the urine, to know whether it was the urine incorporated with the coagulum, or that which surrounded it, which produced this effect, the following experiment was made.

Experiment iv. Four ounces of blood were drawn from the arm into a cup, and allowed to coagulate. Four ounces more were drawn into a separate cup. From each of these equal portions of coagulum, at the end of three hours, one ounce of serum was separated and poured off. To one of them fresh urine was added ; to the other common water. The urine and water were changed night and morning.

The water was tinged of a bright red colour throughout the whole experiment, and deposited no sediment. On the eighth day the coagulum was rather looser in its texture. On the thirteenth day it began to break, and by the twentieth day it was nearly dissolved. The progress corresponding with that of the coagulum in *Experiment* III.

The urine the second day of the experiment was clear, but the bottom of the bason was covered with red globules undissolved.

On the fifth day, the urine poured off was tinged of a bright red colour similar to the water taken from the other coagulum ; and after standing some hours a white sediment was deposited.

On the thirteenth day it was looser in texture, and more dissolved than the coagulum in the water. It continued to tinge the urine of a bright red colour, and what was poured off deposited a white sediment in greater quantity. On the eighteenth, the coagulum was nearly dissolved ; so that the coagulum immersed in the urine dissolved two days sooner than that in the water.

From this experiment we find, that it was the urine incorporated with the coagulum in *Experiment* 11. that prevented the red globules from dissolving, and preserved the coagulum for so long a time, since these effects were not produced by urine while simply surrounding the coagulum.

If we compare *Experiment* 11. with the result of the case, they agree so entirely, that it leaves no doubt of the process carried on in the bladder being similar to that which took place out of the body. The patient was unable to make water for twenty-four days, although the passages readily admitted, during the whole of that time, an uncommonly large instrument, which could not have been the case had there been any obstruction in them; for six days more he voided it with difficulty, but afterwards made water very well.

The coagulum out of the body was reduced in twenty-five days to the size of a cherry, and in four days more it was completely dissolved.

The patient's urine became darker, from the red globules mixing with it, in nine days. In the experiment this took place in five days.

The white sediment was first observed, in both instances, about the twelfth day; it continued to be deposited till the patient got well, and to the end of the experiment.

That the blood is capable of uniting with a quantity of urine equal to itself, so as to form a firm coagulum; that the red globules do not dissolve in a coagulum so formed; that an admixture of urine prevents the blood from becoming putrid; and that the coagulating lymph breaks down into parts almost resembling a soft powder, are facts which may have been before ascertained, but we have not been acquainted with them.

They are certainly not generally known, and one object of the present paper is to communicate them to others.

These facts, considered abstractedly, may not appear of much importance; but when compared with what takes place in the living body, and found to agree with the process the blood undergoes in the urinary bladder, they become of no small value, since they enable us to account for the symptoms that occur in that disease, and lead to the most simple and effectual mode of relieving them.

CASE I.

Hæmorrhage from the Use of the Caustic.

A gentleman, forty-six years of age, who had been many years in the West Indies, had a stricture which brought on occasional attacks of irritation and discharge, that were treated as symptoms of gonorrhœa. In one of these he used an injection, and took large doses of the balsam copaiva ; while under this treatment he had a suppression of urine, and from that period, which was above two years before he applied to me, he had frequent returns of strangury.

In 1796 he put himself under my care.

Upon examining the canal, two strictures were met with, one at $3\frac{1}{2}$ inches, the other at $5\frac{1}{2}$. The caustic was used; one application relieved the first stricture, and three more allowed the bougie to go through the second, and pass on to the bladder. As the bougie met with no obstruction, nothing more could be done, and he went into the country. He continued well for three months, and then had a suppression of urine; but from the time he left town, the stream of urine had been gradually diminishing.

On examining the canal, it was found that the second stricture had returned, but readily gave way to the use of the caustic. A stricture was now discovered at seven inches not before met with. This at first could not be readily understood; but it appeared that the removing of the first stricture had taken off the spasm from that next the bladder, so that the bougie was admitted to pass through it; but as soon as the parts were left to themselves it, contracted again.

This stricture, which was the original one, required fifteen applications of the caustic, before the bougie could pass through it; an hæmorrhage followed, which was so great that it rather lowered him. As the bougie did not pass with ease, the caustic was again applied; it gave a good deal of pain, but that soon went off. On the same night he walked home, about twelve o'clock, the thermometer standing below 30°, after having sat the whole evening in a hot room. This imprudence brought on a return of the bleeding, which continued several hours, and was followed by a suppression of urine. In the course of the day they both went off. He was very low and languid; nothing therefore was done for a week; a bougie was then passed, and went with ease into the bladder. Five months after, the same bougie passed equally readily, and he continued free from any return of spasm. He then caught a gonorrhœa, which had the usual symptoms, but did not bring on any spasm or difficulty in making water, nor did it reproduce the stricture. He never afterwards had a return, and died of a fever in France in 1803.

CASE II.

A gentleman, twenty-seven years of age had a gonorrhœa four years and a half ago, unattended with violent pain or chordee; injections were used, but brought on no unpleasant symptoms; ever since that time he had a discharge, but no difficulty in making water. He put himself under my care in January, 1797. On examining the urethra it was discovered that he had a stricture at six inches from the orifice, which was removed by the caustic, and another at seven inches, which after three or four applications gave way. Immediately after the bougie passed through, the parts bled a good deal. This he was told was of no consequence, and should it continue he was not to be alarmed, but to remain quiet. After going home, a distance of two miles, the bleeding returned, and was very profuse; it continued four hours, which alarmed him, and made him send for me. He was faint and low, but the bleeding was nearly stopped. The quantity of blood lost he supposed to be several pounds; but when it was explained to him that the urine coagulated along with the blood; and as in these cases there is a frequent desire to make water, a good deal of urine is mixed with the blood, which in that state is all taken for blood, his alarm was removed, he remained quiet, and had no more bleeding. Six days after, a large sized bougie passed readily into the bladder; and at the end of seven weeks the same bougie passed with ease.

This gentleman caught a gonorrhœa four months after, which was severe; after he got well, the same bougie was passed that had been used before, with ease into the bladder.

In this case there has been no return of the disease in eight years.

CASE III.

A gentleman, forty-four years of age, had at different times slight symptoms of stricture, though not sufficient to call his attention to that subject ; but in the year 1797, having a discharge for which it was difficult to account, he put himself under my care. A stricture was met with about six inches from the external orifice ; this was treated by caustic; and from an anxiety to get into the country, after four applications it was used every day ; this had been done twice when the first stricture gave way, attended by a bleeding, which lowered him a little, though in small quantity.

The caustic was now only used every other day. Another stricture was met with, and after the second application to it, which was severe, he dined in company, and was afterwards dressing to go to a party, when an hæmorrhage came on at ten o'clock at night, nearly twelve hours after the application. It was very profuse, and lasted till four in the morning, which was six hours; and when it stopped, a violent irritation came upon the bladder, with difficulty in making water, which only came away in the quantity of half an ounce at a time. This state of irritation was relieved by an opiate glyster, and he had several hours rest. His water was very much tinged with blood. In the evening the irritation returned, and was very severe; but by throwing up a glyster of warm water, and, after the bowels were emptied, an opiate glyster, this abated. On the second morning the frequency of making bloody water continued, and he voided at intervals small clots of blood, parts of them white upon the surface; this continued through the day. The greater number were discharged in making water at the time of going to stool. On the third morning some more of these came away, after which the bladder was easy, the urine clear, and the times of making water as usual in health. He continued weak for a few days, but had no return of these symptoms; ten days after, when the parts had recovered themselves, the bougie was found to pass readily into the bladder, and there was neither discharge nor irritation in the parts.

In this case the blood had coagulated in the passage in small masses, and afterwards gone into the bladder, which kept up this irritation till it was all voided. The blood did not pass into the bladder in a fluid state; for in that case it would either not have coagulated at all, or formed one mass.

When the patient had perfectly recovered the effects of the bleeding, which was in fourteen days, a full sized bougie passed readily into the bladder, and he was entirely relieved from the symptoms he had felt before the caustic was used.

This gentleman has had no return of the disease in eight years.

CASE IV.

A gentleman aged twenty, very athletic and active, had a stricture about six inches from the orifice; for which he had in vain used the bougie several months, and therefore had recourse to the caustic. The first application gave little pain; but upon the second application, the pain at the moment was so severe as to bring on a cold sweat, and the soreness when he made water (which he did immediately after) was excruciating; the second time he made water he fainted away with the pain. This went off next day, and he took a long walk; before his return he felt blood trickling down; but as he had been told bleeding was not of any consequence, he continued his walk, and afterwards went out to dinner. After drinking some wine, the bleeding increased so as to terrify him; and he lost about three pints. Two surgeons who lived in the neighbourhood were called in; and both took the alarm, and begged he would send for me. At the time of my arrival, the parts were entirely covered with coagulated blood. He was desired to make water, and have the parts washed; hut no bleeding followed these exertions. He was then to go to bed, and keep himself quiet, as there was now no apprehension of a return; but if the parts should bleed, to encourage fainting: this he said he never had done, from loss of blood; that once from the use of a bougie he had lost a great deal of blood, although nothing to compare with the present quantity, but no faintness was produced. He bled a little in the night, but next day it was completely stopped. He was extremely lowered by the loss of blood; four days after, a full sized bougie readily passed into the bladder. He then went into the country. Three months after he called upon me; said he had been living very hard, drinking two bottles of wine a day, had caught a gonorrhœa, and believed the stricture had returned; but upon trial the same bougie passed readily, and without pain, into the bladder. Since that time, no accounts have been received of him.

CASE V.

A gentleman, of a florid complexion, stout and healthy, twenty-two years old, had a stricture, to which the caustic was applied ; it neither gave much pain, nor produced the smallest irritation ; the stricture was about six inches from the external orifice. The third time the caustic was applied to the stricture he had more pain, and in half an hour got into a stage-coach, and travelled ten miles in a very hot day, a good deal crowded in the carriage. While he remained in the coach, he felt a trickling of blood down his thighs ; and when he got out the bleeding increased so much as to alarm his friends, and at last he fainted away ; it was supposed that he lost above a quart of blood. When he sent for me, the bleeding was entirely stopped, and he looked very pale. He was allowed to make water, which he had been afraid to do, lest it might bring on a return of the bleeding. He was requested to keep himself quiet for two or three days, and then return to town. There was no more bleeding, but a serous discharge, which went off in three days ; on the fifth day a full sized bougie readily went into the bladder, nor did it give much pain in passing along the canal.

Frequent opportunities have occurred of seeing him, and there has been no return of stricture in two years. This gentleman afterwards died of a fever, and on inspecting the body no appearance of stricture was seen.

These were all the cases of this kind, that had come under my observation when the former edition of this work was published ; and having found from them, that whenever a violent bleeding took place, the stricture was invariably removed, and the hæmorrhage itself attended with no danger, it became no longer an alarming symptom, but one which afforded me the greatest satisfaction, as it enabled me to inform the patient of our complete success; and in no instance, that has since occurred, has any bad consequence resulted from it, or has there afterwards been any remains of the disease. In one patient, who took the management into his own hands, it was productive of considerable alarm from his improper conduct, but of no real danger; and the circumstance is now mentioned to prevent others from falling into the same error. This gentleman, who was a naval officer, finding the bleeding violent, made a bandage of considerable length, and contrived by crossing it on the perinæum, to produce sufficient pressure there to prevent any blood coming forward, consequently it all went back into the bladder, and produced a suppression of urine. When this information was brought to me, from being clear that there was no contraction remaining, he was informed of his error, and told to drink freely, so as to float the coagulum, and remove it from the neck of the bladder, which would enable him to make water; as soon as the bladder was full the water flowed; but for three days none passed till that was the case, but there was no occasion to use any other means for his relief.

Under similar circumstances several surgeons, from their alarm, have attempted to restrain the bleeding by pressure, but very fortunately for their patients they did not succeed, for if they had, the consequence would have been a suppression of urine.

I I

SECTION III.

STRANGURY SOMETIMES A SECONDARY EFFECT.

IT is not common for the caustic to produce strangury ; on the contrary, in many instances it removes it, by taking off spasmodic action from the stricture. It does however occur, that those patients who are subject to occasional suppressions from the use of the bougie, are not less so while the caustic is used, and sometimes have them in a still greater degree.

This symptom is more an effect of the passing the bougie along the canal while in a state of irritation, than of the caustic being applied to the stricture ; and commonly comes on after one stricture has been removed, from the bougie passing over the surface where it had been. It also has in several instances taken place after the last stricture has been destroyed, and the bougie passed through it into the bladder.

Although strangury in such instances is a secondary symptom, almost always the effect of some imprudence on the part of the patient, or some irritation brought on by passing the bougie over tender parts, it is right to take it up as a separate subject, so as not to be misunderstood in what has been said upon the effects of caustic in removing strangury; and that this circumstance when it happens may not mislead the practitioner. It is generally on the days when the caustic is not employed that this symptom takes place. Sometimes after exercise, or retaining the water unusually long, it comes on the same day. Taking laudanum, remaining quiet, or passing a small bougie, will in general, either singly or combined, remove it.

The dose of laudanum is to be proportioned to what was required for its removal when brought on by other causes. In some patients 20 drops are sufficient, in others 50 or even 100 every two hours till the water flows, are necessary.

The only instances in which it has been attended with any trouble, or been of long continuance, are subjoined.

CASE I.

A young man, from Lincolnshire, twenty-five years of age, had been subject to frequent attacks of strangury, which lasted for many hours, and were relieved by the warm bath, the internal use of opium, and glysters of warm water. Some of these were so violent as to endanger his life. He came to London in 1796, and put himself under my care. The caustic was applied to a stricture about three inches from the external orifice, which readily gave way; a second at $5\frac{1}{2}$ required four or five applications, and when removed brought on a strangury; this, after having continued four or five hours, was relieved by a glyster of hot water; the irritation upon the bladder however continued for two days. When this went off, and the canal was examined, another stricture was met with at $6\frac{1}{2}$ inches; the caustic was applied to this four times before it went into the bladder. He was so circumstanced with respect to his private business, that as soon as the strictures were removed, he went on the same day into the country. There were accounts of him six months after, and he continued perfectly well, having had no return of irritation in the bladder or suppression of urine.

CASE II.

A gentleman, aged twenty-six, eleven years ago, had a severe gonorrhœa, which was treated by injection; the inflammation extended to the perinæum, with severe chordee, which was very slow in going off. From that time there is reason to believe he had a stricture beginning to form, which increased so as to require the occasional use of bougies for several years past.

In May, 1797, he put himself under my care, and a stricture was met with about six inches from the external orifice, which readily gave way to two applications of the caustic, without his feeling much pain, although he had suffered very severely from a caustic applied to the skin of the arm, some years before; and the passing of the urine appeared to be improved. There was another stricture about $6\frac{1}{4}$ inches. When the caustic was applied to this he had a temporary spasm, which went off on passing a small bougie; a second application was made, after an interval of three days; this was followed by spasm in a greater degree. After the third application, which was on Monday, a spasm came on in the evening, and the bougie could not pass; he went into the warm bath on Tuesday forenoon, and in an hour after the bougie passed, and the urine flowed. On Tuesday evening at eight o'clock he made some water, but did not empty the bladder; he passed a very restless night, the irritations being very frequent; the bougie could not now pass, and not a drop of water came. In the morning the bougie was attempted to be passed, but without success; it went very readily down to the stricture at six inches, but no further. The caustic was then applied, and he took, at ten o'clock, thirty drops of tincture of opium, and had a glyster of warm water, without any benefit; at twelve o'clock an opiate glyster was injected, which remained half an hour, and thirty drops of tincture of opium were given by the mouth. At four he took forty drops of tincture of opium, at six used the tepid bath; then went to bed, and sweated profusely. At ten o'clock he passed a tea-spoonful of water, and was easier; a bougie was introduced down to the stricture, and was followed by a table-spoonful of water; this relieved the bladder. He took camphor, five grains; from this time till four in the morning he had a straining every seven minutes, and half an ounce of water flowed at each effort; but at four, the strangury became complete. He then fomented the perinæum with spirits and vinegar for twenty minutes, after which the urine passed in drops. At five bathed his feet, and passed a bougie down to the stricture, which was followed by a quarter of a pint of urine. Passing the bougie was repeated after every irritation, and brought away about the same quantity of water. At twelve, the urine came without the use of the bougie, and continued to do so through the day. During the whole of the time that there was a complete strangury, which was twenty-four hours, it was unattended by fever or violent agitation, and in the intervals he was perfectly composed.

This attack of spasm had been brought on each time, by using too much exercise after the caustic had been applied; and it appears that the spasm was on the stricture at six inches, probably brought on by the irritation of the bougie passing through it, before the parts had recovered themselves.

The caustic was applied at the end of ten days, and he had a connection the same night, which appeared to sooth and quiet the parts; but unluckily he repeated the connection before morning: this brought on a return of the spasm, which lasted for twenty-four hours, without his being able to pass a drop of water, and then went gradually off.

He was afterwards more prudent, and had no return of spasm, although the caustic was applied twelve times before this stricture was completely destroyed. In eight years there has been no return of the disease.

CASE III.

A French gentleman, aged fifty, had long been troubled with a difficulty in making water. Six years ago he was reduced to the dreadful situation of being separated from all his family. In August,

1795, he came from Germany to England, and arrived in November. Before he left Germany, he had a great discharge of matter from the urethra; but the fatigue of his journey, and a voyage of fifty-two days in a ship, with bad accommodations and coarse provisions, brought on a slight inflammation of the bladder.

For these complaints he took various medicines, during five months, without benefit, and in June he consulted me. At that time the symptoms increased, he made water with great pain, in a small stream, and had a discharge from the urethra.

Upon examination, the complaint proved to be stricture in the urethra. The treatment by caustic was adopted, and after sixteen applications two different strictures were removed, and he appeared to be materially relieved.

When the bougie went through the strictures and passed on to the bladder, it gave a good deal of uneasiness; this was followed by pain in the region of the bladder, and frequent desire to make water. He told me next day that he had made water thirty times in the night. Under these circumstances he was directed first to take opening medicines, then camphor and opium internally, and opiate glysters; but they afforded no relief, and the symptoms increased under this treatment. After this had gone on for four days, the bladder was found to be very much distended: a flexible gum catheter was passed, which readily went into the bladder, and drew off three pints of water. This led to an explanation of the quantity he had voided in the day; and the thirty times he before mentioned to me, were only efforts that had been ineffectual, which, from being a foreigner, he had not well explained, and called it making water. From this error, the strangury brought on by the bougie passing over the recently removed stricture, had been allowed to continue four days undiscovered, and brought on a paralysis of the bladder, attended with inflammation of its internal membrane. When his water was drawn off he had pain, and the last drops were followed by a discharge of matter. The bladder was emptied by means of the catheter once in twenty-four hours ; but this, after two days, was found not to be sufficient, and it was repeated every six hours. Under this treatment, the pain abated, the quantity of matter became less, and in three weeks he was free from any uneasiness, and made water without the instrument.

Cases in which the strangury could not be relieved by any mode of treatment, and an operation became necessary, will be found in the second volume.

SECTION IV.

AGUE.

THAT the application of the caustic to a
stricture should bring on a regular paroxysm
of fever, is an effect that could not be expected, and one for which it may appear
difficult to account. It is most frequent
in patients who have been long in hot climates, and has in general been occasionally
a symptom of the disease in its early stages,
when the patient was under the influence
of any temporary indisposition. This symptom however, is met with in patients who
were never out of England, and had no
recollection of having before experienced it.

The paroxysm of fever seems to arise
from the stomach sympathizing with the
stricture, and purgative medicines are the
most effectual means of carrying it off; nor
is there occasion to have recourse to any

other treatment. In no instance have any serious consequences arisen from these attacks, although in several cases they have been very violent. In general they come on when a stricture is destroyed; being found to occur less frequently at any other time.

The instances in which this symptom has occurred have been very numerous: the following cases were the only ones in which it was very severe.

CASE I.

A gentleman, aged fifty-four, twelve years ago had symptoms of stricture, having a difficulty in passing his water, which was relieved by the introduction of the bougie; there was no other symptom, neither discharge from the canal, nor local uneasiness at any other time. These attacks were not frequent, they only came on from occasional colds, and were readily relieved by the use of the bougie. For the last two years they had become more frequent and more severe, and his colds upon exposure to damps brought on aguish attacks; the strangury was relieved by applications of hot flannels to the perinæum, and tincture of opium taken internally; but once he remained four hours in the tepid bath before the strangury went off. In March, 1797, he put himself under my care; the caustic was applied to a stricture which was $4\frac{1}{2}$ inches from the orifice; this gave way to two applications; there was another at six inches, which was removed by four applications, but when it gave way an ague came on in the evening, and there was a return next day; it then went off. A third stricture at seven inches required three applications; but it never gave the same pain, or produced constitutional affections, as the other had done. As soon as this was removed all the parts were at ease, and the bladder recovered its natural state.

CASE II.

A gentleman, twenty-eight years of age, a native of Jamaica, had lived in that island until he attained the age of nineteen, in the enjoyment of tolerable health. At this time he was afflicted with a violent gonorrhœa, which continued on him for about six months, and then disappeared without his having taken medicine, or gone through any sort of treatment whatever. He then went to Spain, and lived in the southern parts of that kingdom for the term of nine years.

For two years before he left Spain he was afflicted with successive venereal gonorrhœas, from which his imprudence never allowed him time to be relieved, and which at length brought on stricture. He was then recommended to come to this country, and undergo a course of bougies.

On his arrival he put himself under my

care. Upon examining the canal, a stricture was met with at $5\frac{1}{2}$ inches from the orifice; to this the caustic was applied.

On the third application this stricture was destroyed; but in half an hour he was seized with a violent shivering, attended with a severe fever. These fits not only returned on every succeeding application, but also when he exposed himself to cold, or underwent any bodily exertion. He was so much reduced by them, that it was thought expedient to suspend for a while the process of his cure.

About three weeks were allowed him to recover his strength, which he did tolerably well before the recommencement of the process,

On returning to the use of the caustic, sometimes after the application there was a tendency to shiver, which manifested itself on cold days; but went off on going immediately to bed, and getting into a perspiration. He was then desired to stay in the house; and by this precaution was

K k

relieved from these attacks. One day he was tempted to go to a coffee-house, an hundred yards from his lodgings, and in an hour after being there, a shivering fit came on : this induced him to give up going out till he was quite well.

The use of the caustic was continued for four months, three times a week. In all about seventy applications.

There was an irregularity in the canal, which did not allow the bougie to pass readily into the bladder; but a flexible gum catheter was then made use of, with a stilet to give it firmness; this was used three times, with the interval of a fortnight at each time, and was passed without any difficulty into the bladder.

This gentleman afterwards went to Jamaica ; he had no return of his complaint while he remained in this country. It is remarkable, that a brother of this patient had the same disease, which was removed by the caustic ; but there was not the least disposition to paroxysms of fever. This led me to inquire what difference there had been in their mode of life; and it was found that the brother had left Jamaica at five years old, and remained in England for many years, so that his constitution was naturally less irritable.

This gentleman died of the yellow fever at Jamaica, four years after being under my care.

CASE III.

A gentleman from Holland, thirty-five years of age, a native of that country, who had been subject to agues, and at those times to suppressions of urine, for several years, consulted me on account of a difficulty in passing his urine. The canal was uncommonly small, and a stricture was met with at the distance of $3\frac{1}{2}$ inches from the orifice; this had the caustic applied to it three times, after which the bougie passed through it. He was then taken ill with a .

K k 2

severe ague, which he attributed to having taken cold. This went off with a very copious perspiration. Another stricture was met with at $5\frac{1}{2}$ inches; soon after the application of the caustic, an attack of ague more severe than the last, came on; when this went off, it was in eight hours succeeded by a slighter attack, which left him very weak: in neither of these attacks was there any suppression of urine, and the only medicine given was a draught, composed of infusion and tincture of senna, with soluble tartar.

There was still another stricture at $6\frac{1}{3}$ inches, which required several applications of the caustic, and when this was destroyed an attack of ague, more severe than the others, was brought on, and did not terminate as they had done; it was attended with delirium, which lasted twenty-four hours, and for several days the fever, in some degree, continued; but upon his getting out into the air it went off. After his recovery the bougie was found to pass into the bladder, and he made water with more ease than he had done for many years. His business called him over to Holland, as soon as the cure was completed.

CASE IV.

A gentleman, aged fifty-one, who had lived thirty years in the West Indies, had for two years, at short intervals, attacks of ague, and during these attacks difficulty in making water, and in some of them a total suppression ; he came to England in 1796, at which time he consulted me. Upon inquiring into the nature of the difficulty in making water, it was discovered that he had several strictures, the first of which was within three inches of the external orifice. To this the caustic was applied, which gave no pain ; indeed he was scarcely sensible of the application. He had had a fit of ague the day before, and another the following day ; but the caustic being applied a second time, there was no return of the ague. It was applied to a second stricture at six inches, and after seven applications the bougie passed into the bladder. He had the next day an attack of fever without the cold fit, and a swelling in perinæo, extending towards the anus. This abated in twenty-four hours, and in three days went off. Upon passing the bougie at this period, it stopped at a stricture at seven inches, which had been relaxed by the destruction of the one next to it, but not destroyed; this required seven or eight applications of the caustic, the effects of which brought on severe attacks of ague; at last it was subdued, and the full-sized bougie went into the bladder. After the last application of the caustic, which made the stricture give way, he was attacked with a rigor, which was not followed by a complete sweating fit; next day the cold fit returned, and the fever was extremely violent, the sweat uncommonly profuse, and when it went off left him in a very languid state; he was several hours without any perceptible pulse, although able to speak and take nourishment; but this gradually went off. It was a fortnight before he recovered his strength.

The stricture was now found to be destroyed, and six months afterwards it had not returned.

SECTION V.

THE EFFECTS OF THE CAUSTIC, WHEN BY
ACCIDENT IT REMAINS IN THE CANAL OF
THE URETHRA.

WHEN the use of the caustic was first introduced, a variety of objections were made
to this practice; one which had very great
influence upon many patients, was the dread
of the caustic remaining in the canal. Such
an accident was supposed to be worse than
death.

That such an accident has happened cannot be denied ; but the effects have nothing
very alarming in them, as will appear from
the following cases; and the mode which
has now been adopted for arming bougies,
puts it in the power of every practitioner in
future to avoid the possibility of meeting
with this accident.

It is right at the same time to state the

effects which the caustic, when so left, has produced, to point out what should be done when such an accident happens, so as to turn the accident as much as possible to the advantage of the patient.

CASE I.

In April, 1796, a gentleman had a stricture to which the caustic was applied above fifty times, in different trials to subdue it; and in all these attempts the caustic had never given any severe pain, or brought on irritation. Finding the common means ineffectual, the caustic was allowed to remain a long time at the stricture (which was at seven inches); the bougie became so soft that the caustic dropped out: the pain was not very severe. He passed some urine, but did not bring away the remains of the caustic; about half an hour after he made water more freely, and a small portion of the caustic that was undissolved came away; there was a pain and tenderness in the canal for three days, after which time it went off entirely. As the patient knew all the circumstances, and his mind was naturally alarmed, the pain not being considered as much more than usual, was a sufficient proof that it had not been very great.

CASE II.

A gentleman had a stricture about three inches from the external orifice, to which the caustic was applied fourteen or fifteen times, of a large size, without subduing it; and not gaining any ground, a caustic two sizes larger than that generally employed, was used and kept some time at the stricture; it came out of the bougie, and remained in the urethra: he did not make water, but went home without knowing that any thing particular had happened. He was told that the application had been more than commonly severe, and therefore he had better remain quiet.

Nothing was done for two days; on being asked if the pain had been great, he said it lasted longer than usual, but made no other remark. As he did not know that the caustic remained, his mind was not influenced; nor was the difference so great as to enable him to make the discovery, or even to take notice of any difference till he was asked, and then he only said that it lasted an hour longer than common. The stricture was more acted on by this application, and he felt himself evidently better after it, and only made water twice a-day, which he had before done much more frequently.

CASE III.

A gentleman whose sufferings from stricture had been for many years extremely severe, being subject to attacks of irritation that were frequently brought on, and much increased, by passing calculous matter, had the caustic applied to a stricture, three inches from the orifice, fourteen or fifteen times, with little effect; it neither gave much pain, nor produced irritation; the size of the caustic was therefore increased in proportion to the want of effect. The sixteenth application of the caustic was continued for a considerable time; and when it was attempted to be withdrawn, the urethra acted so strongly upon the bougie as to pull off the caustic, with some of the wax of the bougie, and retain it. The alarm on the patient's mind was very great, almost such as to make him faint. That we might take advantage of this accident immediately, a bougie was passed down to the caustic, and pressed against it, to prevent it from leaving the stricture it was intended to act upon.

The pain was not severe, and after the bougie was withdrawn he made water. His mind did not readily recover itself; but, on being told that it would not be necessary to see him for three days, as we could not go on with the caustic for that space of time, and the present accident required nothing being done, he was in some measure composed; and afterwards confessed that the pain was not great, even augmented as it was by his apprehensions. The passage was irritated by some calculous matter lodging near the bulb of the urethra, which had remained there four days ; lying in that part at the time the accident happened, it was probably the cause of the spasm which occasioned it. We were able in five days to proceed with the caustic, and the stricture was in a degree benefited by this unintentionally violent application. Some time after this the caustic passing through another stricture, and being allowed to remain a little time, a spasm came on, and, in attempting to withdraw the bougie, the caustic was again retained. This brought on more inflammation than the former, and it was fourteen days before it went entirely off; it did not, however, prevent the patient from persevering in the use of the caustic, which removed the stricture, but he afterwards died of the stone in the bladder.

In addition to these facts, the following is mentioned, although of a different kind.

A gentleman who, in a state of intoxication, had been carried at night into a house of bad fame, in the morning was much astonished at his situation; alarmed for the consequences of his imprudence, he expressed so great an anxiety respecting his health, that his female companion told him to make his mind easy, she would give him an injection that prevented all infection; by mistake she gave him the caustic alkali undiluted, instead of a weak solution of it in water. He injected it, and brought on very great pain; but fortunately the urethra did not allow it to pass far, and neither suppression of urine nor irritation on the bladder followed; local soreness and pain in making water were the only consequences. The membrane to which it had been applied came off in form of a slough.

CHAPTER VIII.

CIRCUMSTANCES UNDER WHICH THE USE OF THE CAUSTIC HAS PROVED UNSUCCESSFUL.

WHEN these observations were first published, my experience was very limited, compared with what it has been since that time; as will appear from the variety of circumstances attending this disease, which are now registered in the Cases.

In the first edition of this work every difficult case was stated which had come under my care. In the present the same plan is followed; but the number of cases has been too great, to allow me to do more than to select those that explain some circumstance respecting the disease, or mode of treatment; and the number which have appeared to me necessary for that purpose is so great, that there is more reason to fear the reader will think it unnecessarily large, than too small.

It is no small commendation of this mode of practice, that every untoward circumstance which has occurred in the use of the caustic, and every case that has had an unfortunate termination, has a place in the present work.

In those cases where the caustic gradually removes the stricture, and brings the urethra to a size that allows the patient to make water perfectly well, if there is any return, it is not to be attributed to the failure of the caustic, but to the want of proper management, either from the caustic being too small, its use left off too soon, or the part being afterwards allowed to become indolent from not having been occasionally relaxed by the use of a bougie; but all such cases are within the power of being cured by the caustic, if its use is recurred to when that is found necessary.

Several cases have occurred in which the caustic has failed of success; these will now be taken notice of, mentioning the circumstances under which the failures took place; and to render these more distinct, they will be made the heads of separate sections.

SECTION I.

CASES OF STRICTURE IN WHICH THE CAUSTIC
FAILED OF PRODUCING A CURE, IN CONSE-
QUENCE OF THE INFLUENCE OF GOUT.

So much is the urethra, in its natural
state, under the influence of gout, that it is
sometimes affected by it, on the coming on
of every attack, with all the symptoms of
inflammation; as pain in making water,
and a purulent discharge; and as soon as the
gout fixes itself in the foot, they entirely
disappear. It has even been asserted, that
regular attacks of gout have fallen upon the
urethra, exactly similar to those on any other
part; this may undoubtedly happen, but no
such instances have come within my own
observation.

This natural susceptibility of the urethra
to be influenced by gout, appears to be much
increased when that canal is in a diseased

state, so as to increase all its symptoms, and when they have gone off, to produce a recurrence of them, and prevent the disease, to which it is liable, from being completely removed. This is generally true ; there are however cases of stricture in the urethra in gouty habits, which do not at all appear to be under its influence, and therefore are to be ranked among the ordinary cases of the disease, where no gout is in the constitution.

The following cases will shew the manner in which gout affects stricture in the urethra, and explain the recurrence of the disease, even after it has been removed by caustic ; and therefore prevent the surgeon from persevering with this mode of treatment, after it is found to be counteracted by gout.

CASE I.

A gentleman, between fifty and sixty years of age, who had strictures for twenty-years, had also frequent attacks of gout; at those times there was a difficulty in making water, and he was obliged to pass a bougie of a small size. His stream of urine was always small, but the passing it in general not attended with difficulty; while in a warm climate he had been a year without using a bougie; this he was at other times obliged to do occasionally, sometimes once a day, or once in two or three days.

He put himself under my care in the year 1797, and had the caustic applied to a stricture at six inches; this was removed by three applications; when this stricture was destroyed, the bougie passing through it brought on a strangury, which was removed by the warm bath. Another stricture was met with at seven inches. After four applications this second stricture was destroyed.

The bougie passing into the bladder produced irritation, attended with frequency in making water, which lasted for half an hour. When this went off he felt himself very well, and had an ease about these parts which he had not felt for years.

Two months after, the same bougie passed into the bladder, but with a degree of difficulty, which induced me to apply the caustic again; this brought on a good deal of irritation at the moment, and was followed by a suppression, which went off while the patient was in the warm bath. The irritation subsided, and he was very well; but soon after he had an attack of gout, which again brought on suppression, and required the use of the bougie. When the gout went off, he made water very well, and a bougie passed readily into the bladder.

The gout in this case acted on that part of the canal, producing a spasmodic contraction, in the same manner as a blister applied to any part of the body, in many people brings on strangury.

In the course of four or five years, in each of which there was generally one or two attacks of gout, the stricture returned, requiring the occasional use of the bougie, in the same manner as before the caustic had been used, and in future attacks of gout, a strangury was brought on in consequence of a spasmodic contraction taking place, while the constitution was under the influence of gout, which continued to recur even after the gout went away.

In this case the stricture appeared to have received no permanent relief from the caustic, and eight years afterwards it was as difficult to dilate it with the bougie, as other strictures of the same standing.

CASE II.

A gentleman, about forty years of age, had strictures for several years, which required the use of a small bougie occasionally; but generally in the spring he had a severe attack, attended with suppression.

In 1796 he put himself under my care. The urethra was very small in itself, and there was a stricture three inches from the external orifice. The passing the bougie gave pain ; but the caustic was so little felt that he doubted much that any thing was really applied ; this stricture was removed by three applications of the caustic, and afterwards other two strictures in succession, the whole of them requiring about twelve applications of the caustic.

As the urethra was small, it was explained to him that he was more liable than others to a return of the stricture. Three months after, the same bougie passed into the bladder, but not with perfect ease. It was then proposed to him to have the caustic applied again ; but he continued so well that he did not attend to my advice. In the following spring he had the gout flying about him, and all at once was taken with a difficulty in making water, and great irritation in this part, which induced him to send for me. An attempt to pass the former bougie gave so much pain in going along the canal, before it came to the seat of the first stricture, that he was unable to bear it, so extremely irritable was the internal membrane at that time. One of a smaller size, still gave pain ; this was much greater than that produced by the caustic, which was immediately after applied to the second stricture that had become spasmodically contracted. Two applications of the caustic removed the strangury, and it was then proposed to do nothing more, as a fit of the gout was come on, but to leave the parts to themselves till the influence of that disease was gone off. Since that time no accounts of the patient have come to my knowledge, but there is no reason to believe that the complaint was materially benefited by the use of the casutic.

CASE III.

A gentleman, about thirty years of age, applied to me for relief from a stricture. To ascertain that such a disease existed, a bougie was passed; this gave a very uncommon degree of pain; and as there was a stricture at five inches, the caustic was applied to it. The pain he expressed was beyond what is usual. He said it was insufferable. Two days after he called upon me, his hand much swelled from a violent fit of the gout. This explained to me the very severe pain he felt from the bougie, and also from the caustic. He was therefore desired to leave the treatment of the stricture, till the gout was entirely gone off.

Six months after, the treatment of the stricture was renewed; the caustic gave pain, but by no means very severe, and its use was continued till the strictures, which were two in number, were destroyed; for this purpose it was applied twenty times. Two months after, the canal was perfectly free from any obstruction, but he had not in the interval been attacked by the gout; so that it remains to be ascertained whether it will have any effect on the seat of the stricture.

Since that time there have been many severe fits of gout, and in all of them a temporary difficulty in making water, but having had no opportunity for several years of passing a bougie, no report can be made respecting the real state of the urethra.

CASE IV.

A gentleman between fifty and sixty years of age, who had laboured under a stricture in the urethra for twenty years, and had a fit of the gout regularly every spring, at which times the difficulty in making water was increased, and often became very troublesome, put himself under my care, and unfortunately the time chosen was the spring of the year. He had not the gout, at the time the use of the caustic was begun ; but after it had been applied three or four times, the gout came on, so that we were obliged to wait till it went off; but on resuming the use of the caustic, it returned; and in this way it was found that no real benefit was to be derived from this practice, at that season of the year; he therefore returned into the country, since which time no particulars respecting his case have come to my knowledge, but he did not receive the smallest benefit from the use of the caustic.

SECTION II.

FAILURES FROM THE STRICTURED PART HAVING BECOME SO HARD, AND THICK, AS NOT TO BE DESTROYED BY THE CAUSTIC.

IN some patients the strictures are so obdurate, that the use of the caustic is necessarily persevered in for a longer time than the parts can bear its application, irritation therefore comes on and stops the progress of the cure; and, when the same means are resorted to again, the same thing takes place; so that it requires a greater degree of perseverance on the part of the surgeon, and a longer attendance on the part of the patient, for the accomplishment of a cure, than are often to be met with.

Under these circumstances twelve different cases have come under my observation, which have not been removed by the use of the caustic. After the detail which will be found in the second volume, in the Chapter, " On Strictures which require an unusual number of applications of the armed bougie for their removal," a more particular account here, of those cases in which the patients declined perseverance in the mode of treatment, would convey no new information; it is however necessary to state the small number of this kind that have been met with.

In such cases it is to be regretted that we have not a more active caustic, capable of being with safety applied to the urethra, since that is all which is required for their removal; and when the stricture becomes ligamentous, or almost cartilaginous, the lunar caustic makes less impression upon it than could be imagined from any preconceived opinion on the subject.

SECTION III.

FAILURES FROM EVERY APPLICATION OF THE
CAUSTIC PRODUCING A REGULAR PAROXYSM
OF FEVER.

IN some constitutions, where the patients
have resided long in warm climates, every
time the caustic is applied to a stricture a
regular paroxysm of fever takes place, and
that so violent as to render it impossible to
pursue this mode of treatment. Of this there
have been three instances. The disposition
for fever was considered in the former
edition as the effect of climate, and not of
any natural peculiarity of constitution, as a
gentleman who formed one of the instances,
had been in a warm climate, and a brother
of his, who had not, showed no similar disposition; this is found upon a more enlarged
experience not to be true, since many who
have been long in a warm climate have not

acquired it ; there is however every ground for believing that such a natural disposition is greatly increased by long residence in warm climates.

As the symptoms of this attack of fever have been already fully explained, and are of such frequent occurrence in the cases interspersed through these volumes, there is nothing deserving of notice in this place, but that in some rare instances, the returns are so frequent, and each return is of such increased violence, as to make it necessary to desist from the prosecution of the cure by this mode of treatment.

In the winter and spring, many constitutions are more liable to these attacks than in the summer, and autumn ; attention should therefore be paid to this circumstance.

SECTION IV.

PAROXYSMS OF FEVER FROM THE EFFECT OF
THE CAUSTIC ARE LESS FREQUENT WHEN
THERE IS A FISTULA IN PERINÆO.

THE circumstance of strictures being rendered less irritable after a fistula in perinæo
has taken place, appears of so much importance, and so contrary to any preconceived
opinion upon the subject, that it is placed
under a distinct head.

It is natural to expect that where there is
a fistula in perinæo, the part of the urethra
where the fistula opens into it will be liable
to inflammation from any cause that irritates the stricture which is almost close to
it, and this is found to be the case; but inflammation in this canal hardly ever produces these attacks of fever; they most commonly arise from urine lodging behind an

obstruction upon an irritated surface, and producing an abration there, or from its passing over an abraded surface ; so that when the urine is allowed to escape by means of a fistula, although its passage is painful to the patient, no fever arises in consequence of it ; but if a fresh abscess forms and breaks, the urine passing over the ulcerated surface shall immediately be followed by a paroxysm of fever.

These observations are confirmed by the cases already stated of strictures attended with fistula in perinæo ; in none of them was there any paroxysms of fever except where a stricture had been destroyed, a circumstance which always renders the constitution liable to such an attack.

That a fistula in perinæo to a certain degree relieves the parts beyond it, and prevents a suppression of urine from taking place by letting it pass off by that channel, are self evident propositions ; to me, therefore, this symptom is always rather satisfactory than otherwise, in the cases that come under my care; but that its presence should make the patient less liable to paroxysms of fever, certainly never occurred to me, and nothing but the following case could have induced me to believe it was capable of having that effect.

CASE.

An officer, twenty-two years of age, in the year 1782, after walking a mile, was seized with a great desire to make water, and on attempting to void it was seized with the most excruciating torture. These pains returned in a less degree at different times for the five following days, when he passed a stone the size of a pea, which gave him complete relief, and he continued well till 1783, when there was a return of frequency in making water, attended with pain and difficulty. In the spring 1784, he was put under a course of bougies, and while using them, passed several small sharp pointed calculi. He went on passing occasionally

M m

bougies till 1789, when he went to Jamaica, where from the the effect of climate and the free use of wine, he had frequent stoppages of urine, and a constant desire to make water. This, together with attacks of fever which he became liable to, and a hurt he received on board of ship, made him return to England in June 1793. He went on with the use of the bougie, and in 1795 returned to the West Indies : he had not been many months in that climate when he had an attack of fever, and a return of all his former symptoms, and gradually lost his health, so as to be rendered unfit for the duties of his profession. In this state, in 1797, he was advised by some of his military friends to come to England and put himself under my care, which he intended doing, but was ordered to St. Domingo, and could not procure leave of absence ; he was there attacked with a fever, from which he suffered so much that he was advised to embark in the first vessel that was to sail, which proved to be an American, and carried him to Philadelphia, where he suffered very severely, and arrived at Liverpool in September; from whence he came by slow stages, much oppressed by his complaint, and in five days arrived at Derby, and was confined there under the care of Dr. Darwyn, from the end of October 1797, to April 1798.

He arrived in town the 30th of April, and put himself under my care on the 1st of May. The use of the caustic was taken up, and applied to a stricture $4\frac{1}{2}$ inches from the external orifice. After fifteen applications a violent attack of fever came on, which left him so low and languid, as to make it necessary for him to go into the country for the recovery of his health.

At the end of five weeks he returned to town, when the use of the caustic was resumed; after four applications the attack of fever returned with greater violence than before, and it became necessary for him again to go into the country, where he remained till the end of August, improved both in his general health and strength. A

this time the first stricture had been destroyed, and the caustic was now applied to
one at 6 inches.   The first application relieved the symptoms of the stricture very
materially, and now it was expected that we
should meet with no further interruption ;
but the second application brought on a
return of the paroxysm of fever ; this however was slight compared with the others.
In ten days he recovered from it, and the
caustic was applied again, but it brought on
so violent an attack of fever, that it became
absolutely necessary to give up all idea of
persevering with the caustic.   He went into
the country, where he remained all the
winter, which was very severe, and encreased all the symptoms of his complaint,
nor did he recover his strength.   In the
following summer he got better, and recovered strength, but in January 1800 he
had a severe attack of irritation in the
bladder, and was advised to go to a warm
climate.   He therefore returned to his regiment in Jamiaca, where he had only one

attack of fever, and went on tolerably well till the 6th July, 1801, when a suppression of urine took place, and a large abscess formed in perinæo, which broke externally, forming a fistula in perinæo. At this time his strength was so much reduced that he was not expected to live, and remained in a weak low state till the end of October, when he began to get better, but was unable to leave his room till February 1802. He was detained in the West Indies till the 8th of June, 1803, when he sailed for England, and arrived the 23d of August. In the beginning of October he again put himself under my care. Such was the alarm upon the patient's mind of the caustic producing attacks of fever as before, and indeed the same dread was upon my own, that it was resolved to try every other means before it was had recourse to. The common conical bougie was employed; but after a fortnight's use nothing was gained, as one of the smallest size could not be passed into the bladder, on account of the irregularities formed by the orifices leading to the fistulæ; small silver sounds, in a curved form, were then tried, but with no better success. A month was consumed in these attempts, during which the patient dragged on a very miserable existence; he made water every hour in the night, and was never more than two hours without doing it in the day. Half or three parts of the urine voided passed with pain through the fistulæ, and it was necessary to introduce a small bougie about five inches, and let it remain a minute, before the water flowed forwards. Under these distressing circumstances he was told that there was now no choice, every other means having failed, we were called upon to try the caustic, and should it be attended with violent attacks of fever, it was then time to give it up. He assented to this proposal, and in the beginning of November the caustic was applied to a stricture at five inches, and we had the satisfaction to find that it brought on no distressing symptoms. The application was repeated every third day;

the patient confined himself entirely to the house; and after three applications he had no occasion to pass his small bougie, had less effort in making water, and a greater proportion passed forwards. When this stricture was destroyed there was a slight paroxysm of fever, but it went off without being followed by a second attack. The second stricture at 6 inches was then destroyed, and when it yielded there was another attack of fever; this was also the case upon the giving way of the third at 7 inches. In May 1804 the strictures were removed, but from the irregularities of the thickened parts where the fistulæ had taken place, a bougie could not be conducted into the bladder; a small silver catheter was found to pass; this was repeated every other day, and in June all the fistulous orifices were healed, he made water freely, and could pass the catheter himself so as to draw off the water; and with a view to exercise this part of the canal by relaxing it, he was advised to pass the catheter once every second day. In this state he retured to the West Indies.

CHAPTER IX.

OF THE TREATMENT OF STRICTURES IN THE ŒSOPHAGUS.

THE œsophagus, as it is required to be wider at one time, and narrower at another, to adapt it to the different kinds of food that are necessarily conveyed into the stomach, is nearly under the same circumstance, with respect to the formation of stricture, as the canal of the urethra.

Cases of stricture in this canal are, for very obvious reasons, much less frequent than in the urethra; they are however, more common than they are generally supposed to be, and the symptoms they produce are even more distressing and more dangerous than those mentioned in the former part of this work.

To convey to the reader a distinct idea of the disease, for which it is meant to propose a new mode of relief, it will be sufficient to state those facts on which my own knowledge of it is founded ; these will be met with in the histories and dissections of the two following cases, which came under my care before my mind had been applied to the consideration of strictures, or the effects of the caustic in the treatment of that disease in the urethra.

A lady, about thirty-six years of age, and naturally healthy, had no difficulty in swallowing till a twelvemonth before her death ; at that period this complaint first came on, and gradually increased, which alarmed her exceedingly, and made her apply for medical advice. She was directed to take the cicuta to a considerable extent. Mercury was used, and a salivation kept up for some time, but without the least benefit. In consequence of the effects of the mercury, there appeared to be an enlargement of the thyroide gland, and the lymphatic glands in its vicinity, which continued in an enlarged state till her death.

Ten months after the commencement of this complaint she first applied to me; this was in December, 1789; the œsophagus did not admit at that time any solid food to pass down, and even fluids passed with great difficulty, and in very small quantity, attended with considerable pain, which was continued along the fauces to the basis of the skull, and through the eustachian tube to the ear. This pain returned at intervals when no attempt was made to swallow, and lasted for about an hour; the periods of its return were irregular, and no cause of their recurrence could be ascertained. For some months she had little or no thirst, although formerly she was as much liable to it as people commonly are; this circumstance, a very fortunate one, might arise from the saliva not escaping from the mouth and fauces by the œsophagus.

A long bougie, about the size of a goose's quill, was passed into the fauces, but did

not go beyond the cricoide cartilage; one
with a very small point passed considerably
lower down in the œsophagus, and when
withdrawn was covered with a thick mucus; this appeared to ease the throat at the
time, but brought on so much irritation afterwards, as to prevent its use being again
had recourse to. Tincture of opium was
now given upon sugar, but did not relieve the irritation, which was worse at
night; it was then tried in glysters, but
with no better effect, and produced head-
aches.

As the œsophagus hardly admitted nourishment in a fluid state to pass in sufficient quantity to support the body, attempts to give medicines by the mouth
were entirely relinquished, and they were
exhibited in form of glyster.

Jan. 12th, 1790, fifteen grains of musk
were thrown up three times a day, which
seemed rather to soothe and lessen the irritability and general uneasiness, but not in
the least to relieve the swallowing This

was continued till the 18th, when it was left off, as it appeared to have lost its effect.

Jan. 18th, a glyster of twenty grains of the extract of hemlock was thrown up three times a day; it brought on giddiness, but did not effect the disease.

Jan. 19th, it was repeated, with only ten grains in each glyster, and then left off.

Jan. 21st, four ounces of decoction of valerian, and one dram of the powder, were thrown up the rectum, and the throat fumigated with factitious cinnabar. The valerian glysters were repeated three times a day, for three days, without benefit; the fumigation seemed to give temporary relief to the throat, and she thought that she swallowed rather better after it; although upon the whole she certainly became daily worse.

Jan. 25th, the use of the valerian was continued, with fifteen grains of camphor, three times a day; this certainly gave more ease than the other medicines. The camphor was employed for three days, but her throat became now so much oppressed with phlegm, that she was obliged to clear it frequently to prevent being choked ; and as the camphor gave a disposition to sleep, which prevented the phlegm collected in the œsophagus from being brought up, and gave her violent head-aches, she was induced to leave it off.

Jan. 31st. at bed-time, two scruples of Dover's powder were thrown up by glysters in consequence of a cough, and heat upon the skin, and some degree of fever; they had similar effects as when given by the mouth; brought on perspiration, and gave considerable ease both to the pain and cough, and procured a good deal of sleep. This was repeated on the 2d, 4th, 5th, and 7th of February, and produced the same effect, viz. perspiration and sleep.

Her throat became more and more oppressed with the phlegm, till at last she could not clear it at all ; for six days she could not swallow any thing, and was

entirely supported by nourishing glysters.
On the 9th of February she died.

Upon examination of the parts after death,
the disease appeared to be confined to the
coats of the œsophagus, just behind the thyroide cartilage; at that part they were so
much contracted as nearly to obliterate the
passage; about half an inch lower down,
there were two spots, like ulcerations, just
beginning to take place.

The thyroide gland, and the lymphatic
glands in the surrounding parts, were hard
and swelled, but seemed not to have in the
least obstructed deglutition.

At the time of her death, the muscles of
the neck were all rigid from spasmodic contraction.

A lady, fifty-nine years of age, had been
remarked from her infancy for having a very
narrow swallow, but at that time it could
not be considered a disease: it increased
as she grew up, and for the last thirteen
years of her life was very troublesome; but

even before that period she was unable to swallow any substance the size of a pill, and was obliged to masticate her food thoroughly, and swallow it with great caution ; for when she swallowed in a hurry, or was off her guard, it brought on a spasm upon the œsophagus, and she had the sensation of being choked. This effect was more readily produced when her mind was at all agitated, and at the periods of menstruation. These affections or spasms were relieved at different times by rubbing the throat externally behind the cartilages of the larynx, by smelling eau de luce, and swallowing a few drops of tincture of opium, which passed down to the stricture, remained there, and removed the spasm. These attacks lasted sometimes only a few minutes, at others thirty-six hours ; they went off always in an instant, and communicated the sensation of something giving way ; they appeared to herself to be brought on by the wind from the stomach opposing and stopping the morsel, and the removal appeared to take place from the wind escaping, and permitting the morsel to pass.

Thirteen years before her death, she had a considerable uterine hæmorrhage, which lowered her very much, and from that time this complaint in her swallowing became evidently worse; the returns of these affections were more frequent and more violent, and when free from them, the passage of the œsophagus was permanently contracted in a greater degree than before; when the attacks of choking came on, the opium and volatile salts were now of no use. She could swallow very little solid food, not being able to give passage to any thing larger than a pin's head.

Eight months before her death, she was seized all at once with a fixed pain a little above the pit of the stomach, under the breast bone, and a coldness in the stomach with chills down her back; this went off gradually, but returned in a month much in the same way, and never afterwards could be said to have gone away altogether.

At this time the disposition to choking seemed to be diminished, the morsel passed down some way without much pain, but when it was dropping into the stomach, she was thrown into agony from the pain; it was very acute and greatest at the first attempt, but less severe upon repetition; this lasted about a fortnight, when it gradually abated: during this period, and for the remainder of her life, she was unable to attempt swallowing solid food. Besides the fixed pain in the stomach, she had for some time after the sensation of an acid in the stomach, and violent retchings; these symptoms gradually and uniformly increased, and for the last six weeks she had an increase of the secretion of saliva, spitting about a quart a day. This produced retching, and what came up from the stomach gave her the sensation of being very hot in the mouth: latterly she brought up a brown coloured fluid, like the broken coagulum of blood; this came after retching. Sometimes when she attempted to swallow nou-

N n

rishment, it appeared to pass down to the orifice of the stomach, and then returned with some of this fluid, which looked like coffee grounds.

A little time before death, the debility and merasmus was extreme; there was a considerable difficulty in breathing; she had likewise, for the last month, an appearance of aphthæ in the mouth, which before death spread over all the fauces and tongue: worn out by these symptoms, and want of nourishment, she died.

Upon examining the body after death, there appeared to be no disease in the stomach itself.

The inside of the mouth was covered with aphthæ, which did not reach beyond the fauces. The œsophagus, directly behind the first ring of the trachea, was so much contracted that the orifice did not admit a common quill. At this part there was no apparent disease, the parts were in no respect thickened, and the internal membrane had the natural appearance, only contracted, forming a regular annular stricture. For about an inch lower down, the œsophagus was externally as small as common in the greatest degree of contraction; after which it became a little larger, although still much smaller than we generally find it. The coats at this part were thinner and less muscular than natural. The whole internal surface of the œsophagus, below the bifurcation of the trachea, was, for three inches in length, in a state of ulceration, and the parts surrounding it at this part, were all consolidated; this ulcer had two sinuses extending some way into the lungs, but these did not appear to communicate with the air cells; the aorta at this part adhered to the œsophagus, but was not itself at all affected by the disease.

The ulceration seemed to have begun only eight months before death, as the pain from food passing into the stomach came on at that time, which seems to fix the period of the inflammation that necessarily preceded the formation of the ulcer.

N n 2

It does not at first sight appear in what way the stricture in the upper part of the œsophagus should produce ulceration in that canal nearer the stomach; and yet this effect resembles so exactly what is met with in strictures in the urethra, ulceration taking place behind the stricture, that it is difficult to suppose the ulceration in the œsophagus unconnected with the stricture. It is probable that in such cases the frequent retching arising from the phlegm collected between the stricture and the stomach, produces the same consequences as the ineffectual straining of the bladder, to get rid of the urine.

The examination of these two cases afforded me an opportunity of ascertaining, that there are obstructions in the œsophagus similar to those in the urethra   Since that time these facts have naturally led me to consider this disease in the canal of the œsophagus, and of the urethra to be similar, and that any observations made on the treatment of the one, are applicable to the other.

Whenever consulted in cases of stricture of the œsophagus, recourse has been had to the use of the bougie ; and if that mode of treatment failed, to the application of the caustic. In some instances the use of the bougie has answered, in others it has failed, as will appear from the following cases.

CASE I.

A woman, about twenty-five years of age, of an irritable habit, but in very good health, came over from Ireland in the packet ; the motion of the vessel made her extremely sea-sick, and she retched for several hours ; the effects of the retching were a difficulty of swallowing, and tenderness in the whole canal of the œsophagus. The difficulty in swallowing increased, and in some months after was so great, that she consulted me about the best mode of relieving it. A bougie was passed, the point of which was nearly the size of the little finger, becoming gradually larger towards the other end; this, with some difficulty went into the stomach, and the next day she swallowed much better. As the stricture, from this examination, proved to be principally spasmodic, she was advised occasionally to have a bougie passed; not considering the obstruction sufficient to make the use of the caustic either proper or necessary; and by following this mode of treatment she has been very much relieved.

CASE II.

A gentleman, twenty-six years of age, had from his infancy an occasional difficulty in swallowing; this increased as he grew up, and has been at times very distressing, rendering him unable to get even fluids into the stomach without much uneasiness, and then in very small quantities at a time.

These attacks came on without any

previous cause that could be ascertained; and lasted a few days, after which they gradually abated; but even in the intervals he could only swallow very small morsels of solid food.

This gentleman was very subject to the gout, and had several severe fits of it in his feet; but there did not appear to be the smallest change at those times in the complaint in the œsophagus. He had tried a great many different medicines of the nervous and spasmodic kind, without the least advantage. An emetic once seemed to relieve him, but at another time did the very reverse; so that it was never afterwards had recourse to.

It is curious, that whenever he was made sick, by drinking too much bad Port wine, so as to retch severely, he was relieved for several weeks. When he first consulted me, with the view of ascertaining whether the stricture was only spasmodic or permanent, a bougie of the size of the finger was passed; it met with no obstruction, and went readily into the stomach. It became evident from this circumstance, that there was no permanent stricture, at least none sufficient to authorize the use of the caustic. It was then proposed to try the effects of mercury, which had not been used. He went through a course of mercurial frictions : during this course he derived no immediate benefit from it ; but ever since the effects of the salivation abated, he has been much better than he was before. Six years after he was killed by a fall, but in that time the complaint had not materially increased.

CASE III.

A gentleman, aged forty-three, of a very irritable habit, extremely nervous, and readily agitated by casual occurrences, in March, 1796, had for the first time a difficulty in swallowing, which increased gradually, and was attended with symptoms of great irritation ; as quick pulse, hot skin, fits of choking, sickness, and bringing up great quantities of mucus from the stomach. In this state the bougie was had recourse to ; and although the point of the bougie passed through the stricture, it rather increased the irritation. Its use was persevered in for six weeks ; but the complaint became so much worse in that time, as to raise apprehensions respecting the patient's life. Under these circumstances he came to London in June, 1796, attended by his surgeon, to see what chance there was of the use of the caustic affording relief.

At the time he consulted me he was in a state of great irritation, with a quick pulse, hot skin, great hurry of spirits, almost approaching delirium ; his voice not reaching much beyond a whisper, a great degree of impatience in his temper ; and any attempt to swallow attended with convulsive spasms in his throat, and at those times a great deal of phlegm was discharged. The stricture was situated nearly behind the middle of the thyroide cartilage ; it did not admit the end of a bougie, the diameter of which was five-twentieths of an inch. As he could not live in his present state, all risk was out of the question, and the only thing to be considered was, whether there was a chance of relief from the caustic. The fair answer was, that the caustic was not likely to aggravate the present symptoms, and that it was highly probable it might remove the obstruction. From these assurances, the patient very willingly submitted to its being tried.

The caustic was applied by means of a bougie, in the same manner as to a stricture in the urethra. The common bougie was passed down to the obstruction, and while there, the part opposite the cutting edge of the fronth teeth of the upper jaw was marked, to determine the exact distance of the stricture; this bougie was then withdrawn, and the curve it had taken carefully preserved. The same curve was given to the armed bougie, upon which the exact distance was marked; it was then introduced, and the caustic allowed to rest for about half a minute against the obstruction ; it gave little or no pain, brought on no local inflammation, and in the course of the day there was less spasmodic affection of the œsophagus when he attempted to swallow. This gave encouragement to repeat the use of the caustic, and it was applied four times, once every other day : each application gave evident relief.

After the fourth application, he could swallow fluids without any difficulty, and could get down morsels of meat with more ease than he had done since the beginning of his illness. The armed bougie did not pass through the stricture, there was therefore no reason to believe that it was wholly destroyed ; but the confinement to the house in London, in addition to the effects of the caustic, brought on a fever, which made it necessary to discontinue the use of the caustic ; the fever went off in a week, and he swallowed with little difficulty, had less phlegm collected in the œsophagus, and his voice was more distinct. It was thought right to attend to his general health, and with that view he went immediately into the country, where he recovered strength, and was able to walk two miles without fatigue. He went to the sea in the autumn, in which situation his health was still more improved. He did not attempt bathing.

He returned to London in March, 1797. He had not lost any ground respecting his swallowing since the caustic was used, his voice was more distinct than last year, his fits of choking less frequent, and the quantity of phlegm collected in the œsophagus not so great as before, although he was still sometimes liable to it.

It is remarkable, that whenever he was sick and retched to vomit, there was no difficulty in bringing up the contents of the stomach, that action relaxing the stricture.

With a view of relieving his complaint still further, which it was not thought prudent to attempt in the state of irritation, that he was in the year before, the caustic was again applied ; but enlarged to the full size, in which the sticks are cast for the common purposes in surgery, which is more than double the size of that formerly used ; the bougie was of necessity also much larger. The caustic was first applied on March 18th ; it gave violent pain ; but the sensation produced by it remained for half an hour, and then went off. On the 22d it was repeated ; he had caught a cold, which at that time was very general in London ; this increased the quantity of phlegm formed in his mouth and throat, but did not prevent us from prosecuting the use of the caustic. The 24th, the armed bougie passed through the stricture, and immediately some thick phlegm was brought up, which appeared to have been lodged in that part of the œsophagus. 25th, he swallowed considerably better, and his voice was distinctly louder than common ; this was evident to all his friends. 26th, the application of the caustic was repeated, and the armed bougie again

went through the stricture. Having gained
so much, it was not thought prudent to attempt further enlargement till it should be
ascertained, after leaving the parts some
time to themselves, that it was absolutely
necessary; and he went into the country,
London not agreeing with his general health,
and his cold being rather increased. The
accounts received, at several different times,
were, that he continued better than at the
time he left town, and swallowed very
comfortably. Some years after he died of
an inflammation in his bowels, without
having experienced any return of difficulty
in swallowing.

CASE IV.

A gentleman, aged fifty-four, for twelve
years felt occasionally a pain in his stomach,
and in the last two years of that period the
returns became more frequent, attended
with violent retching, without bringing off

any thing from his stomach but phlegm. In November, 1795, after a very severe attack of this kind, he found a difficulty in swallowing morsels of the usual size; this increased so much, that in March, 1796, he was unable to swallow meat. In June the difficulty was so alarming as to require medical assistance. On the 20th of June, a bougie smaller at the end than the point of the little finger, was passed into the œsophagus; it met an obstruction behind the cartilages of the larynx, but was pushed beyond this tight part. It was passed regularly for thirty-two days, but did not produce the smallest improvement in the act of swallowing. On July 18th, he put himself under my care; at that time, he could swallow liquids a little at a time, but even this required caution; bread and butter, and sopped bread, were often got down with more ease than liquids. He swallowed better at one time than at another, and could tell from his feelings, without making the attempt, whether he could swallow better or

not. He was subject to occasional fits of
irritation, and at these times brought up a
great deal of mucus and phelgm. As the
bougie had failed, the use of the caustic was
proposed, to which he readily consented. The
curve from the mouth to the œsophagus was
ascertained by passing a bougie of a large
size down to the stricture; an armed bougie
was then moulded into the shape in which
the other came out; it was passed down to
the stricture, and allowed to remain there
some seconds; it gave no pain, brought on
no irritation, and he swallowed some water
immediately afterwards with more ease than
usual; next day he eat one morsel of roasted
veal without difficulty. 20th, the caustic was
again applied for half a minute; the pressure
made use of gave pain. He swallowed some
water immediately after, and got down two
gulfs at once, which he remarked he had
been unable to do before. 21st, he eat
a small piece of mutton, and thought he
swallowed better; 22d, the caustic, was applied for a still longer time; he drank some

water, which readily passed the stricture' but stopped somewhere near the stomach, before it went into that viscus; 24th, the caustic was repeated and gave less uneasiness; 27th, the armed bougie passed through the stricture, to which it had now been applied five times. August 1st, he swallowed tolerably well, but the food met with an obstruction near the stomach, which was now so much increased, that the morsel was forced up again.

It was attempted to pass a long bougie down to this obstruction near the stomach, but it was too large to go through the first stricture; 3d, the caustic was therefore again applied to the first stricture; when he swallowed gently, the morsel got into the stomach, but any hurry brought on spasm near the cardia, which made him retch and bring it up again: 4th, this stoppage at the orifice of the stomach had been so great, as to prevent any thing getting into the stomach, although it readily passed down to that part.

O o

This led me to believe that there was a disease near the orifice of the stomach, of which the stricture in the œsophagus was only a consequence, similar to what happens in the urethra. A stricture near the neck of the bladder, producing a contraction in other parts of the canal.

As this disease, of whatever kind it might be, was out of the reach of surgery, the assistance of a physician was required, and Dr. Pitcairn was called in.

It was proposed that a blister should be applied to the pit of the stomach, and that the patient should go through a course of mercurial frictions, using nutricious broth clysters. For two or three days he could not swallow at all ; on the ninth, some food passed into the stomach, but it could not be retained there. 12th, he was able to retain twelve ounces of asses milk, given in small quantities through the day; his pulse was more regular, but very weak. While the gums were sore from the mercury, he thought he swallowed better, and worse when the effects of the mercury went off.

September 1st, he grew weaker; the use of the mercury was therefore left off. He now retained scarcely any thing upon his stomach, and that principally wine; he brought up occasionally a great deal of mucus mixed with matter.

On the fifth of September he died. This happened in the country, and the nature of the disease in the stomach was not permitted to be ascertained by an examination after death.

EXPLANATION

O F

THE PLATES.

IT appears essentially necessary for the proper management of strictures, that the surgeon should be perfectly acquainted with the natural form of the canal of the urethra; its shape, size, the course it follows, the particular situation of the bulb of the urethra, and of the prostate gland. Not having seen any engravings by which all these circumstances are accurately illustrated, the two following Plates are laid before the public.

PLATE I.

This Plate represents two casts of the urethra, which were made by injecting that canal in two different subjects with wax, and afterwards removing the wax by cutting open the urethra; so that they form bougies of the exact size of the canal, impressed with all its natural inequalities.

Fig. 1. This cast, which was taken from a subject about seventy-five years of age, is represented in the engraving of its exact size. The dimensions of the different parts are accurately given in the third Section of the first Chapter of the work, so that it is not necessary to repeat them here.

Similar casts from the urethra of subjects at different ages, resemble those represented in this figure.

a, A portion of the bladder.

b, The neck of the bladder.

c, The canal which passes over the prostate gland, and extends from *b* to *d*.

e, The caput gallinaginis, where the seminal ducts open, imprinted upon the wax, and a ridge leading from it, along the sides of which the semen passes forwards towards the reservoir formed for that purpose, which is called the bulb of the urethra.

f, The membranous portion of the urethra.

g, A natural constriction of the urethra, directly behind the bulb, which is probably formed with a power of contraction, to prevent by its action any part of the semen from passing back when the acceleratores muscles, in the orgasm, propel it into the vagina.

h, the bulb of the urethra, or reservoir, where

the semen is collected previous to its expulsion.

i, A portion of the canal which appears to be narrower than the rest, and nearly of the same size as the constricted part at *g.*

k, A natural enlargement of the canal, three-fourths of an inch from the external orifice.

l, The external orifice, which in some instances is smaller than the rest of the canal, but in others is of the same size.

Fig. 2. Is the representation of a cast taken from the urethra of a man thirty years of age, the dimensions of which have been also given in the third Section of the first Chapter. As this cast is similar to the last, the same explanation may be applied to its different parts. The express purpose for which it is here represented, is to shew the part at *g,* which in the former figure was in a natural state, but in this had formed a stricture; and the impression made by the stricture gives a better idea of the effect that disease produces on the canal than can be formed even from are presentation of the morbid parts themselves. It also shews the situation in which this disease is most commonly met with; and if it be true that this part is naturally employed to shut up the canal on particular occasions, it satisfactorily explains why it should be the most liable to this disease.

It is a strong circumstance in favour of the supposition that this part is so employed, that a number of patients who have irritable urethras, or strictures in that situation, find the part so much affected by having connection with women, that if it takes place more than once in the night, a spasmodic affection is brought on, inducing strangury.

PLATE II.

This Plate represents a cast of the urethra and bladder, in which is seen the exact curve of the urethra, from the part where it is a, fixed canal, to its termination in the bladder.

a a, The cast of a portion of the bladder in its distended state.

bb, The ureter of the right side terminating in the bladder.

c, The cast of the canal which passes over the prostate gland.

d, The membranous portion of the urethra.

e, The bulb of the urethra.

ff, The canal of the urethra leading to the external orifice, in the same situation respecting the bladder, in which it is placed when the penis is in an erected state.

PLATE III.

Is a representation of the cavity of the bladder of a patient who had a stone which adhered to its internal membrane. The particulars of the case and dissection are related at length in the third Section of the fifth Chapter, to which the reader is referred.

The patient had undergone the operation for the stone, and the wound was not healed up at the time of his death ; it was therefore considered as the best mode of opening the bladder to do it laterally, by an incision from the opening made in the operation, towards the fundus of the bladder.

In this way the cavity of the bladder was exposed, without any portion of its coats being removed ; and neither the urethra, nor the wound made in the operation for the stone, were in the smallest degree injured.

The fundus of the bladder, which was in a perfectly natural state, was removed, as its being kept could not convey any information respecting the disease.

a a, The portion of the bladder towards the fundus, which was in a natural state.

b b, The cut edges of the coats of the bladder, separated from each other as much as the parts admitted of it.

c, The surface of the fistulous canal, leading from the bladder externally in the perinæum, formed by the wound made in cutting for the stone, which had never healed up, but had become covered by a smooth membrane. In the natural state the two sides were close together, but in this view they are separated from each other.

P p

d d, The edge of the external integuments in the perinæum.

e, The corpus cavernosum penis.

f, The canal of the urethra, where the penis was cut through to remove the superfluous parts. The urethra terminates towards the bladder in the wound made by the gorget in cutting for the stone. There is not the smallest appearance of prostate gland ; it must have been very small, and the inflammation brought on by the operation had consolidated all those parts, so as to prevent the cut edges of the prostate gland from being distinguished.

g g g g g, A number of very irregular projecting portions of coagulating lymph, loose and detached on their external surface, but fixed at their base by a firm union to the internal membrane of the bladder ; the surface to which they adhere includes the whole circumference of the bladder, and extends for three inches towards the fundus.

Before the bladder was opened, if the parts could have been examined, this exsudation of coagulating lymph must have formed a zone just above the neck of the bladder, to which the stone, previous to the operation, was connected by the projecting parts being imbedded in its substance. They are still incrusted with calculous matter in a soft state.

END OF VOL. I.

Printed by W. Bulmer and Co.
Cleveland-row, St. James's.

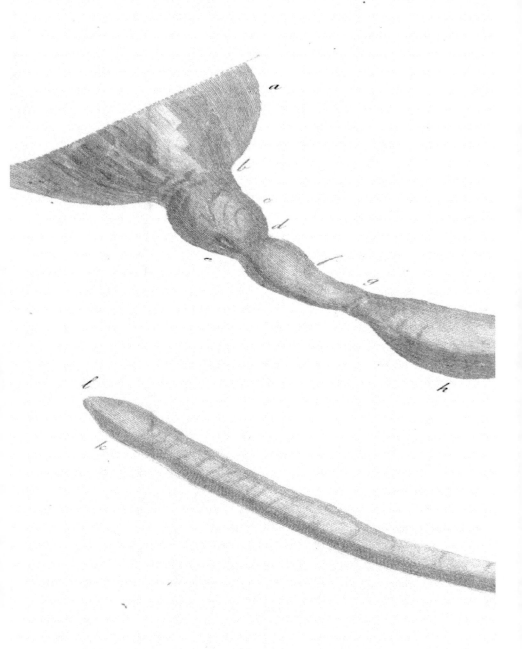

Plate 2.

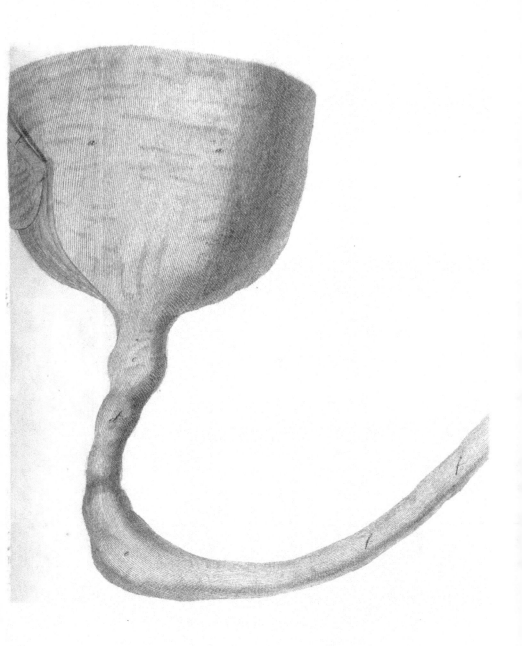

Plate 3.

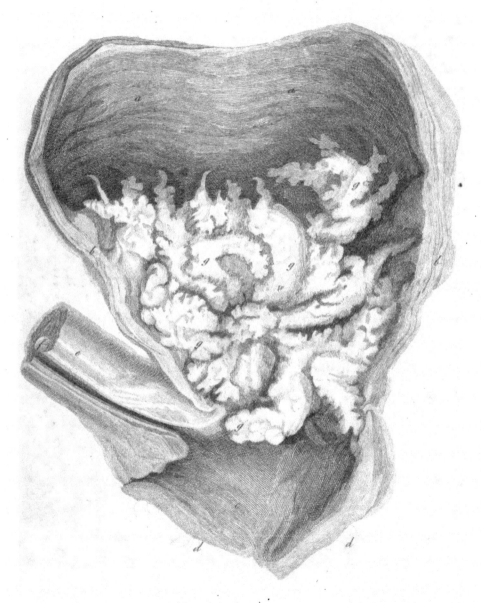

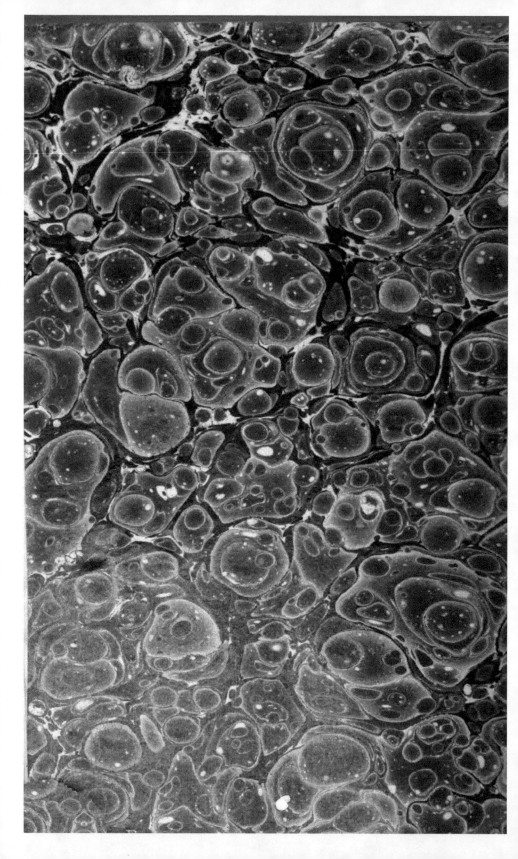

CPSIA information can be obtained
at www.ICGtesting.com
Printed in the USA
BVHW041015280819
556932BV00018B/2616/P

9 781407 635842